When Hope Rises

A Memoir By

TAMMY DOVE

Trilogy Christian Publishers
A Wholly Owned Subsidary of Trinity Broadcasting Network
2442 Michelle Drive
Tustin, CA 92780

Cover design by: Cornerstone Creative Solutions
Original Artwork by: Brian Oeisted

For information, address Trilogy Christian Publishing
Rights Department, 2442 Michelle Drive, Tustin, Ca 92780.
Trilogy Christian Publishing/ TBN and colophon are trademarks of Trinity Broadcasting Network.

For information about special discounts for bulk purchases, please contact Trilogy Christian Publishing.

Manufactured in the United States of America

10 9 8 7 6 5 4 3 2 1

Library of Congress Cataloging-in-Publication Data is available.

ISBN 978-1-64773-967-6 (Print Book)
ISBN 978-1-64773-968-3 (ebook)

Dedication

This story of hope is dedicated to the Frenchtown Volunteer Fire Department crew who "just happened" to be on site the night Doug died. To Missoula Emergency Services, Inc. and the team who fought valiantly to keep Doug alive on the way to the hospital. To the Emergency Medical staff at St. Patrick's Hospital who took the baton for the next leg of the race, fanning the flicker of life in Doug's seizing body despite the grim prospects. To the many doctors, nurses, and the ancillary staff at St. Patrick's Hospital, Providence Rehabilitation Center, Nebraska Medical Center, Methodist Hospital Omaha, Quality Living, Inc., Omaha. To Valerie Chyle APRN, PLLC, who has tirelessly worked with Doug to ensure the best possible care and provision during the recovery process. To Dr. William "Bill" Bekemeyer, who showed up even when he didn't have to. To our families, especially my mom, Patty Sayler, my rock in the storm. To my brother Eric, your assistance was always so timely—no phone call necessary. To Dave and Connie Murray, whose steadfast support and compassion were invaluable. And especially to Dan Vander Zwagg. Without Dan's quick thinking, there would be no story to tell.

Contents

Acknowledgements

To the Father, Son, and Holy Spirit, who created Doug and me "for such a time as this." You carried us when we were unable to go any further in our strength.

Dan Vander Zwagg, you arrived just in time to save Doug's life. You were God's man for the hour that night. There are not enough words to express our gratitude for your selflessness—especially knowing how many sleepless nights you suffered afterwards. You did exactly what you were supposed to do. A better friend we couldn't ask for.

Dave and Connie Murray, you were not obligated to share the burden of Doug's recovery as beautifully as you did. Yet you faithfully showed up to hold vigil as often as you could spare the time. Your heartfelt tears, compassion, love, strength, and gifts were much needed and appreciated during this trial of life, death, faith, and hope. Our family circle was enlarged as you joined your strength with ours in travail for Doug's life. We are truly blessed to call you friends and family.

My mom, or Mother Dear as I fondly call her. Your example of grace and strength were invaluable gifts. More than once, while growing up, you indirectly taught me by example how to rise up and be strong when necessary. Little did I know how desperately I would need those very gifts you shared with me until I was faced with the reality of Doug's death. Once again, you chose to sacrifice what you were doing to be by my side when I needed you most. Not for just a day or two did you sacrifice your time and resources; you continue to do so to this very day. I may have been able to fight this fight of faith without you, but it would have been significantly more challenging without your strong presence and steadfast love.

Eric, a sister couldn't ask for a better brother. You plowed snow, hauled firewood, and repaired vehicles and equipment. A phone call away, I could always count on your help and listening ear. "Thank you" seems so inadequate for all you have done for us. We are truly grateful for your love and assistance.

Steve and Pam Jackson, you were my Jesus with skin on. Your love and support kept my faith burning bright. Every word of encouragement was fuel for hope. You had my back in prayer, for which I am ever grateful.

Josh Yakos and Clark Fork City Church. Our spiritual family, you circled the wagons of prayer and fought the fight of faith for us. As our Aaron and Hur, you kept our hands up as they did for Moses, enabling us to defeat the enemy of death. The victory is yours to celebrate.

Terry Geber, you who are also familiar with tragedy and recovery were quick to step in and care for my horses. Housing and feeding them as if they were your own, you relieved me of a great burden in looking after them as well as plowing snow for us. You were a good neighbor!

The many intercessors who stood alongside us in prayer, many of whom we have never met. Your prayers turned the scale in our favor, soundly spanking the enemy. We are forever indebted to you.

My former co-workers at Western Montana Clinic who sacrificed vacation pay to ensure my financial responsibilities were met with ease; your generosity relieved a huge burden. I pray you are doubly blessed for your sacrifice.

I am sure there are many more of you who deserve to be acknowledged. We couldn't begin to name all our friends, family members, the medical community, the EMTs, our co-workers...by name here, but we are grateful for and love each one of you. I ask for your forgiveness if you feel left out and remind you that our Father in heaven sees and acknowledges you.

I would be remiss if I didn't mention those who helped this first-time author learn the ropes of writing a book. The entire team at Trilogy Publishing, Wendy Walters at Release the Writer, Charity Bradshaw at Launch Author Coaching, Danica Winters at Self-

Publishing Services, Lysa TerKeurst, She Speaks Conference 2019, and Carolyn Master of Carolyn Reed Consulting. Carolyn, we have spent a year together while you gently and tirelessly guided my thoughts and words to craft our message of hope. I am so grateful for divine guidance to your gift and wisdom.

Writing seems to be warfare, and my intercessors battled on my behalf. Cathy Jo, Michelle, Jennifer, Allie, and Paige, my sweet sisters, you are mighty warriors, thank you for going to battle for our story.

Doug, without you, there would be no story. You, my love, persevered when most believed you wouldn't. You have always risen to the battle and never looked back. Because of your grit and steadfastness over our now thirty-eight years of marriage, I am a better woman because of your example. Despite learning to adapt to your new limitations, you have been mostly patient with me as I attempted to adapt as well. I am grateful for the grace you extended to me as I grappled with finding my footing in the storm. God seemed to know what He was doing when He put the two of us together.

Praise for When Hope Rises

We were honored to have been a stop on Tammy and Doug's recovery journey. It was inspiring to hear how their faith was the foundation of their healing. We are hopeful their story may serve as a beacon of hope for other families who are enduring similar struggles.

Jill Vollmuth and Laura Bergevin, two of the many members of Doug's QLI team

[/vc_row_inner]

Foreword

This is a story about an industrial accident that never should have happened. By the grace of God, I am here to tell about it. In my haste to complete the demolition job I needed to do, I apparently misjudged the risk I was taking and was almost demolished instead. As a result, I find myself the recipient of a miracle. If not for divine intervention and quick thinking, my story may have turned out much differently.

Since my accident on January 3, 2012, I have learned God is faithful despite circumstances, which may indicate otherwise. Despite the seemingly slow progress in rehab and many setbacks, He has been faithful to encourage me and stand by my side, giving me the strength to go through the arduous trials that are a part of recovering from a traumatic brain injury. Many times, I have found myself flat on my face in a pool of blood, angry and frustrated, yet determined to overcome the limitations I was faced with.

This has truly been the "Refiner's Fire." I can relate to Job when he was tested by God. Despite the severe trials, I can still say God is good; I know He is for me and not against me. Though He slays me, I will praise his name.

I praise Him for another day to live. I praise Him for His faithfulness. His provision. His healing power, believing He is not done with me yet. I praise Him for giving me a wife of strong character who chose to stand by my side when it would have been easier to quit and walk away.

My story has given me the opportunity to give hope to those who are struggling to find any good in the midst of their difficulties. This world has become increasingly dark and filled with adversity in the years since my accident. I believe you will find a measure of hope and encouragement in the chapters ahead as you read about a God who still does miracles. He still raises the dead.

Introduction

Have you ever received a phone call confirming your greatest nightmare has just become your reality? If you have, you know it's a moment that stops time in its tracks as the world around you fades to black. You are not prepared to hear the words, "There has been an accident. Your husband is unconscious, his heart has stopped beating." There's nothing anyone can say or do to stop the gut punch that seemingly occurs in that kind of moment. You are left without air to breathe or articulate the grief, which has instantaneously engulfed your being.

In an instant, God had changed our lives forever. We were both called to our purpose. Suddenly our faith was being tested. Did we truly believe Romans 8:28 (NRSV)? "We know that all things work together for good for those who love God, who are called according to His purpose." I was now being challenged to believe and trust in God—the man Jesus who is capable of miracles. The One who set the heavens and earth in place. The God who spoke and the universe came into being. The God who took dirt and formed man.

As humans, we continue to grow in our faith. We learn to draw from every experience in life. Experiences, which form us into the beings we are, shaped by the many trials we encounter throughout our lifetime. When we come face to face with the challenges of life, we must dig down into our spirit man as David did when he faced the giant Goliath. David said, "The Lord who saved me from the claws of the lion and the bear will save me from this Philistine!" (1 Samuel 17:37). Sure enough, the Lord delivered David from the giant. Just as He is willing to deliver us from our giants if we trust Him to do so. However, even in the trusting, He calls us to the battle, to stand before the giant with our knees shaking, our guts knotted up, and our bowels a wreck as we hear the mocking voice of the enemy telling us there is no way this will turn out the way we desire. He cackles, "You will never win!"

God takes us to the place of pain and agony, the unknown, to the place where you hold on to hope by a thread, praying for the faith to trust in the fragile gossamer strand of hope to hold strong and fast. However, the doctor you've known for twenty years, you respect, and trust tells you there is *no hope*. He tells you Doug's brain was oxygen-deprived long enough he is most likely brain-dead. Survival is highly improbable. If by a miracle Doug might possibly survive, he would essentially exist in a vegetative state. The enemy reinforces the doctor's words with shouts, "No hope, no hope, you'll never win!"

Sometimes you must push your faith to the very limit, believe in the impossible, and pray for miracles—which may or may not be granted. You must trust that God is good, and He wants the very best for you—despite what circumstances are dictating. When we trust and abide in His will, we can experience peace while the storm is raging around you.

Courage transforms the emotional structure of our being. This change often brings a deep sense of loss. During the process of rising, we sometimes find ourselves homesick for a place that no longer exits. We want to go back to that moment before we walked into the arena, but there's nowhere to go back to. What makes this more difficult is that now we have a new level of awareness about what it means to be brave. We can't fake it anymore. We now know when we're showing up and when we're hiding out, when we are living our values and when we are not. Our new awareness can be invigorating—it can reignite our sense of purpose and remind us of our commitment to wholeheartedness. Straddling the tension that lies between wanting to go back to the moment before we risked and fell and being pulled forward to even greater courage is an inescapable part of rising strong.

Brené Brown[1]

[/vc_row_inner]

Let's Start at The Very Beginning—It's a Very Good Place to Start

I have never not known Doug Dove. He has been a part of my life for as long as I can remember. We grew up together in the 9-Mile Valley, a rural mountainous area west of Missoula, Montana. Doug is three years older than I am. He was four years ahead of me in school. We rode the same school bus, which my mom drove. Our families weren't especially close, but in such a small community, neither were we distant.

Doug's parents, Jack and Peggy, lived across the driveway from his grandparents, where my family used to buy milk and cream regularly. Whenever we picked up milk, the adults chatted, oftentimes catching up on the local gossip, while we kids explored the farm and played.

Over time, Doug and I grew in familiarity with one another, and by the time we were teens, it was clear we were also developing a romantic interest for one another. During the summer of 1977, when he was a month shy of eighteen, and I was stuck in the middle of fourteen and fifteen, I clearly remember how the spark of romance quickly ignited. The heat of the summer air was hot, yet our youthful, passionate blood was burning hotter still. The temperatures began to escalate, and we were heading into an inferno—one with the potential to derail, if not destroy, our lives.

As lightning caused fires in the surrounding wildlands, the need for firefighters grew in conjunction with every acre burned. Doug was hired to battle those blazes. Suddenly, our personal inferno was reduced to embers. Our summer days of flirting, fun, and frolicking at Kreis Pond came to an abrupt halt. It was as if a tanker load of fire retardant had been dropped on our relationship. My young heart ached with loneliness in his absence. I spent the remainder of the summer daydreaming of Doug's return. I was ever so anxious to pick up our romance where we had been interrupted. However, fate had other plans. This country bumpkin of a boy was now in the company of worldly, rowdy, alcohol-imbibing men. The lure of partying with the big boys was much more attractive than the lull of a naive girl back home with four years of high school to complete.

Days turned into weeks. Weeks rolled into months. Summer was over far too soon, and school was starting once again. It was time to shift gears and get back to the daily grind. There were no more long horseback rides, lazy days swimming and sunbathing, and much less time to daydream of my all too short summer romance. Between basketball practice, games, and my studies, one would have thought I wouldn't even have any time to think of Doug. However, my romantic, dream-filled heart wasn't to be deterred. At last, when the long-awaited high school yearbooks were finally delivered that September, I dutifully picked up his and had his junior classmen sign it for him. I even wrote some silly, gushy nonsense as only a lovesick girl would do, affirming my undying love for him.

Commitment apparently was not on his mind when he showed up at one of my first basketball games with a blonde bombshell on his arm. I was shell-shocked, pun intended. My heart was shattered. A million bloody shards laid everywhere. I went from lovesick to just plain sick, hoping I wouldn't vomit on the court. Doug had committed an unthinkable foul against me. I found it impossible to focus on the game. Tears blurred my vision as the blonde confirmed my insecurities. I was just a summer plaything. The voice in my head whispered loudly that Doug had seen through my façade. He had discovered I was damaged goods.

You see, I had a terrible secret. I had been sexually exploited as a child and erroneously believed the incident was my fault. I had been corrupted, and I was no longer worthy of love or acceptance. Those piercing nails of rejection fortified my proverbial prison for years.

And now, seeing this blonde on the arm of my mighty knight, I felt shame, rejection, and humiliation wash over me once again like a rogue wave almost knocking me off my feet. I angrily asked myself, *How could you have been so foolish as to trust him with your wounded heart?* I genuinely thought he was special, perhaps even "the one." Doug proved to me, though, he was no different than the rest of the guys. He only cared about his needs.

I handled his betrayal and my mangled heart in the same way I handled my other negative emotions. I buried them beneath a copious amount of food. It seemed rational in the moment to eat until I was miserable, rather than dwell on whatever was causing me pain at the time. Unfortunately, I hadn't yet learned that coping with emotional pain this way doesn't work. Instead, it only exacerbates the problem. Shame, guilt, self-condemnation, and self-loathing thrive when fed profuse amounts of fuel. I can just picture a witch sprinkling a bit of each into her cauldron. The contents growing exponentially. Bubbling and boiling over the sides. Cascading into the fire. Smoke billowing. Emanating a putrid stench. Her cackles echoing the taunts of the bullies who had teased me while growing up, "Fatty, fatty two by four, she can't fit through the kitchen door."

Eventually, the smoke cleared. The pain receded. Life moved on. I threw myself into school activities and long horseback rides through the forest. My black mare, Sass, was a great listener. I would pour out my heart to her, watching as her finely sculpted ears moved gently as if she was catching my every word. I cried countless tears into her mane as I laid sobbing over her neck, pouring my heart out to her. I was participating in equine therapy before it became a thing. I am certain that little horse saved my life. She allowed me to heal as I shared my struggles with her. Sass also gave me something else to focus on as we practiced for events, rather than dwell on the less desirable circumstances in my life. As Winston Churchill said, "There is something about the outside of a horse that is good for the inside of man."[2] The inside of me changed over the next few years. It was time to close this chapter of my life and move on to the next.

The next chapter would include a part-time job in addition to school. I decided to give up basketball. I did not grow up in a sport-loving family and hadn't developed a passion for the game. It also became quite obvious my less than petite, five-foot-two build was not advantageous in basketball. So, when the opportunity to wash dishes at the 9-Mile House Bar and Restaurant was presented, it was a no-brainer for me. I jumped at the chance to earn some cash. I much preferred to get paid to race between tables and gather dirty dishes than run up and down the court.

I quickly went from washing dishes to helping prep food and making salads. I already had a strong interest in cooking. My Easy-Bake Oven had gotten a regular workout when I was little, and I could make a Jell-O parfait like a pro. This promotion would give me an opportunity to further develop my culinary skills.

Waiting tables was a natural progression at the restaurant. The tips were an added incentive for a girl with clothes to buy, a horse habit to support, and college looming on the horizon. And as an extrovert, I loved the social aspect of waitressing. One could count on the locals showing up like clockwork on given nights. Doug's family were among the regulars, requiring me to see him often. We kept the conversation between us casual and generic. He would ask me things like "What's new?" or "How's the weather?" *Cold as ice like my heart,* I remember thinking.

Yet, the embers of desire still carried a little heat. Like a lightning strike smoldering in the timber, patiently waiting for the breeze to fan the glowing coals into a flame, the winds of change were beginning to blow. On April 25, 1980, two and a half years after breaking my heart, Doug asked me to go out on a date with him. I was in a quandary because while I really did want him back, I most definitely did not want to be rejected again. I was about to say no, but my lips seemingly had a will of their own, saying yes instead. My foolish heart skipped a few beats, optimistic this time could be different. We were older, after all. I was all of seventeen, a junior in high school. Doug was twenty and working at the local paper mill. It was one of the best paying employers in the area, so he was quite doing well for himself financially. My brain was arguing with my heart, screaming, "Danger, danger," attempting to remind my heart how painfully excruciating our last encounter was. My stubborn heart reasoned. *Your mom was married at sixteen and is doing well, there is nothing wrong with "young love."* Lots of people get married young.

I prepared for this date with great attention to detail, trying on a dozen outfits or so before settling on the perfect one. I can still see those black corduroy pants with a green top. I may have looked like I was cool as a cucumber on the outside, but I was a hot mess of emotions on the inside. I was terrified he wouldn't show up and terrified he would. I was scared he would hurt me once again, yet optimistic we could start over.

I didn't have too much time to pace the living room while tormenting myself with my many thoughts because Doug was punctual, arriving to pick me up exactly when promised. I would later learn he took punctuality very seriously, believing that you rob someone else of their time when you are late. Being quite the gentleman, he held the door for me as I climbed up into his blue 1976 Ford 4×4 pickup truck. Even without a lift kit, getting in was a stretch for my short legs. (Later, he would take great delight in putting his hands on my backside and boosting me up into the truck.)

Our first date consisted of burgers and a drive. We talked for what seemed like hours. It was as though we had never been apart. It soon became obvious there was still chemistry between us. Smoldering coals of passion were ignited once again, and it was hard to slow down the desire, which was rapidly building like steam in a runaway freight train. I may have been sitting on the passenger side of the pickup when I first got in, but it didn't take long for me to slide across the seat where I could easily feel the warmth of his body and readily see the twinkle in his eyes. In my innermost being, I knew that night Doug was the man I would marry. I fell hard and fast. Giving little thought to the pain he had caused me years earlier, fueled with fresh passion, I anticipated the joy to come.

From that night on, I never wanted to be away from him for a moment longer than absolutely necessary. If I wasn't at school or work, I would go to the woods with him while he processed fence post and rails out of the trees he cut down. Doug had very little spare time because he was working more than forty hours a week at the paper mill in addition to working in the woods during whatever time was left. I was impressed by his work ethic, but this left us with little time to spend together. To occupy my time while he was busy working, I usually brought along a book to read. One day while sitting in the shade of a tree with my book, it occurred to me, if I helped Doug load the posts on the truck, he would have more time to hang out with me. I would also benefit physically by getting a great workout in at the same time.

I was self-conscious at first as I attempted to wrestle the six and a half foot logs onto the truck without getting filthy. Eventually, I quit worrying about my appearance. Covered in sawdust, dirt, and sweat, I began what would turn into years of wrestling posts. Soon, I was spending every spare moment I had working shoulder to shoulder with Doug and his dad, Jack. Jack laughed at us, lovebirds. We would sit smashed so close together, almost like Siamese twins, in the pickup truck as we drove to and from the post-sale (the acreage of timber Doug had purchased from the US Forest Service to process into fence post and rails) or anywhere else for that matter.

Head over heels in love, I doodled his name all over my notebooks as silly girls do. My mom took notice and said, "If you are still together a year from now, I have something to tell you." I know now she didn't want to get my hopes up, but a year later, I went and asked her, "So, what is this something that you wanted to tell me but had to wait a year?" She said, "If you had been born a boy, your name would have been Douglas Edward just as his is." I could see why she waited to tell me because hearing this made me believe we were simply meant to be!

Douglas Edward proposed to me in December of my senior year. My parents consented with the condition we would wait to get married until I had attended a year of college. Having married so young, my mother wanted me to have the opportunity to further my education before I settled down. We agreed, not knowing how arduous it would be to wait. This was especially trying once I moved to Spokane, Washington, to attend Kinman Business University for ten months. Those ten months felt like an eternity for us. Missing each other desperately, we burned up the telephone lines and a good portion of money talking for hours on the phone.

Doug asked me not to work from the get-go because he wanted me to be able to come home as often as possible or to be able to spend time with him when he could find the time to come to Spokane. He willingly paid my living expenses after my savings had run out to ensure my time would be his. My heart and future were back in Montana. I could hardly wait for school to be finished.

All I could think about was Doug. I imagined his strong arms holding me close, the mischievous twinkle in his gold-flecked green eyes as he laughed with ease and a lifetime of oneness. I was far more interested in planning a wedding and a future together than finishing business college. However, I made myself buckle down, determined to complete my education and honor the commitment I had made to my parents.

At long last, or so it seemed, I had my diploma in hand. I could now progress to a marriage certificate. The date was set. My dress was purchased. All the details, which could be completed beforehand, were checked off the list. I was more than ready for eleven o'clock in the morning on September 11, 1982.

The day before our wedding, the sun, which had been shining so brightly, disappeared behind dark grey rain-laden clouds. This turn of the weather threatened to hinder our festivities, but after a much-needed refreshing rain on the summer sun-scorched land, the rain relented, providing a mostly dry but damp cool day for our wedding.

The day may have been cool, but I was heating up with anticipation as the eleven o'clock hour drew near. I didn't know if most weddings start on time or not but wanting to become Mrs. Douglas Dove sooner than later made me determined that mine would. However, when the clock ticked past eleven due to unforeseen circumstances, impatience began to set in. At 11:10, the entire wedding party was finally present, and I, in my beautiful dress with flowers in hand, bellowed in a very unladylike fashion, "Let's get this show on the road."

It was the moment I had long dreamed of; I was marrying my knight in shining armor. I had lost him once, but fate brought him back to me. You can bet I was not going to let him slip through my fingers a second time. The rainbow shimmering in its radiant glory over the meadow after the wedding ceremony suggested hope-filled dreams do come true.

The Salvation of Marriage and Souls

Fast-forwarding ten years. I had made the decision to go back to college and further my education in the healthcare field. A year and a half into my schooling, Doug had the opportunity to take over a friend's fence post and rail manufacturing business. We were already supplying the raw material to this business; therefore, it seemed like a reasonable decision to take it over. After discussing what it would take to get this process going, I agreed to put my education on hold at run the manufacturing end of the business.

My days were no longer filled with education and socialization in a climate-controlled classroom, but instead, I spent the majority of my time alone with the exception of the men delivering raw material and an occasional customer. No longer protected by walls, windows, heat, and AC, I was at the mercy of Mother Nature and her whims. To ensure the success of our business, I would have to work regardless of the temperature in rain, shine, wind, or snow.

I knew my years of helping Doug and his dad wrestle posts had developed a better-than-average amount of strength for my female body. I assumed it would be sufficient to enable me to meet the demands of handling hundreds of posts and rails every day. I was wrong. I was working my tail off in the heat and freezing temperatures against the protest of my maxed-out muscles at the post yard as well as trying to maintain our home and business records. In the meantime, Doug was working in the woods he so loved and getting his social needs met at work. He was living the dream.

I, on the other hand, was slowly losing my identity and dying inside. I missed the socialization and the beautiful clothes I enjoyed wearing in a professional business setting. Doug was often frustrated with my lack of physical strength. He failed to understand that he possessed a Herculean type of strength and was actually nicknamed Hercules by his co-workers as a result. As time went by, I found myself increasingly depressed and regretting my decision to help run this business. When I mentioned my frustration to him, he would ask me to be patient with him, promising to hire someone to help me. The flame of passion I had for him was quickly being extinguished. I didn't like the person I was becoming. Eventually, I sought out counseling once thoughts of suicide began to occur in my head frequently.

The counselor suggested I quit living the life my husband wanted and begin to live the life I wanted. Rather than return to the University of Montana to continue pursuing a degree in Physical Therapy, the counselor suggested I apply to the School of Radiologic Technology at St. Patrick's Hospital. He informed me I would be able to complete schooling in two years rather than another four or more to complete my PT degree. I could feel hope rise within me that day. I determined to pursue this course of action whether Doug agreed to it or not. My life was at stake, and I needed to do an intervention for my future well-being.

Doug was not happy with my decision but agreed to the transition back to school. The next several months were emotionally rocky as we endeavored to hire someone to replace me in the post yard. At one point, I said to Doug, "I don't like myself right now, and I really don't like you." I then informed him I was going to visit friends in Arizona and would be gone for a week. "I think we both need some time apart to determine if we have a future together," I explained. "I am no longer willing to live my life feeling as if my value to you is dependent on how much I can contribute to your business." Our relationship had become one of codependence. I was putting all my energy into meeting his needs while few of mine were being met. Counseling gave me the gumption I needed to speak up and move my life into healthier places, and I was doing it...no matter what.

My trip to Arizona was instrumental in saving both my marriage and my soul. While there, I did some deep soul searching. I also read books on Indian Spirituality. As someone who sometimes has dreams that come to pass, I was fascinated by the stories I was reading about the spiritual significance of dreams and visions from the native perspective. My desire to know more increased with each book I read. I knew in my heart of hearts, something spiritual was missing in my life and was most likely a solution to the misery I was currently experiencing.

The time in Arizona passed all too quickly. It was time to return home to Montana to see what kind of future awaited me. I wondered if Doug and I would be able to sort through our differences and salvage our marriage or if I would find myself divorced, single, unemployed, and living as a student once again. It was a long drive home as my brain processed the many possibilities awaiting my future. Divorce was not what I wanted. I wanted to reconcile and move forward with each of us being fulfilled in our employment and giftings. Driving through the endless darkness, I recalled how angry Doug was when I left, causing my optimism to dim at the thought, much like the clouds obscuring the stars that night.

As I got closer to home, the snowcapped mountain peaks of the 9-Mile Divide took my breath away as they welcomed me. They sparkled incandescently in the spring evening sun. The meadows were verdant, lush, and dotted with wildflowers as spring was unfurling her glory. I was in awe of the beauty. My heart expanded as I took in the familiar sights. I remember thinking how I would miss this scenery if I had to move out. If I recalled correctly, Doug would not be home that evening when I arrived because he was working a night shift. Answers would not be immediately forthcoming. I would have to wait until morning to find out what his decision was regarding our future. As a result, sleep was elusive as, once again, my all too busy brain was trying to offer me a myriad of possibilities.

The next morning when he came home, neither one of us wanted to broach the subject. I don't recall exactly how it all played out, but I do remember the most important thing Doug said. "After spending a week without you and thinking about our circumstances, I realize how important you are to me, and if you're willing, I want to work this out." My mouth was dry with emotion, my voice cracking as I replied, "I am willing as well. However, my willingness is on the contingency. I am no longer obligated to work in the post yard, and I still get to go to school." Doug agreed. He pulled me into his arms, burying his face into my neck; he held me tightly. It was obvious he had missed me. I was greatly relieved; however, I was not yet convinced he would stay true to his word. Having me taking care of business was just too easy. In addition, I had always deferred to his desires when it came to developing our business and increasing our income. As a result, I was not able to fully surrender to his embrace. Regardless of my concerns, we were both greatly relieved to know we would not have to endure the pain of a divorce. We had no idea at the time how God was working mightily in the midst of our mess.

A week after returning home, I was in town at the grocery store, and I bumped into an acquaintance I knew to be a Christian. Excitedly, I began to tell her about the books I had been reading about Indian Spirituality. With matched enthusiasm, her face beaming, she asked me, "Do you want to know about Jesus?" Having grown up with minimal knowledge of Him, through Christmas and Easter church services and along with a short stint of Youth Group, I was curious.

Looking back now, I can see I was very ripe fruit for the picking. I would soon find out the missing piece I was looking for in my life was Jesus Himself. I had a God-sized hole in my heart that only He could fill. My friend's face lit up even brighter like a thousand-watt bulb. Grinning from ear to ear, she said, "Great, I would be happy to introduce you to Him." With great anticipation, I then asked, "When can we meet?" Somehow knowing this would be a pivotal moment in my life, I hoped she would have time the next day. However, her response was not what I had hoped.

"I am in the middle of finals right now, so I won't have time for two weeks." I was crushed and couldn't believe I would have to wait to meet this Jesus. After all, her initial response led me to believe this introduction would be eminent. In expectation, I had ridden the emotional rollercoaster to the highest point. Without warning, I was now crashing downward in disappointment. Not to be deterred, I asked, "What day and where?" We set a date for May 28, 1992, at her home.

I showed up promptly at the agreed-upon time, eager to hear more about this mystical figure I had learned about as a child in the occasional Sunday school classes I had attended. I knew my friend had a sense of peace and joy I wanted and seldom saw in others. She illuminated a room when she walked in, and I wanted what she had. She was more than willing to share this gift of love she had received years before. She explained to me it was God's selfless extravagant unconditional love for each one of us that compelled Jesus to give His life on the cross to ensure we may live eternally with Him in heaven. God was not the ogre I had mistakenly believed Him to be after all. While struggling to fathom this wild, crazy kind of love, I decided to go all in. I would sort out the details later. The peace I felt after inviting Him into my life is not possible to describe in words. The hole in my heart was now filled. There was a satisfying snap as the missing piece of the puzzle was finally put in place.

Unsure of Doug's response, I shared my news with mixed emotions. It was a shot of excitement laced with trepidation. His response was, "I certainly hope you don't go and get one of those dumb fish symbols and put it on your car!" I reassured him I hadn't planned on it.

I was disappointed by Doug's reaction. I knew he had grown up in a Christian home. His sister went to Bible College, and Doug's Grandma Mary was the godliest woman I knew. She was soft-spoken and kind. Her long gray hair was always braided, coiled in a tight bun, accentuating her weathered face, which wrinkled deeply as she smiled. She always had her Bible open to where she had been recently reading.

Once the shock wore off for Doug, he said to me, "I have often laid in bed at night worried whether you would make it to heaven or not if you died." I was incredulous and asked why he hadn't said anything. He mumbled some lame excuse, not having a good explanation.

I immediately joined my friend on Sunday mornings at her church. Back then, it was known as Clark Fork Christian Center. It was not like anything I had experienced growing up. They didn't have an organ or a choir, and they didn't sing songs from a hymnal. Instead, there was a band, and the music was uplifting and fun. I did not know a church could actually be enjoyable. Soon I was attending on a regular basis. Doug came along whenever he felt like it. It was six months before the Holy Spirit convinced Doug to attend regularly, and once he did, there was no looking back.

Soon we began serving in several ministries. It didn't matter what ministry or how many hours we served, we always felt we had to do more to assist and advance the Kingdom of God. We would look at other people God had chosen to partner with in healing ministries or others who were miraculously feeding, clothing, and educating the poor, the orphans, and widows, wondering why our service didn't feel as significant. We wanted to be world changers too.

As we have matured in our faith, I have come to understand the reason our labors felt insignificant is because they were. Doug and I were working, hoping to earn God's favor, believing our good works would grant us access to heaven. We had yet to understand that it is His loving grace, which opens the Pearly Gates. We would never be able to work long enough or hard enough to get there. Nor would we ever be "good" enough. Belief in Jesus Christ is the key to heaven's gate. It cannot be earned. It is a simple but costly gift.

Knowing Jesus laid His life down as an example for us to follow, when guest speakers asked, "Who is willing to lay down their lives, or should I say, 'selfish will and comfortable lifestyle,' to serve others in the most depraved places?" we raised our hands like Isaiah and said, "Here I am, send me" (Isaiah 6:8 NLT), meaning every word. In retrospect, I don't believe either Doug or I had fully considered the extreme sacrifice and personal cost of completely surrendering ourselves to God in service to His creation. When we observed others whom God was empowering mightily as they laid down their lives for the betterment of humankind or read stories of the great pioneers of our Christian faith, we seldom stopped to ponder how much they sacrificed. Nor did we fully comprehend the amount of suffering they endured to get to a place where God decided they were battle-worthy. David had to kill the lion and the bear before he was ready to face Goliath.

Doug and I would have told you back then we thought we had long since passed through the Kingdom boot camp and were battle-worthy as we managed to keep our marriage intact while experiencing the many challenges of building a house and business together. We somehow managed to survive the ensuing emotional shrapnel of his mother's unpredictable moods and financial betrayal when she emptied the business account and disappeared with the money for which we had worked so hard. Several years later, on December 14, 2009, when the paper mill Doug had worked at for almost thirty-two years decided to close down without warning, we received another financial hit. My dad had died just six weeks earlier, making this blow much like a one-two punch. We had barely gotten back on our feet, and *bam!*

I could not help but think of a story I had heard years before about how when a baby giraffe is born and finally makes it to its feet, the mamma giraffe immediately knocks the baby down. She does this repeatedly until the baby giraffe jumps up instantly as soon as it hits the ground. This is done to prepare the baby to be able to run as soon as possible to avoid being eaten by a predator.

While navigating life's obstacles during our twenty-nine years of marriage, we had no idea we were being trained to get up as soon as possible in preparation for the next attack. Nor did we know when or how the next one was to come. But what we do know now is that every minute detail of what we had experienced in life up to that point was critical in our preparation for what was looming around the corner. In the many times we offered up our lives in service to God, it seemed the offer had been declined. We were not living in a far country as missionaries. We were not healing the sick, feeding the poor, or raising the dead. We began to think that He hadn't heard us or worse, we weren't worthy. We soon would learn, God had listened. The problem was His timing was much different than ours, as were His ways.

Warning! Curves Ahead

Looking back, it is obvious I have had a lifetime of preparation for the tragedy my husband and I were about to encounter. Apparently, however, I required some last-minute encouragement. On the morning of December 7, 2011, during my quiet time, I read *Jesus Calling*, a devotional written by Sarah Young. She said, "I am with you in all that you do, even in the most menial task. I am always aware of you, concerned with every detail of your life."[3]

God, I know that to be true! It's just like Brother Lawrence's book, Practicing the Presence of God. You are there when I am scrubbing toilets and when I am picking up the dog poop in the kennel. I get it, Father, You're in all I do!

After reading my Bible and journaling, I knew I needed to get on with my day. I started by scrubbing the shower, finding it much easier to incorporate the cleaning with my shower. Afterwards, I glanced up at the mirror as the steam was evaporating. I was shocked to discover the steam had formed a cross shape on the mirror over Doug's sink. Certain it must be a figment of my imagination, I looked at this foggy cross on the mirror from every angle possible, trying to see if I could make the cross disappear. But no matter what direction I looked from, the cross remained on the mirror for almost an hour and a half—even with the vent fan running and the rest of the bathroom being free of steam. At the time, I didn't realize the significance of this miraculous sign. But in the following month, I would look back and recognize this was the beginning of the many clues that a life-altering event was careening our way.

A week or so after the cross appeared, I stumbled upon the book *Outwitting the Devil* by Napoleon Hill. The concept that reverberated most in my spirit was, "Satan will use fear and discouragement to keep you from achieving God's best for your life."[4] Prior to that, in a conversation between Hill and the devil, the devil told him:

> I am powerless to influence or control you because you have found the secret approach to my kingdom. You know that I exist only in the mind of people who have fears. You know that I control only the drifters (Laziness + Indifference = Procrastination = Drifting), who neglect to use their own minds. You know that my hell is here on earth and not in the world that comes after death. And you know also that the drifters supply all the fire I use in my hell... You have become my master because you have mastered all your fears... I cannot control you because you have discovered your own mind and you have taken charge of it.[5]

[/vc_row_inner]

The devil also told Hill:

> Every failure brings with it the seed of an equivalent success. But the seed will not germinate and grow under the influence of a drifter. It springs to life only when it is in the hand of one who recognizes that most failures are only temporary defeat, and who never, under any circumstances, accepts defeat as an excuse for drifting.[6]

[/vc_row_inner]

I never fully understood how failure could be used for growth. Throughout my school years, it had become deeply ingrained in me that failure of any kind meant I was flawed. I was less than unworthy, unlovable, and without value. Perhaps I, too, fell into the devil's trap and failed to reach for the stars because I might fall short of the mark. My athletic skills fell dismally short in the sports of basketball, softball, and track, in which girls in our small school customarily competed. In other words, I was a failure at sports in general, or so I thought.

My shortcomings were confirmed regularly when I was one of, if not the last person, to be picked to be on a team. I can still feel the sting of humiliation as my cheeks turned red. It felt as though every skin cell on my face was igniting with fire. The seed of rejection was planted even deeper in my soul with every game played and every mistake I made. Teasing words were like fertilizer. Rejection sprouted vigorously, like Jack's beanstalk. Its vines encased my heart and lungs, threatening to choke the breath and dreams out of me. Or perhaps it was me choking back a sob, wishing just one time I would be accepted just as I was.

After reading *Outwitting the Devil*, I realized I had been duped. The Holy Spirit gently reminded me of Psalms 139:13-16 (MSG):

> Oh yes, you shaped me first inside, then out; you formed me in my mother's womb. I thank You, High God—You're breathtaking! Body and soul, I am marvelously made! I worship in adoration—what a creation! You know me inside and out, you know every bone in my body; You know exactly how I was made, bit by bit, how I was sculpted from nothing into something. Like an open book, You watched me grow from conception to birth; all the stages of my life were spread out before you, The days of my life all prepared before I'd even lived one day.

[/vc_row_inner]

Years ago, I did a word study and discovered this Psalm says God is in awe of how He created us, and He respects us as His creation. It was time for me to come into alignment with God's perception of who I was. It was time to stop settling for a Lois Lane life. I needed to become a Holy Spirit empowered "Super Woman," as God had created me. Just because I didn't excel in the "normal" games kids played didn't mean there weren't many other places my gifts and talents didn't shine.

It was time to stop "drifting," as Hill put it, in fear of what others might believe about me or of failing in some way. I determined if God said I was marvelous, I must be. I knew I essentially needed to transform the way I thought about myself. I wanted to fully participate in all that He had prepared for my life and to turn my back on fear. Considering I had spent most of my life directed by fear, this was not an easy task. As I mentioned, I was afraid of rejection, which led me to be a people pleaser so I could find acceptance. I also feared failure, so I rarely took risks or tried anything for which I wasn't confident I would succeed.

However, over time, I finally started to believe that I would never be alone in battle because Jesus was right beside me, and "the one who is in you is greater than the one who is in the world" (1 John 4:4 NIV). Soon I would be going toe-to-toe with the devil himself to fight against my worst fears. And unbeknownst to me, preparation for the biggest battle of my life was occurring. I began having prophetic dreams again. On Christmas morning, I woke up at 3:00 a.m. after having a dream in which there was a preteen boy with spiky blond hair. He was wearing a gold-colored rugby shirt and blue jeans. Unfortunately, I didn't recognize the boy or understand the significance of this dream, but I knew this dream was way more than a simple dream.

As Doug and I were walking into church later that morning, the McClurg family was walking ahead of us. The father, Aaron, was wearing a gold-colored rugby shirt and blue jeans, exactly like the clothes on the boy in my dream. I remember feeling perplexed at this revelation and pondered its significance.

During worship, God told me the dream was for Aaron, and he gave me an interpretation of the dream. I wrote the revelation of the dream as fast as I could, trying to capture every word. I was overcome with emotion, seeing God express His tender love and compassion toward Aaron. Tears fell faster than the words I was writing. Ink, water, and salt stained my paper, creating a swirling blue composition.

Once the service was over, I shared this word with Aaron and his wife, Nicole. I was surprised to see this broad-shouldered, well-muscled, burley, tough guy quaking like leaves on an aspen tree. Aaron was moved to tears as he took in how much God loved him through my message. When he gathered himself, he confirmed my word was congruent with what was happening in his life at the moment, so he believed what I shared was indeed a word from the Lord. This was a very powerful and moving moment; it seemed as though the tangible presence of God was felt as peace and joy filled our souls. I immediately felt our connection with Aaron and his family intensify.

On our way home from church, I remarked to Doug that I felt like I had recently walked into a new spiritual dimension. That night I had another dream, which pertained to Aaron accompanied by the interpretation of the dream. I wrote down the dream and interpretation to send to him but never had a chance to get it in the mail. It was quickly becoming obvious, though, that the Holy Spirit was moving in and through me in new ways, and I was overjoyed to be empowered in this way.

But even though I could sense a greater presence of the Spirit, I didn't sense anything necessarily foreboding on New Year's Eve day in 2011. However, sometime mid-morning, I had an overwhelming need to take my Christmas tree down. I never take my tree down until the sixth of January, my birthday, and the twelfth day of Christmas. I wrestled with this feeling. Yet, I found myself standing in front of the tree with ornaments in my hand, having removed them despite my reluctance to break tradition. *What's wrong with you, Tammy?* I put the ornaments back on the tree. There were more important things to be done, such as washing the dishes or tackling the mountain of laundry. However, I found myself back at the tree several times during the day, taking the very same ornaments off once again only to return them back to the tree. I finally gave in to this compelling urge and removed the remaining decorations from the tree. The evening arrived quickly, or so it seemed. I decided to wait until the next day to remove the lights.

The next day was New Year's Day. After enjoying a leisurely morning of reading and sipping coffee, it was time to finish taking down the tree. Knowing I would be busy with the tree for a while, Doug decided to take the dogs for a walk. As they headed out the door and up the mountain, I climbed up the ladder to begin the arduous task of untangling the lights from the branches of the towering tree. I was getting as good of a workout as it was with my many trips up and down the ladder. I really dreaded this part of the decorating process, but I couldn't have the joy of the beautiful tree without the drudgery of the dismantling process. This seems to be the paradox of life; we can't know love without loss, joy without pain, or rainbows without rain.

At last, the lights were off the tree and boxed up. I was sweaty from the cardio-inducing ladder climb. My fingers were sore from the pricking needles and sticky with sap. I was feeling a sense of accomplishment and puzzlement at the same time. It felt good to have the deconstruction process complete with the exception of taking the tree to the burning pile, but I still failed to understand my need to take the tree down a week earlier. It didn't matter, and dwelling on it wasn't going to change anything. Besides, Doug was back. I was anxious to get the tree outside so I could clean up the dry needles from the floor. I loved everything about the Christmas season, but I was always ready to get the furniture back to its "normal" place. It was finally beginning to feel like we may have a sense of normalcy in our life once again after the last two years of turbulence.

We each grabbed an end of the tree, hauling it out of the house. Then, we ceremoniously tossed the tree onto the burning pile. We paused, taking a moment afterwards to reminisce our Christmas tree party feeling grateful for the enjoyment it brought us and others. It was then that Doug told me with excitement dancing in his hazel eyes, he had an overwhelming sense God was going to do something huge in our lives in the next year. He described this overwhelming feeling as "extreme pregame jitters" or a "beyond butterflies" feeling. The next day, he said the same sense was still with him.

Little did we know, the following evening, January 3, 2012, he would be dead.

As I Breathe, I Hope

In September 2011, Doug had the opportunity to go to work for Industrial Technologies, Inc. doing demolition at Smurfit-Stone Container, a paper mill he had worked at for almost thirty-two years until it shut down unexpectedly in January 2010. Prior to September, he was working as a pipefitter/welder in Prudhoe Bay, Alaska, which required traveling out of state for weeks at a time. Neither one of us enjoyed having him away from home for so long. We know many couples who live this lifestyle and do well, but we were used to having a lot more together time. Doug was so happy and relieved to be working locally again, and I hesitated to tell him I had a very bad feeling about the work.

At the job site, he was using a gas-fired torch to cut large pieces of metal into smaller ones to be salvaged. He was going through coveralls rapidly because of sharp metals that would tear the cloth and hot slag that often burned holes in the fabric—and sometimes Doug. All I could envision was him being ripped apart.

January 3, 2012

Doug was working nights that week. I can't remember if we had talked earlier that evening, but I do remember getting a call and recognizing the phone number—it was Dan Vander Zwagg, Doug's co-worker. My gut knotted up as my brain rapidly fired suggestions of what this call could mean. The worst possible scenarios flashed across my mind in rapid succession like machine-gun fire, each scene being worse than the one before.

Doug and Dan were the only ones working the night shift. Dan ran the excavator while Doug was on the ground using a cutting torch. I hurried to answer, but our call didn't connect. As I was trying to call Dan back, his wife Katy's number showed on my caller ID, confirming my fears that something was wrong.

I answered her call, trying not to panic, but my racing heart and the nausea welling up indicated otherwise. She blurted out, "Doug has been hurt, and it is really bad!"

I could hear the anguish in her voice as she went on to explain that a sheet of metal weighing in excess of 300 pounds had fallen on him, pinning him underneath. His heart had stopped by the time Dan had found him, but the EMTs got his heart beating again with CPR. Doug was now on the way to St. Patrick's Hospital.

My legs felt like they had turned to rubber as I tried to take in the news. In a moment's time, my world slowed to a halt, but just as quickly, I felt a weighty presence envelope me, and I was overcome with a sense of peace and strength.

After I hung up the phone, God spoke to me in what I understood to be an audible voice. *Tammy, this will be the hardest journey of your life, but if you will trust Me, Doug will be okay.*

I knew I had a choice. I could either trust God to watch over Doug, or I could let fear take hold and control my outlook on the future. At this point, I had nothing to lose in trusting our future to the One who formed us from the dust and numbered our days. I was not going to allow the devil to defeat me with fear and discouragement. The verse 1 John 4:18 (MSG) filled my heart. "There is no room in love for fear. Well-formed love banishes fear. Since fear is crippling, a fearful life—fear of death, fear of judgement—is one not yet fully formed in love." After all, love is the perfect antidote to fear!

Before leaving, I called my mom to tell her the dreadful news, and we decided to meet up and make the rest of the twenty-six-mile drive into the city together.

> "It is great to be faced with the impossible,
> for nothing is impossible if one is meant to do
> it. Wisdom will be given, and strength. When

the Lord leads, He always strengthens" (Amy Carmichael).[7]

As I drove to meet my mom, I praised God for His will being accomplished in our life. As I was praying, my words changed into a dialect I have never spoken before. I thanked Him for all He was doing as His Spirit filled my car, and I had the most amazing time of worship and prayer. It was incredibly powerful! The peace and strength only increased, the farther I drove and the more I prayed. Every time my mind tried to go to the negative "what if" place, I kept reminding myself of all the great and wonderful promises of God. As I would soon find out, reminding myself of God's promises along with praise, worship, and prayer would be my lifeline. They all kindled my flame of faith.

My mom and I arrived at the meeting point at the same time. As I got into her car, we both commented how this was like déjà vu. Seventeen years earlier, my brother Eric was crushed by a piece of hydraulic railroad equipment, and just like Doug, he was unresponsive when they found him. After doing CPR, Eric was resuscitated and flown to the University of Tennessee Medical Center in Knoxville.

He was in a coma for thirty days with multiple life-threatening complications. His liver and spleen were damaged from laceration resulting from a railroad spike tearing into them. His lungs were bruised so badly the oxygen would not move through them, so he had to have ventilator assistance to breathe. Even with the ventilator assistance, it was doubtful his body would get enough oxygen.

The company Eric worked for sent a private jet to fly us from Missoula to Knoxville. The flight to Knoxville gave us a long time to play out the many possible scenarios of Eric's injuries and future. Thankfully, Eric survived.

Fortunately, the drive this night would not be so long. All we could do was hope God would give us another miracle.

Hospital to Heartache

When we arrived at St. Patrick's hospital, I told the receptionist who I was and whom I was there to see. I heard her say to someone, "Go get the chaplain." I immediately wanted to vomit as I struggled to swallow the bile rising in my throat. *Doug must have died before I could get here. I thought You said if I trusted You, Doug would be okay.* My faith sprouted wings and flew out the window.

When the chaplain came to greet us, he immediately ushered us into the special waiting room where Doug's employers, the Murrays, Dan, and the mill manager, Tom, were waiting for me to arrive. The chaplain then told us Doug was still alive. However, it was questionable if he would survive. He explained Doug was on his way to surgery for intubation[8] and PICC line[9] placement. In the meantime, we would have to wait for the surgeon to give us the latest update.

The surgeon stopped by before heading to surgery to give me an idea of what to expect. He said the CT showed a possible subdural hematoma, and the X-rays showed four broken ribs along with two old rib fractures. The surgeon did his best to appear optimistic, but it was obvious by the grim look on his face the outcome for Doug's survival didn't look good. Despite the news and all his injuries, I believed deep down there was hope for Doug to pull through. It was time to trust and firmly believe in the God of Heaven and Earth.

I was numb with shock, though. It was hard for me to see the grief on the faces of his employers and co-workers. Everyone was struggling with their emotions while trying so hard to be strong and keep their tears in check. I wanted so badly to take their pain away, to alleviate their suffering all while numbed by mine.

Family, friends, and our church family came to show support, offer encouragement, and pray for us. It was heartwarming and life-giving to see the family of God laboring in prayer on our behalf. At one point, the waiting room was full of people anxious for the news that Doug was stabilized, which would allow me to finally see him and get an update on his condition.

While we waited, the story of the accident began to unfold. Apparently, Doug was cutting a 4×11-foot sheet of metal, which was in a vertical upright position. The eleven-foot upright portion of metal was attached at a ninety-degree angle to the base, which was concaved. In essence, it was an upside-down "T." Except the "T" had a curve on the top instead of being straight. The metal stuck up like a mast in a ship, and the bottom piece may have been able to rock somewhat. No one knows for sure what happened, but Dan returned from the shop to find Doug lying on his left side with the eleven-foot sheet of metal on top of him.

Initially, Dan thought Doug was playing a trick on him by lying under the metal. However, he quickly realized that Doug was not joking when he saw that his face was purple, and his tongue was hanging limply out of his mouth.

Frantically, Dan attempted to extract Doug's lifeless body out from underneath the metal. Empowered by adrenaline, he was able to hoist the massive sheet of metal up and off of Doug. However, because it was still attached or hinged at the base, Dan was not able to move it away from Doug. Despite the superhuman strength created by the adrenaline, it wasn't enough to hold the metal up with one arm and pull 236 pounds of Doug out with the other arm. He wasn't Popeye, in as much as compassion compelled him. With his thoughts racing to find a solution. Dan quickly recalled he had seen the Frenchtown Volunteer Fire Department on site while returning from the shop. Realizing if he was to get the assistance of the fire department, he had no other option than to set the sheet of metal back on top of Doug. Begrudgingly, he did so as gently as possible and dashed off to get help.

It would seem, by divine providence, the Frenchtown Volunteer Fire Department had been called to put out a small fire at the paper mill where Doug and Dan were working. We were later told this fire could have been easily put out with a bucket or two of water or by the fully charged fire hose laying nearby. For reasons unknown, the security guard called the Fire Department to come and put out this small fire.

Dan caught them just as they were climbing into the trucks getting ready to leave. Panting heavily after his sprint, Dan managed to get the words out between gasps of air that his partner appeared dead and stuck under a sheet of metal. Someone immediately called for an ambulance while the rest of the crew ran to extract Doug's limp body from under the metal, at which time, they found no pulse or breath. They promptly began CPR while hooking him up to a defibrillator. His heart was responsive and restarted with basic chest compressions, but he was unable to breathe on his own. As soon as Doug's heart started beating, he started having seizures and continued as they transported him to the hospital by ambulance. It was estimated that Doug had been without oxygen for anywhere from five to fifteen minutes. The odds were stacked against him with very little hope for survival.

"And sometimes, against all odds, against all logic, we still hope" (Unknown).

Still Waiting

Our group waited anxiously for news on Doug's progress. Every half hour or so, someone would ask me if I was going to ask for an update. I calmly told them the best thing I could do was allow the doctors and staff to do what they needed to make sure he was getting the best care possible. Because of my medical background, I knew interrupting them would distract them from giving Doug their full attention and would not benefit any of us in the end. When they were ready for me to see Doug, they would come and get me. Nonetheless, the wait seemed like an eternity!

It was after midnight before I got to see Doug. I was told by the nurse I could take two additional people in with me. How could I make this tough decision with so many wanting to see him and be assured of his well-being? As his employer and friend, I felt Dave Murray, Doug's boss, needed to go with me for sure because he felt so responsible. I wanted him to have as much peace as possible. Doug's sister Connie, with whom he had a strained relationship at the time, was there as the sole representative of Doug's family that night. I made the executive decision, regardless of what had transpired between them in the past, she needed to see her brother that night.

As we walked into Doug's ICU room, I was astonished and relieved to discover he was not as ravaged as I had envisioned. As a matter of fact, he looked just fine! If it hadn't been for him being on a respirator and hooked up to all sorts of monitors and IVs, it would be hard to tell he had just been through a potentially fatal accident. This, combined with my experience in healthcare, made seeing him much easier than I had imagined.

"Hey, Dougie, it's Tam," I said as I walked into the room, not knowing what to expect. I wanted to assure him I was there, thinking it would comfort him. However, my voice alone caused him to react. I didn't even have the opportunity to give him a reassuring touch. Instead, I watched in dismay as my greeting was returned in the form of a seizure. His body violently spasmed, jerked, and bounced on the bed.

Despite watching him seize, which was awful, I was able to remain calm, trusting in God's promise that Doug would be okay. As the seizures continued, the doctors and nurses, in what seemed like unison, firmly and loudly asked me not to speak as Doug was so sensitive to my voice. This whole scene took a matter of seconds, even though it felt like slow motion. Though it was a good sign, he was able to recognize my voice, having seizures was obviously not good for his brain.

I believe it was at this point the nurses told me they would be starting hypothermia protocol on Doug. He would be covered with special cooling blankets, which would drop his body temperature significantly, thus allowing most of the blood to go to his brain instead of supporting the organs. Increasing the blood supply to the brain increases the amount of oxygen in the brain, which enhances healing. He would be kept "on ice" for twenty-four hours and gradually warmed back up to normal temperature. After he thawed out, the doctors would have a better idea of Doug's prognosis. With this information, I left his room and returned to the waiting room and sent Dan, my mom, and our pastor, Josh, to see him.

I was exhausted, and though many holding vigil with us had opened their homes to me, I knew I needed my own space to process the events of the evening. The animals would need to be fed, so I declined the invitations to stay in town and decided to drive back home instead. I knew I probably wouldn't get much sleep, if any, but at least I could shower, change clothes, and try to relax as best I could.

My mom returned from visiting with Doug, and I explained my thinking about heading home. She agreed to leave with me, but before we left, everyone gathered around us to pray. It was so comforting to have such a strong support network.

The ride home was cold and beautiful. The cloudless sky was filled with millions of diamond-like stars, all which glistened against the blackness of the night.

The animals were confused by my early morning arrival. Despite their confusion, I was greeted warmly by my furry family. I took great comfort from them as the dogs wiggled and squirmed for attention, barking with excitement to have me home. The cats wanted their fair share of attention as well, meowing in anticipation of treats while rubbing against my legs, hindering my ability to stay upright. After everyone was properly greeted, I went through the steps of preparing for bed.

Numb and exhausted, I finally crawled under the blankets. My body may have been worn out, but my brain was in overdrive. It was busy trying to find answers as quickly as possible. One solution would pop up, and it would immediately race off to find another. Sleep was elusive. My throat ached. The tears wouldn't come. My stomach felt like I had been kicked by a mule or as if someone was tying my intestines in tight knots. Still, no tears. I could feel nausea grow from deep within, eventually bringing forth nothing but bile. Wave after wave of retching, I attempted to purge myself of the grief I couldn't express in tears.

I was completely spent. In complete surrender to God with the future of my husband and my life, I finally dozed fitfully, tossing and turning. Dreams wove together as my brain continued to reconcile what had just happened.

Day 2

The next morning, Mom and I got to the hospital shortly before the shift change, and it was quiet and eerie without the usual hustle and bustle I was used to seeing during the day shift hours. A multitude of thoughts and emotions were racing through my head as we walked down the familiar hallways, a labyrinth, leading towards ICU.

Did I hear You, God? What if the hypothermia protocol didn't work? Then what? What if he dies? What if he is brain-dead? I don't know if I have the fortitude to pull the plug. He is an organ donor, so many might benefit from his death. He would like that—knowing his death gave life to others.

Thoughts like these plagued my mind, and they were weirdly morbid and comforting at the same time. My mouth was dry as I swallowed hard to push fear away. Mustering up the strength to face the unknown, I pulled my shoulders back and lifted my head as I pushed open the ICU doors. I was clinging to hope[10] as tightly as I knew how while praying for the gift of faith[11] necessary to walk the path being laid out before me.

When my mom and I got to Doug's room, he appeared to be contentedly sleeping. However, it wasn't long before his body would start to twitch, tremor, and spasm violently with seizures, his body bouncing on the bed. The nurses came racing in and gave him Propofol, a strong drug to paralyze him and stop the seizures. Apparently, the anticonvulsants normally administered to control seizures were not enough to stop the severity of the seizures he was having, much to the consternation of the medical staff.

His sedation afforded me time to sit quietly and pray by his side. I also got to visit with the many people who, one by one, made their way to Doug's room to support us with offers of help, prayers, and words of encouragement. Watching so many people break down in tears was difficult for me. I wanted to relieve their pain, particularly the tough guys', as they saw Doug lying helpless in bed, with tubes and monitors everywhere. Doug was a down-to-earth, hardworking, simple man, and it soon became clear he was loved by many. With this many visitors, my gift of hospitality kicked in thinking I somehow needed to take care of them in their pain. It was a great distraction in some ways, but there was no way I could continue at the pace I was going. My brain was rummy, and my body was far beyond tired.

The medical staff kept reminding me I needed to take care of myself, saying, "This is going to be a marathon, not a sprint. You need to be able to endure for the long haul."

I had no options other than to wait, pray, and trust the Lord for the very best outcome possible.

"She holds onto hope for He is forever faithful" (Unknown).

Defrosting

Day 3

At some point during the night before, the cooling blankets were removed from Doug's body to allow it to return to normal temperature. The plan was once Doug was thawed out, he would be taken off the Propofol paralytic early in the morning, and by eight o'clock in the morning, he should be responsive. Filled with hope and, admittedly, a bit of apprehension, my mom and I hurried to the hospital only to see discouragement and disappointment written all over the faces of the medical staff that greeted us. Apparently, when the medical team took Doug off the paralytic, he started to seize violently. So much for the hypothermia protocol! This was not encouraging at all. According to the doctors, this indicated the possibility of severe brain damage.

What now? God, what are You doing?

Thankfully, we were told the trauma team would be meeting with us at ten o'clock to tell us what our options were.

> "Someone's life may depend on what you believe"
> (Graham Cooke).[12]

There is nothing like a crisis to bring people together. Doug's employers Dave and Connie Murray, their son Kyle, Dan, and his wife Katy, and our family were becoming one big family. Dave Murray stood at the foot of Doug's bed in tears, begging Doug to come back. Dave told me he would be willing to trade places with Doug if at all possible. I watched and listened in amazement. God was molding lives through this event, and I could see the evidence all around me in visitors and staff alike. I felt like a spectator, watching others cry in their pain and on Doug's and my behalf.

All the while, I stayed dry-eyed. I was filled with equal parts of anguish and hope, hanging on to every promise of God's faithfulness I could recall. I found myself wishing I had been a bit more disciplined when it came to memorizing Scripture because I knew it could have provided more ammunition to fight this battle. Thankfully, I found God isn't concerned if we get the words right; what He is concerned with is the heart being transformed by the words.

It was time to meet with the trauma team to hear what our options were going to be regarding Doug's prognosis. My mom and I were ushered into another small drab room filled with the medical team responsible for Doug's life. I surveyed the room, recognizing some of the familiar faces I had worked with, hoping to find a glimmer of encouragement. Instead, I saw the exact opposite. I saw grief, resignation, and compassion.

The attending ICU physician finally broke the silence. His kind brown eyes looked so sad and tired. His dark mustache seemed a bit droopier than I remembered. The words he seemed reluctant to speak were so quiet. "Your husband most likely will not survive this accident."

I was sure I heard wrong. I choked out the response, "Excuse me?" in disbelief as I leaned closer to hear him say just slightly louder, "Your husband most likely will not survive this accident," a second time.

I inhaled violently in shock as my body recoiled from these grievous words. My chest felt as though my heart was being ripped out. My guts were tormented. I am not sure how I remained standing, but I did.

He continued, "In my opinion, having Doug seize as violently as he did after we woke him up is an indication of such severe brain damage that will most likely result in death. Even if Doug should somehow miraculously survive this traumatic event, he will remain in a vegetative state for the rest of his life."

This was not at all the diagnosis I had been expecting. This diagnosis was exactly in opposition to the words I heard God speak to me! *Didn't people live for months in a coma to wake up and do exceptionally well? Who is this doctor to say Doug will never live? Wrong answer!*

I struggled to breathe, let alone think clearly, as my exhausted brain attempted to process this horrific news. What I wanted to say to him was, "Get behind me, Satan," because surely this was not from God. Hadn't I heard him say that I needed to trust Him, and Doug would be okay? Had my imagination played tricks on me? I felt doubt creeping in like a thick fog, attempting to dampen my faith. After all, Eve herself succumbed to uncertainty when the serpent questioned her integrity by twisting God's instructions regarding eating fruit from the tree of knowledge of good and evil. "Now the serpent was more crafty than any of the wild animals the Lord God had made. He said to the woman 'Did God really say, 'You must not eat from any tree in the garden'?'" (Genesis 3:1 NIV).

My faith resurfaced when I heard the Holy Spirit whisper, *Trust Me. Don't give in to fear. Stand strong.* I pulled up my big girl panties and stood strong. I collected my wits, or what was left of them, and asked if we could get a second opinion remembering what I had recently read in *Outwitting the Devil.* Satan can and does use wonderful, highly educated, and competent people to do his dirty work.[13] I was confident this was exactly what was taking place. I was convinced the staff at the hospital were unwitting pawns in a game of life, death, and faith, but the attending doctor agreed to contact a neurologist to consult with us.

The Rainbow

How can I trust You to deliver Doug from a death sentence with the verdict I've been handed?

Trust Me, was whispered repeatedly in my spirit.

God, I know You are good in the midst of all of this. Just because what the doctors were telling me doesn't add up, it doesn't mean You aren't good. I know deep down I can trust You for the very best in our lives.

The Murrays came in from the job site to check in and tell us the guys Doug worked with had seen a short chunk of rainbow appear over the iron pile they had been cutting. These men, for the most part, were not what I would consider deeply spiritual men. They were hardworking and harder drinking fellas who believed this rainbow was a sign to them that Doug would be okay. What made this rainbow so intriguing was the sky was cloudy and grey all day long. There was no rain or sun around to create this rainbow.

In the Bible, God used a rainbow as a sign of his promise to never flood the earth again (Genesis 9:12). The rainbow was a gift to Noah for his faith and perseverance as he stood in the face of adversity, daring to believe in the impossible. Noah was willing to endure forty days and forty nights of torrential rain while never having even heard of rain. I believe because of Noah's tenacity, God honored him with a glimpse of His glory. This reminded us, we need to "hold fast the confession of our hope without wavering, for He who promised is faithful" (Hebrews 10:23 ESV). Perhaps this rainbow above the iron pile *was* a reminder to hold fast to our hope.

Still trying to process the grim words of the doctor while grasping for a glimmer of hope, I looked at my brother Eric. He was now standing in Doug's ICU room after his own healing seventeen years before. Recalling his and other people's testimonies of beating the odds helped me remain determined not to give up on Doug.

Lord, let it be done unto us according to Your will. I can and will accept dead if You need to take Doug home. However, I won't like dead much, but I know with Your help, I will get through the pain and loss. Father, I don't know if I can handle a vegetable, but if a vegetable is how Doug remains, then I will trust You for the grace to walk it out. But Lord, if there is any conceivable way I could have Doug back whole and in his right mind, please restore and protect him.

In my selfishness, I was more terrified of Doug remaining a vegetable than the thought of him dying. I knew my life would be greatly impacted if he was impaired in any way. I couldn't imagine spending the rest of my married days with him in a coma hooked up to life support equipment. Despite having made vows of "in sickness and health," the thought of spoon-feeding him and changing diapers multiple times a day wasn't appealing to me. As a result, I was very forthright and honest with God about my feelings and desires.

Ironically, Doug and I had recently discussed this very issue. He had been adamant, saying, "If I can't have the quality of life, I would much rather be dead." Knowing how strongly he felt about living a life with mental or physical limitations, I didn't want to be responsible for making any decision, which could possibly hinder his quality of life. As I tried to comprehend the complexity of our circumstances and our future, I kept hearing in my heart, *This is for My glory.*

Soon, I began to get a gut feeling that we would know whether Doug would live or die in twenty-one days from the accident. The powerful Bible story of Daniel was being played out in my mind. Daniel went before God in prayer and fasting on behalf of Israel and Jerusalem, seeking His mercy and forgiveness for their sins and rebelliousness. He patiently waited twenty-one days for the angel Gabriel to appear with the answer to his prayer.

I shared this unction freely with others, telling them I had the sense God was giving Doug an "upgrade on his hard drive," and once He was done, Doug would wake up. This got a lot of laughs because Doug had never been remotely interested in computers; give him a chainsaw, pipe wrench, or welder any day. But in my spirit, this made complete sense. If God was redirecting Doug, He would have to knock him down to get him to pay attention.

God is not above the hard way, particularly if He feels His children will benefit from the experience. "For the Lord corrects those He loves, just as a father corrects a child in whom he delights" (Proverbs 3:12 NLT).

While we were waiting for the neurologist to come, Brad, a friend from church, came to me and said, "Aaron McClurg called and wanted to know if he could come and pray for Doug." Aaron was the guy from my dream, so I immediately said yes because I wasn't about to turn down prayer. After all, you never know which one will tip the scale with the desired answer.

After receiving the call to come, Aaron arrived at the hospital looking rather disheveled. He appeared exhausted, his eyes red and swollen from crying. Aaron explained to me he was supposed to be at work, but after hearing about Doug's accident, he was overwhelmed with a burden to intercede for Doug's life. He had spent hours on his face in tearful prayer, unable to get off the floor for some time until the burden finally lifted from him.

Aaron explained to me that his father-in-law was in as critical of a condition as Doug was after having a stroke, but he couldn't pray for him with the fervency he had for Doug. Aaron's compulsion to pray for Doug was so strong he was unable to ignore it. He later told me he had never experienced such a strong conviction to pray for anyone ever before. And further, Aaron felt he was to lay hands on Doug and pray for him.

I expressed my gratitude to Aaron for his obedience and compassion as I walked him to Doug's room. Aaron practically grabbed the front of Doug's gown as if to get his attention as he prayed for him. He told Doug God was not done with him yet and commanded him to get back here. Aaron also prayed for "doctors with hope," and then he left as quickly as he had come. I marveled at the coincidence in which I had an encouraging word for Aaron two weeks earlier, and now here he was speaking life over Doug.

The arrangements were made for Doug to have a secondary examination This would be with a neurological specialist. When the neurologist on call who was to give the second opinion strode into the room, he confidently said, "It really disappoints me when doctors and people give up hope this early in the game. There is always room for hope."

Say what? Way to go, Aaron! Yay, God! I think all of us in the room let out a collective sigh of relief at the neurologist's optimistic outlook and declaration. My mom and I looked at each other as relief was expressed through our eyes. *He has no idea what he just said.*

I have nothing but absolute respect for the doctor giving the initial prognosis. His experience as a pulmonologist is substantial and was a critical component in Doug's care. However, Doug required a team to support his medical needs, and neurology was an essential part. I was reminded of God's promise in Proverbs 15:22 (TPT). "Your plans will fall apart right in front of you if you fail to get good advice. But if you seek out multiple counselors, you'll watch your plans succeed."

When we left the hospital that night, our hearts were filled with hope for a brighter future.

Glimpses of Goodness

As the days wore on and Doug remained unconscious in the hospital, good things came in the form of blessings from God. Neighbors stepped in to take care of our animals and plow the snow from our driveway. Flowers, cards, prayers, and gifts arrived from friends. We even received a gift basket with a beautiful note attached. It read, "We heard about Doug's accident and thought this might make your hospital stay a bit better. Signed, The Fishers. P.S. You don't know us."

We have yet to meet them in as much as we would like to, but they did not fully identify themselves, so we have no way of contacting them. The contents in the basket would suggest they, too, had experienced an extended hospital stay.

Day 8

The neurologist ordered an MRI of Doug's brain because he was perplexed as to why Doug was not responding to the tried-and-true treatments he had prescribed. The results from the MRI came back normal. Astonished, I asked him to repeat himself. He responded by repeating the MRI results were normal and showed no indication of anoxic brain damage due to a lack of oxygen, as thought to be the cause of the seizures, much to his surprise. He told me he would be contacting colleagues at Mayo Clinic for further insight due to the uniqueness of Doug's symptoms. He thought they may have more experience in this area than he had. As gifted as our doctors are, Montana's limited population does not provide the multitude of patient exposures, as do the much larger metropolitan areas.

My friend and sister in Christ, Sarah, worked the night shift in the hospital's ICU, so she offered to care for our dogs during the day. Each morning, I dropped my dogs off at her house before coming to the hospital and stopped by on my way home to pick them up. I usually gave her the update in the evening as to how the day had gone. When I got to the hospital the next morning before she got off shift, she would update me about how Doug did through the night.

One morning, Sarah approached me as I walked through the doors of the ICU, and said, "Tammy, the doctors and nurses have been talking amongst themselves, and they said they don't know how you have been able to maintain such a positive attitude during what must be the very worst time of your life. They also said you encourage them when they should be the ones encouraging you. Two of the nurses even said they saw an aura around you."

My heart swelled with joy as I realized in awe that others were recognizing the strength and peace I was experiencing as I allowed the Holy Spirit to work through me. God was indeed being glorified in the midst of my trial.

Sarah went on to say we both knew why I could stay so strong and positive when everything around me seemed to be so difficult. I thought to myself, *God, You have been telling me over and over this is for Your glory.*

Later, I read in *Jesus Calling*:

> As you live in close contact with Me, the light of My Presence filters through you to bless others. Your weakness and woundedness are the openings through which the Light of the knowledge of My Glory shines forth. My strength and power show themselves most effective in weakness.[14]

[/vc_row_inner]

I knew that what they were experiencing was the glory of God. As I pondered the significance of this, I was in awe that He would choose Doug and me, such broken vessels as we were. I was all too familiar with our shortcomings and my far-from-sinless life. Being an example for others to follow seemed like a daunting responsibility. But partnering with imperfect people is what He loves to do—He takes the broken and brings forth a restored vessel. It is through our cracks and flaws that the light of His glory gets filtered through so the world may see Him in us.

In one of His many messages to me during this journey, He said, *I have chosen you to carry My Glory to dark places. If you will allow Me, I will take you to places that you would rather not go, you can shine for Me there.*

He was right. This was a place I would have never chosen to go had I been given a choice, but His ways are perfect (2 Samuel 22:31). I knew He had Doug and me exactly where He wanted us.

Holding Out In Hope

Doug was still having seizures. Therefore, one of Doug's ICU physicians determined it was time to place a PEG tube into Doug's stomach to provide nourishment for his healing body. At the same time, a tracheotomy would be done to reduce the risk of infection. The PEG tube was placed, but we would have to wait a few days for the trach tube. It was my understanding both would be done at the same time, but I was now wondering why the doctors waited so long to insert the trach tube, so I inquired.

I was informed the doctors were hoping Doug would wake up, thus negating the need for the trach because once the opening is created in the esophagus, it takes a while to heal if and/or when the tube is removed. However, as gruesome as it sounds, one can breathe easier through the hole in their throat once the tube is removed than they could if they were to have to breathe through their mouth and nose. Thus, the dying process can be delayed due to the increased ability to take in oxygen.

If all efforts to save Doug's life had been exhausted and it was eventually determined Doug was going to remain in a vegetative state (or like a "rutabaga," as Doug puts it), and we then concluded the best option would be to terminate him, dying would take much longer with the trach opening in his throat. I reassured the doctor I had great faith that Doug would indeed pull through. Accordingly, I encouraged him to move forward with the trach placement.

Meanwhile, the neurologist and his colleagues came up with a solution to help with the seizures. In the words of this neurologist, they pulled an old antiseizure drug out of the archives, and Doug was responding quite well to it. What an answer to prayer to finally see Doug's body peacefully resting after days of continuous seizures.

Always looking for ways to bring levity to the situation. I told the neurologist that Doug was an old-school kind of guy and was technologically resistant, so it would make sense they would need an old drug!

Laughter is proposed to be an ancient medicinal remedy, after all.

Day 12

I called and checked in with Doug's nurse before going to church for the first time in two weeks. I knew my spiritual tank was low and in need of a fill-up. I was desperate for a time of corporate worship, knowing it would be the perfect remedy for my depleted soul along with the fellowship. I wasn't disappointed. Arriving at church, I was warmly welcomed and enveloped in loving arms of comfort and encouragement as my church family hugged me with exuberance. All were anxious for a current face-to-face update and for details to enable them to pray strategically.

I cried copiously during worship as the Holy Spirit ministered to my spirit. It was as though I was being removed from my burden and filled again with peace and joy. My tears were the words I couldn't formulate. In essence, they were a holy language unto God alone as I cried out to be refueled with His grace. In the words of pastor and author Dallas Willard, "Grace is God acting in our life to do what we cannot do on our own. Grace is what we live by and the human system won't work without it. The saint uses grace like a 747 jet burns gas on takeoff."[15]

I had been burning through a profuse amount of fuel in the last two weeks. Like a race car driver knowing he wouldn't be able to finish the race without a pit stop, I, too, knew I needed to get my tank filled up and tires replaced. This contest was too important not to take the time to refuel or to risk a blowout on a tire. I was planning on waving the checkered flag, not limping across the finish line, running on nothing but fumes and tattered tires. Refueled and "retired," I went to the hospital to check on Doug.

Day 13

I was pleased to find on my arrival that he seemed to be more alert. Dave and Connie Murray were there as well and agreed with my assessment, so I asked him to open his eyes, and he tried really hard several times. His brow furrowed, and his eyelids would move some, but not enough to open. We felt confident that hope was alive and well!

When the neurologist came in to check on Doug, he asked him to move his eyes, and he complied. Needless to say, we were all stoked, and we may have even done a happy dance! It was now day thirteen, and not only did Doug respond favorably to commands, he was off the ventilator, and another EEG came back with relatively normal results. The only concern the neurologist had was the EEG indicated some spots in the brain were not functioning as quickly as they had to. He said this might have been indicative of brain damage, but he believed Doug would be able to overcome these issues with time.

More encouraging news! Thank You, Jesus.

After getting a good report on Doug, I walked next door to Western Montana Clinic where I worked to check in with my supervisor and give her an update. As I was walking down the hall, my co-worker Becky came up to me with tears in her eyes and said, "If I ever go through something this difficult, I want to be as strong as you are."

I couldn't imagine suggesting this, knowing what it had taken me to become this strong in the Lord. Not wanting her to experience the pain and challenges I had gone through, I hugged her and said, "Do you? Do you really understand what you are asking? Do you have any idea what I have had to go through in my life to get to this place? Be careful what you ask for!"

When I stopped speaking, I saw a mental image of a huge sunflower. I felt the Lord speaking to me. *This is what they see, this huge radiant blossom. But not many understand the root system or stalk required to support something of this magnitude. The flower petals will soon wither, fade, and fall. The seeds will mature, ripen, and spread.*

The growth process would start over once again as the seeds gave way to tender new plants.

He was reminding me we all must die to ourselves to truly live at some point. By overcoming the challenges in life, we develop our character, gaining strength, perseverance, and experience to climb the next mountain in our path.

Later, I shared this revelation with one of my older female patients. She said to me, "Honey, I grow sunflowers, and let me tell you, very few of those seeds ever make it to the ground, the wild birds eat those seeds, and your story is feeding the wild birds!"

Tears formed in my eyes and rolled down my cheeks when I sat at my computer later that day. I felt the Lord's presence around us as if to confirm her words. Shortly after, I read that a person's testimony is a seed to the unbeliever confirming my understanding of God's plan for this all the more. He was continuing to sow seeds as He impressed me to contact friends to play worship music in Doug's hospital room.

Knowing our friends from church, Jim and Suzanne Hartzell, were gifted musicians and worship leaders, I reached out and asked if they would be willing to play for him. Delighted by my request, they came one evening to sing and play the violin and guitar for Doug. His room was full of visitors that night, in particular, Dave, Connie Murray, and their son Kyle as well as Dan Vander Zwagg. As they played, all joined the Hartzells in song, worshipping the Lord with all our heart, mind, and soul. Soon we noticed the hospital staff and other ICU visitors were congregating outside the door worshiping with us. As we continued our praise, the room was filled with the presence of the Lord.

When we finished, everyone had tears in their eyes, and no one spoke—as if we all feared interrupting such a holy and glorious moment. After waiting silently for a minute or two, I thanked everyone for having "church" with us. Right there, in the middle of tragedy, the Comforter came down doing what He does best, dwelling with us in the middle of our pain. He always comes alongside us to comfort us in every suffering so that we can come alongside those who are suffering as well. We can bring them this same comfort that God had poured out upon us. And just as we experience the abundance of Christ's own sufferings, even more of God's comfort will cascade upon us through our union with Christ (2 Corinthians 1:4-5).

Day 14

Doug opened his eyes partway when Dave Murray asked. We were so encouraged and excited he was responding. However, each time we told the medical staff about Doug's responses, they told us not to get our hopes too high because these were natural reflexes, and he needed to do more to confirm progress. Every time we reached what we thought was a significant response from Doug complying with our commands, we were usually told, "His response is good, but not good enough."

Later, the neurologist came in and asked Doug to open his eyes, and this time Doug didn't respond. The neurologist got extremely frustrated and told us he thought Doug was in a vegetative state—able to open his eyes, but not able to comprehend anything. Irritated, he stomped out of the room, saying, "In my thirty years of practicing medicine, I have never had someone fail to respond to treatment to the degree Doug is failing to respond."

So much for hope! I feel like he just poked a huge hole in my balloon. He has been so positive and hopeful with us. This isn't good, God, and You said if I trusted You, Doug would be okay. How could this be?

Wanting to hear a more favorable report, I turned to the nurse who also had been optimistic and encouraging about Doug's chances of recovery. From the beginning, she had told me Doug's strength was obvious. He was relatively young and obviously a fighter. If anyone, he had a good chance of pulling through. When I asked for her opinion, she threw her hands up in the air and backed away from me, indicating she wanted no part in the conversation.

"I am not asking you to diagnose Doug's condition, but I want your opinion based on your experience," I said.

"You are not listening to what we have been telling you," she countered. "Your husband is most likely not going to live, and even if he does, you need to understand that you will never have the man you married back. You are essentially in a living hell right now. You need to find the darkest spot you can, have a really good cry, then find the brightest spot you can and figure out how to live in between."

I have to admit, I was confused and angry by her response. I was quite certain I was not living in denial. I prayed silently for extra grace, knowing I wanted to explode in frustration so badly. I recognized it for what it was. The enemy was working overtime attempting to suck the rest of the air out of my balloon. I wasn't about to let them win this round. I thought to myself, *This sounds like fear and discouragement trying to work its way inside my spirit.* I countered back in my mind, "…the one who is in you is greater than the one who is in the world" (1 John 4:4 NIV).

Feeling God had made me bold for this situation, I took a deep breath, and as respectfully as I possibly could, I said, "I fully understand how bad this situation is; I have twenty-two years' medical experience. I trained as an X-ray tech in this hospital. I have worked in the ER, trauma, and ICU. I fully get it *here*," I said, pointing to my head. Then, I pointed to my heart. "But everything in *here* tells me Doug is going to live, and he is going to be okay. When *this* changes," pointing back to my heart again, "I will change my mind. But in the meantime, I am going to believe with every fiber of my being that Doug is going to be okay!" I stormed out of the room.

"Be strong and of good courage; do not be
afraid, nor be dismayed, for the Lord your God
is with you wherever you go" (Joshua 1:9 NKJV).

I was met by Dave Murray, who was in the hall. "How can you let these people treat you like this?" he asked with anger in his voice.

I looked at him and replied, "Don't worry about me. I recognize what is going on. The devil will use anyone he can to discourage me, whether they mean to or not, and I am not going to let him win this one."

I understood she was trying to help me, not cause me more pain. So many people live in denial when the time comes to let a loved one go. No one wants to suffer the painful loss of someone they love. I, however, don't believe in letting loved ones suffer in order to circumvent the pain of their loss. Not understanding my position, I know many hospital staff thought I was off my rocker and out of touch, but I had to rely on the Lord and my faith to stand firm.

> "As we unflinchingly take our stand on the naked promise, there springs up within us the 'faith of God'…which makes walking on the water a delight" (Dr. Lillian B. Yeoman).[16]

Day 15

I woke during the night with the feeling Doug's spirit had left his body. I felt empty and scared.

Is it true? Did he really die? Is he dead, God?

I hadn't heard anything from the hospital, but a sense of dread fell on me. Pushing fear away, I said aloud, "Let it be done according to Your will, Lord… Not my will, but Yours. I will do dead if dead is what You have for me. I am not going to like dead, but I will do dead. But I want him back as whole as he can be."

Again, I heard the gentle voice of God in my spirit. *This is for My glory.*

The next morning, I went to the hospital to find him still alive and breathing. Nothing had changed for the better, but nothing had gotten worse either.

I went to the trauma team and asked if they could help me make sense of it all. Originally, the neurologist told us there is always room for hope—that Doug should be able to overcome this minimal damage to his brain. But now, he said Doug was in a vegetative state. I needed answers.

Another one of Doug's doctors, who was a part of the trauma team, stepped away to talk with me. "I can't presume to know what the neurologist was thinking yesterday, but I believe Doug could continue to recover. However, there will likely be some limitations. All this will depend on the amount of damage to Doug's brain. In time, he will need to be transferred to a rehabilitation facility to regain his mobility. However, until Doug wakes up, we won't know what his outcome may be."

This doctor did not contradict the neurologist, but then I wouldn't have expected him to do so. In his compassionate manner, he answered as best as he could to provide me some comfort without giving room for false hope.

Whew! This certainly was much more encouraging than the last words I heard from the neurologist. The devil was doing everything in his power to discourage me, so I would have to hang on tightly to my faith.

Power Failure

Day 16

I finally took a day to stay home from the hospital and regroup. I was exhausted and in much need of some quiet time to think and take care of household chores. On top of all of that, we got twelve inches of new snow in the last twenty-four hours. Our neighbors, Terry and Dave, and my brother Eric all pitched in, taking turns plowing heavy snow from our mile-long driveway.

Being outside and doing some physical work was the medicine I needed to help relieve the pressure of the situation we were in. Unfortunately, however, I was feeling some new pressure bubble up since the furnace crashed. I woke to a chilly fifty-two-degree house. Thankfully, I had an old wood-burning kitchen stove I could use to heat up the house. It had belonged to my grandmother, and I learned to cook on it as a child. I designed my house around being able to use this old stove whenever the opportunity arose. Unfortunately, the old stove would only keep a fire for three to four hours, so the furnace would need to be fixed right away.

I could always set up a portable propane furnace to keep the animals and myself comfortable and the pipes from freezing, but I didn't want to leave it unattended during the day and run the risk of a fire. If I had to wait for the furnace to be repaired, it would mean staying home to keep the fire burning. Doug was in good hands at the hospital and would understand if I couldn't come to visit.

After calling around to schedule the repair service, I soon discovered many others in the area were having the same issue, and the furnace repair businesses were so far behind they wouldn't be able to come out for several days. I'd have to humble myself once again and ask for help. Oh, how I hate having to be a nuisance and bother others when I am not able to accomplish what needs to be done. I was feeling desperate. Even though I knew Doug would be fine without me, I wanted to be able to be there for him while knowing our house would be warm and wouldn't be damaged by frozen pipes. Desperate times call for desperate measures, or so they say. It was time to make some more phone calls.

After called my mom and explained my dilemma, she suggested I give her friend's husband a call who was a retired heating and air conditioning serviceman. Dick was more than happy to help out. He said, "I'll grab John Giffin and head out." John, a retired carpenter, is a dear family friend who has always been there for my family, especially the day he held my father's broken, bleeding body as he died on the mountainside after an ATV accident. Doug and John worked together at the paper mill for several years before John left to pursue his love of building houses.

Before John and Dick got to the house, knowing John's fondness for baked goods, I whipped up a batch of cookies as a small token of my appreciation for their prompt response and as an expression of my hospitality. They looked surprised and delighted by the gesture, saying, "You didn't have to make cookies for us. You have enough to do as it is. But we are glad you did, and we won't turn down your offer," as they eagerly reached for the plate of cookies I was holding. I jokingly said, "It's one of my love languages!" Cooking was a long-time passion, and it felt therapeutic to do something normal. My friends loved them and munched away as they fixed my furnace.

What a relief to have that off my mind. After a long and physically exhausting day, I slept soundly for the first time in sixteen days.

The next morning, the Murrays stopped by the hospital to see Doug. Then they dropped by to give me an update and check on me. They said Doug was looking around and pursing his lips like he wanted a kiss. We all laughed, feeling encouraged by his wily ways. Every day more and more of Doug crept out from behind the mask of injury. Undoubtedly, he was making tremendous progress; and yet, with every ray of light, there is always a storm cloud.

The next morning the hospital called to tell me Doug was seizing again. He had to be put back on the ventilator and was given Propofol to control his seizures. He had been stable for nine days. I had hoped we had gotten through the worst, but it appeared we were still in the proverbial woods. Every seizure increased the risk of more brain damage.

I wonder if my lack of support caused him anxiety? Even though I had only missed one day of being at the hospital, I felt guilty for not being there for him. It felt like I had failed to provide the care Doug needed. Within the first few days of the accident, we were educated about the healing properties of frankincense, especially for brain injuries. Frankincense has the ability to cross the brain barrier, helping to reduce anxiety inflammation and help with the oxygenation of the brain cells.[17] Because Doug's brain had been without oxygen for five to fifteen minutes, I thought this might be helpful for his healing. Therefore, I had been administering frankincense essential oil to his body to help with the seizures. I couldn't help but think it was my fault Doug was seizing. But if I've learned anything, it's that guilt isn't always rational in the midst of a crisis, but it will crush you whether it's deserved or not.

Always looking for an opportunity to do harm, it would seem Satan took the opportunity here to land one of his deadly darts.

> When we harbor false guilt, we become a malicious witness, not against our brother (Deut. 19:15-20), but against ourselves. Satan's name means adversary and accuser. He is the accuser of the brothers, and he will answer to Christ for his malicious accusations. (Rev. 12:10). When we accuse ourselves and bear false guilt, we are unwittingly imaging the evil one in the world. False guilt is one of the primary weapons of Satan's parasitic rival kingdom.[18]

[/vc_row_inner]

It would seem I had played right into his web of deceit. I hadn't failed Doug at all. In fact, by taking the time to care for myself, I was actually positioning myself to be of greater help than I would be if I ended up incapacitated due to exhaustion. Before I was trapped like a helpless insect intended for a spider's next meal, I knew I had to quickly eradicate myself from the mental snare the enemy was baiting me into. Jesus died for my freedom. It was time to pull the trump card and remind that slimy little devil, "Therefore, there is no condemnation for those who are in Christ Jesus" (Romans 8:1 NIV).

I had to quit condemning myself. I needed to free up my thoughts and emotions for purposeful use, choosing to hope once again. However, this battle was not going to be a short little scuffle. Instead, it was going to require hunkering down for the long haul after hearing of the fallout from the last bomb, which had been dropped.

After the last seizure, more discouraging news was shared with me. Doug developed pneumonia and a fever. He also had to have fluid removed from his lungs. Due to lack of mobility, he also developed blood clots in both calves despite every effort to keep the clots from forming. I had been expecting the blood clots due to my experience working in the medical field. Blood clots were a common occurrence in immobilized patients, so this was no surprise. Pneumonia is quite typical as well, but I was hoping and praying he would be able to avoid it. Even though I knew how customary these two vagrants were, I was extremely disappointed to hear they were now additional concerns to deal with.

Despite my strong faith to believe Doug could survive this accident, I knew every obstacle he had to overcome lessened his chance of recovery. My brain and heart were at odds with each other as I attempted to process the possibility of Doug having a pulmonary embolism (PE) due to the blood clots. If he experienced a PE, it may reduce the oxygen to his already oxygen-deprived brain or, worse, be fatal.

Pneumonia could lead to demise as well. The dark shroud of death seemed to be stealthily creeping in like a black fog. Faith whispered to me, *Despite how bleak it looks, keep trusting in the Sovereign One who separated the light from the darkness.*

Day 17

> Approach this day with awareness of who is Boss. As you make plans for the day, remember that it is I who orchestrate the events of your life. On days when things go smoothly, according to your plans, you may be unaware of My Sovereign Presence. On days when your plans are thwarted, be on the lookout for Me! I may be doing something important in your life, something quite different from what you expected. It is essential at such time to stay in communication with Me, accepting My way as better than yours. Don't try to figure out what is happening. Simply trust Me and thank Me in advance for the good that will come out of it all.
>
> Jesus Calling, January 20[19]

[/vc_row_inner]

Apparently, the Lord had plans I didn't know about, but then this is usually the case. As He waited for His inevitable destiny on the way to the cross, Jesus said, "Yet not as I will, but as you will" (Matthew 26:39 NIV). If Jesus could surrender His will to the will of the Father on His way to the cross, how much more should I trust the Father with our future. However, I have to confess, I wasn't sure I had the same fortitude at the altar of my sacrifice.

I was struggling. I knew I had a lot of people praying for me. I wanted to trust God to do His best through this, but I won't suggest it wasn't a battle every day because it was. My heart was so duplicitous. One moment I felt confident in my trust in God's work to restore Doug and keep His word to me that he would be fine if I trusted Him. But in the blink of an eye, the smallest setback could send my heart spiraling with fear and doubt.

I was reading in Job and was reminded of the need to endure. When Satan tempted Job in chapter 1, he killed Job's wife and children as well as destroying his livestock. Job was essentially bankrupt, mentally, physically, and financially. It seemed significantly more trying for him to lose his wife and his children than it was for me to sit in a chair in an exceptional care facility with top-notch doctors and nurses, providing my husband round-the-clock care. But there I was, struggling to surrender to the greater narrative God had written for us.

I knew God was sovereign. I knew He was good. And I knew He still performed miracles today, but I had no idea if He would grant us the miracle we so desperately needed if Doug was going to survive. I reminded God how He brought Job through his trial victoriously and even rewarded him significantly for his faith by restoring double for his loss. In an attempt to build my faith, I also reminded myself of how David killed the lion and the bear, which enabled him to kill the giant Goliath in the battle with the Philistines (1 Samuel 17:37). Surely, God could give Doug a miracle!

But just as quickly as those thoughts brought comfort, the devil was quick to torment me with memories of five friends who had died over the last few years despite the prayers of many. He insidiously insinuated my faith wasn't strong enough to spare their lives—and maybe it wouldn't spare Doug's life either.

What makes you think you're so special your husband will live? the devil whispered. Then he reminded me of a conversation my mom had with one of Doug's nurses about my brother's miracle. The nurse responded by saying, "Your family has already had one miracle, what makes you think you should get another one?" I know she was balancing the measure between a sincere question of how things work in the supernatural with sending a cautious message of the reality of our situation. And she was right to wonder and warn.

I, too, had to wonder if God would pour out that much mercy on our little family. And why us and not our friends the Jenkins?

Dave, who was just a few years older than Doug, had been battling cancer for some time and was losing. Dave had children and grandchildren who deserved to have their dad/grandfather as a part of their lives. We didn't have children or grandchildren who would benefit from Doug's survival. *God, this isn't fair!*

Another dear friend, Jill, died of Hodgkin's lymphoma just before her son turned three years old. I wrestled to believe if God hadn't spared Jill, who had so much to live for, why then would he possibly spare Doug? Unraveling the great mysteries of God's sovereignty was not for today, however. I had no doubt that Satan was trying to overwhelm my faith by using this nurse to pierce my hope in God.

In my heart, I whispered to God. *I am a daughter of You, the highest King, and if You want to grant me another miracle, You will!* I quickly commanded myself to soldier-like attention, squashing the "mosquitoish" droning doubts before they could distract me or infect me with their poisonous bite. This was not the time to let reality get in the way of the supernatural.

Shiver Me Timbers

The doctors determined the seizures Doug was experiencing were not actually seizures, which are the result of abnormal or excessive electrical discharges in an injured or scarred area of the brain.[20] Rather, they were "neurological shivers" or involuntary movements and were not worrisome. Doug was back to breathing on his own without the ventilator as the paralytics were discontinued. Slowly he started opening his eyes and looking around. From the huge sigh of relief I experienced, I must have been holding my breath for days. The Alka-Seltzer jingle, "Plop, plop, fizz, fizz, oh what a relief it is," was merrily dancing around in my head as hope once again bubbled up within me. Funny what goes on in one's brain.

Dave Murray kept vigil at Doug's bedside, manipulating Doug's hands and feet, hoping for a response. After watching the doctors test Doug's reaction to pain stimuli, Dave decided to play doctor himself. He twisted Doug's toes to see if he would respond.

Why yes, yes, Doug responded! His face flushed red as it contorted with pain and what could be perceived as anger. He jerked his foot away from Dave's tortuous grip.

Doug has always hated having his feet touched and this time, even with him being in a coma, was no different. Don't touch the toes! Intentionally inflicting pain by twisting the toes on a potentially brain-dead guy in a coma is probably incredibly wicked, but it was truly encouraging to see him react to pain because brain-dead people don't react to pain.

Then, he once again reacted to pain when he tried to pull away from the phlebotomist as she attempted to draw blood from his arm. Once she poked through the skin, she fished around with the needle, trying to locate a vein. All the while, his face contorted with pain as he tried to pull his arm away from her. Some moments, like this one, were difficult to watch as he suffered through the procedure with no way to communicate what he was experiencing. Anger began to boil up inside me as I watched her continue to fish the needle around in his arm. The urge to grab her and violently shake her was escalating quickly within me. *Can't she see how badly she is hurting him?* I wanted to inflict the same pain upon her. In my mind, she suddenly became a voodoo doll, and I was poking her just like she was poking Doug. I made a hasty exit from the room as I stifled the screams for her to stop. I was running out of grace.

Day 19

Doug seemed to respond and look around more than he had been up to then. The neurologist came in and told us he ran some tests, of which Doug responded to some but not others. "Doug's cerebral cortex is not engaging as it should. The cerebral cortex controls functions such as sight, hearing, smell, and sensations, and it controls higher functions such as speech, thinking, and memory. This part of the brain does not tolerate lack of oxygen well, and unfortunately, the kind of damage oxygen deprivation produces may not show up on an MRI immediately."

I replied by asking, "If Doug's cerebral cortex is damaged, why is he responding to our commands by moving fingers or toes, raising eyebrows, and opening his mouth?"

The neurologist replied quickly, "It is likely these responses are simply a natural reflex. The responses have to be a definite reaction to a command." This meant if we asked Doug to move his fingers or toes, it would count as a response to a command. Dave insistently said, "Doug responded to my command to open his mouth." The neurologist again indicated it was most likely a reflex we were witnessing, not an actual response.

We were once again frustrated, confused, and disappointed. Regardless of what the doctor's interpretations were, we were convinced Doug was responding to our commands appropriately.

However, it made sense from a medical perspective to not give false hope when Doug's outcome seemed so improbable.

By this time, Doug's naturally curly hair was getting long and disheveled. I was appalled at the large flakes of dead skin intertwined in his hair. He was in desperate need of a good shampooing at the very least. My cousin is a hairdresser, so she agreed to help me trim him up. Even though Doug's neck was cleared for fractures, he had a cervical collar to support his neck. Nonetheless, we were mindful of supporting his neck when we carefully removed the collar to shave the back of his head.

Up to this point, his face had been a greenish-gray color due to the infection his body was fighting. But as soon as the electric razor contacted his skin, it turned bright red, as if he had a bad sunburn. I don't know if the stimulation of the razor caused flushing or what, but the reaction scared me to death. I had never experienced anything like it when removing cervical collars from patients I had X-rayed. We immediately stopped cutting his hair. With trembling fingers, I frantically put the collar back on. Not knowing what else to do, we let him rest before proceeding to cut the hair above the collar. His face eventually returned to the hideous green color we had recently grown accustomed to seeing. And while Doug no longer seemed to be in distress, we sure were!

I could feel the fatigue and emotional drain taking its toll on me. I was irritable, frustrated, and I wanted to cry. Jaxon, our two-year-old Australian shepherd, needed more exercise than I could give him. My job-share partner hurt her back and couldn't work my shifts. I needed to pay bills, update the checkbook, and file paperwork. And, of course, I didn't know how I was going to take care of Doug, me, and everything in between. I was so overwhelmed, and it seemed like God was nowhere to be found.

God, I am not afraid of Doug dying, but I am afraid of him living or merely existing in a vegetative state for any length of time. I don't know how long to keep him hanging on before tough decisions need to be made. I have been able to remain strong in my faith, believing he will come out of this 100 percent intact. But the longer this goes on, the harder it is getting to keep the faith. I know You can heal him. But will You? God, if

Doug is not 100 percent healed, please give us the grace and strength to overcome whatever disability he may have.

God, I want to honor and glorify You, so is it wrong to ask for double portions of strength and grace? I feel quite selfish, wanting the answers sooner than later. I want my suffering to stop now! I am trying to remember that this is simply a moment in time compared to what You have for us in eternity. Yet Father, let it be done according to Your good and perfect will.

"My grace is sufficient for thee: for my strength is made perfect in weakness. Most gladly therefore will I rather boast in my infirmities, that the power of Christ may rest upon me" (2 Corinthians 12:9 KJV).

Day 21

"If I am ever to be raised up, it must be by the hand of God. God can do nothing for me until I recognize the limits of what is humanly possible, allowing Him to do the impossible" (Oswald Chambers).[21]

This was it. Day twenty-one. It was the day I had been waiting for. The twenty-fourth day of the first day of the month. The day when the angel Gabriel answered Daniel's prayer. Would this be the day I, too, get the answer to my prayer?

I was excited and anxious on my way to the hospital. To encourage myself and build up my faith, I quoted promises from God to myself over and over. *Father, I thank You that You are a good, good Father. You are Jehovah Rapha, the God who heals. I am believing You are going to heal Doug. Papa, You said to trust You. I have trusted You to the best of my frail, human ability to restore Doug's life. Will my little mustard seed of faith move this mountain? Jesus said, "You have not, because you ask not." Jesus, I am asking for Doug's life to be spared and for his brain to be intact. I am asking for a miracle, Lord. I believe You love both Doug and me. I am submitting to Your plan and purposes once again. I am asking all this in the mighty name of Jesus.*

When I walked into Doug's room, one of the trauma coordinators came in to speak with me. "Tammy, it's been twenty-one days, and Doug is still in a vegetative state. He most likely won't ever improve from the state he's in. Our team believes he needs to be moved to a long-term acute care facility."

My heart nearly beat out of my body. I felt the blood drain from my face as a cold sweat began to break out all over my body.

Bile began to form in the back of my mouth as I fought the feeling of nausea well up. *What on earth is going on?* This was not even remotely how I envisioned this day playing out.

"I know this is disappointing, to say the least, but the staff here thinks the long-term acute care (LTAC) facility in Post Falls, Idaho is the best place to send him. However, if you want to keep him in the state, there is an LTAC in Billings. It was implied the care in Post Falls was superior to that of the LTAC in Billings. We just need to know today where you want to send him, so you'll need to make the decision today."

My head was spinning, I wanted to vomit, and my heart was screaming. *God, You said if I trusted You, Doug would be okay.*

I managed to respond to the trauma coordinator, "It is too soon to make this decision."

"Again, I know this is hard, but you *have* been informed prior to today that this day may come if Doug failed to improve. Unfortunately, today is the day the decision needs to be made."

My thoughts immediately went to my brother. He had been in a coma for thirty days but woke up mentally intact. Doug would, too—he just needed a chance. I had thirty days' worth of faith in my pocket I wanted to cash out. I wanted Doug to have thirty days to heal. In my way of thinking, if thirty days worked for Eric, they should work for Doug as well. *Right?*

"I would like Doug to remain in ICU for thirty days. I need some time to make the best decision for Doug." Transferring him to Post Falls would put him 179 miles away, and it would require me driving west over two mountain passes on I-90. Driving over high mountain passes can be treacherous during the winter. The steep road banks and many twists and turns can turn deadly when covered with ice and snowpack. Blizzarding snow and fog were other factors I didn't want to think about. Envisioning having to navigate less than desirable road conditions while traveling in what I imagined would be a state of anxiety and exhaustion in no way appealed to me.

Billings was even farther, with 340 miles east and three mountain passes to negotiate. Of the two options, clearly, Billings was not the best one. If the care in Billings was not of the caliber desired by

Doug's medical team, there was no reason to waste my time or risk my life by driving further.

My thoughts raced, trying to figure out the best option for transportation to and from Post Falls, Idaho. Which vehicle would serve me best for these long drives? My 2000 4×4 Suburban had accumulated a lot of miles over the years as well as wear and tear over the gravel pothole-filled roads on which we live. It needed some repair work. Our 2005 Honda Civic gets great gas mileage, but if the roads are precarious, I won't be comfortable in such a small vehicle.

And besides transportation, how will I work and be available for Doug? Who will care for the animals when I travel? How can we afford this?

I think I staggered out of ICU like a drunk where a social worker was waiting for me. She gave me her condolences. Then, cutting to the chase, she asked me, "What would Doug want?"

"Well, ironically, we talked about long-term care decisions for one another just days before the accident, and we both decided we didn't want to live if we couldn't have the quality of life. The quality, to us, is far more important than the quantity of life because, as Christians, we know we will be going to heaven, so why prolong the inevitable?" She nodded thoughtfully. "Doug was so fit and physically strong that his nickname was Hercules, and there is no way Doug would want to live for any extended length of time in a coma. I am also certain that any limitations will be a challenge for him mentally. I cannot imagine a future for him where he won't be able to do the things that were most important to him before the accident."

I was not at all prepared for her response. "Doug won't recover enough to be the man you married, Tammy. Terminating Doug is totally reasonable under the circumstances. Yes, he is breathing on his own, but he does have a PEG tube, which will have to be pulled, and he will eventually either starve to death or die from lack of oxygen."

Her opinion was no different than any of the others. I'm not sure why I thought it might be different, but I sure wished it was even slightly more hopeful.

"I think it's too soon to make this kind of decision."

"Well, if you send him to an LTAC, they will most likely not allow you to terminate him there. I heard you say you do not want him to live long-term in a vegetative state, so you will need to make the decision today."

But God, I trusted You, and You said he would be okay.

I spent the rest of the day in shock, praying, and agonizing over what to do. I couldn't believe after all we had been through, it had all come down to this. I was so sure I had heard from God, but it felt like I hadn't.

The devil was faithful to remind me the voices were all in my head. *You only thought you heard from Him,* reverberated in my mind.

Friends and family all tried to support and encourage me the best they knew how. Many said they would not want to live as a vegetable for the rest of their lives. Others said they had heard of people who had been in comas only to wake up in their right minds. I still had no definitive answer for the biggest decision of my life. Time was shrinking while the weight of the world was crushing me.

Not even his family had an idea of what to do. Doug's sister Connie told me she and my mother-in-law, Peggy, trusted me to make the right decision for Doug's life. But how could I make the decision to terminate the man I loved?

Oh, God, where are You? What do You want me to do?

If I did end Doug's life, how would I tell everyone who was waiting for a miracle? Dave and Dan had done so much to save Doug's life. How could I look them in the eye and tell them their effort wasn't enough? I believed it would haunt them for the rest of their lives. This was too big a burden for them to bear.

I knew Dave wouldn't be willing to give up yet either. He sat at Doug's bedside and talked to him. He massaged Doug's hands, arms, feet, and legs. He begged Doug to wake up and prove the doubters wrong. He told Doug jokes, and at one point, Doug even seemed to respond appropriately with a laugh. Wasn't this a glimmer of hope we had to hold onto?

The day gave way to evening, and, interestingly enough, no one from the hospital came to me and asked me about my decision. *Maybe the staff is just giving me the gift of a little more mercy...and time. Or maybe God is making us invisible for this moment in time. Perhaps He is here working in the unseen.*

My family, the Murrays, and several others were back in Doug's room, still trying to come up with the right decision, when a pastor friend who was visiting from Mexico stopped by to see us with a pastor friend of his. They had traveled a long way that day and came directly to the hospital to pray for Doug. And though we knew we people were praying all over the world, this confirmation brought incredible comfort. What a blessing it is to belong to the body of Christ. You don't have to know someone to pray for them; you simply need a willing heart.

While Lee was there visiting with us, another doctor came by to check on Doug. This doctor was Doug's pulmonologist for asthma when he was first diagnosed in 1995 and recently retired from ICU rotations on December 31, just three days before Doug's accident. However, being the very dedicated doctor he is, he came to check in on Doug multiple times a day.

He could tell something was wrong the moment he entered the room. "What's wrong, Tammy?"

"I was informed Doug will have to be moved to an LTAC or be terminated." I held my breath and searched his eyes, hoping he would think this was as crazy a predicament as I thought it was.

"It's *way* too soon to make this decision."

I exhaled and felt a rush of comfort wash over me.

"In my opinion, Doug needs to be kept here for thirty days before a decision of this kind can be made. There are too many variables at play before then."

I wanted to throw my arms around him in a bear hug. I couldn't believe it. "Thirty is my number! Years ago, my brother had been in a coma for thirty days before he woke up!"

"I will do everything in my power to ensure Doug is not moved until the thirty days are up."

I stood up to thank him for his offer to help, suddenly my brother and Dave Murray were bellowing behind me, "Tammy, he's awake! He's awake!"

Bill and I turned from the doorway and rushed to Doug's bedside. He *was* awake. Twenty-one days after the accident, on the twenty-fourth day of the month, and almost to the hour from when he died, Doug woke from his coma.

Ever-faithful You are, God! I did hear You correctly! Take that, Satan!

I believe all of heaven and earth were rejoicing at Doug's great awakening!

His room was a flurry of activity and celebration, and family, friends, and staff marveled at this incredible miracle. Of course, the medical staff immediately began examining Doug to evaluate his abilities. It was quickly confirmed that this was not a natural reflex. He was truly awake, right on schedule. Now, we would just have to wait to see if he was in his right mind. My heart was bursting with joy at God's faithfulness to bring sunshine on the other side of darkness.

> "But I know, somehow, that only when it
> is dark enough can you see the stars" (Martin
> Luther King, Jr.).[22]

I believe the stars twinkled like the finest diamonds in the black sky that January night.

The Great Awakening

Day 22

The next morning, I walked into the ICU with many questions, but before I could get to Doug's room, his attending nurse practically ran to greet me. "The neurologist stopped by and said Doug would not be going anywhere until we can reduce the anticonvulsants he is taking. The level he is on is so high Doug wouldn't have been able to respond even if he had wanted."

Apparently, the trauma coordinator and social worker had not read the neurologist's note about this in Doug's chart. Why else would they have told me he was essentially a vegetable and it would be okay to terminate him? In the midst of all that was happening, I had forgotten a conversation with this neurologist days earlier, informing me of the anticonvulsant reduction plan.

As we know from reading scripture, Satan tempted Jesus after He had spent forty days in the wilderness (Matthew 4). Satan has no problem twisting the truth or withholding facts. I believed this was another incident in which good and caring people were pawns in the devil's plan to try to destroy our lives. However, God, as always, had different plans!

> "'…For I know the plans I have for you,' declares the Lord, 'plans to prosper you and not to harm you, plans to give you a hope and a future'" (Jeremiah 29:11 NIV).

As I recalled my earlier conversation with this neurologist, I realized how close we had come to making a life-ending decision, and it was only through divine intervention I didn't.

> Through the valley of the shadow of death, God, in His faithfulness, restored my soul and led me on the path of righteousness. His rod and staff were there to comfort me as I sat at the table with my enemy, but God anointed my head with oil, and my cup was more than half full. It ran over! Surely, goodness and mercy were right there with me and will follow me all the days of my life, and I will dwell in the house of the Lord forever.
>
> Psalm 23²³

[/vc_row_inner]

Many times, I have been told God will never give you more than you can handle. Perhaps that is true, but I also know after reading the story of Job, He has no problem allowing the enemy to push us to the edge the cliff; to the very point where we are hanging on by nothing but our fingernails. One by one, they break until we get down to the last broken, bloody nail before He steps in to show us it's all about His perfect timing, not our perception of what His timing should be.

Jesus, as my nails are broken down to nubs, I have nothing left of myself to offer You except for complete surrender. I thank You for the grace and strength to hang on as You take me farther on this journey. I thank You for teaching me to trust You in greater measure as each new obstacle presents itself. One by one, we are taking down the giants keeping Doug from the promised land. I thank You there is a land of milk and honey on the other side. I thank You for restoring what the locusts have eaten. I thank You for wisdom and a spirit of revelation every step of the way.

I finished praying and walked into Doug's room to find him awake. He locked eyes with me and looked at me as if to say, "Where have you been?"

My heart melted. Doug's spirit was in there just as I had hoped. He was unable to speak as he still had the tracheostomy hole in his throat, but the love expressed through his eyes required no words. It was as if I could feel the arm of God wrap around my shoulders, pulling me in for a reassuring hug. The whisper of *I told you if you trusted Me, he would be okay* was a gentle reminder of His faithfulness. I was overcome with a mixture of awe, joy, elation, relief, and giddiness. I leaned over his bed to give him a welcome back kiss since hugging was difficult, given the remaining tubes connected to his body. Even though he was awake, he was having difficulty getting his extremities to move for the first time in twenty-one days.

And even though the anticonvulsant medications had been reduced enough that Doug was able to wake up, he was still receiving a mega-dose that would need to continue being tapered down as long as he didn't have any more seizures. With such a high dose of medication pulsing through his body, his responses were slow for the time being. Even so, when my friend Barb Jennings came in to check on us that morning, I told her about the birthday cake I made for Doug earlier in July, and he was appropriately grinning from ear to ear.

Doug was working in Alaska at the time and would be coming home days before his fifty-second birthday. I usually threw him a big party and made an extravagant cake, so I asked him what kind of cake he wanted for his birthday this year. He wanted chocolate, which was no surprise because it's his favorite. I can make a chocolate cake in my sleep, so a chocolate cake was no problem. During our next phone call, however, he asked if he could amend his cake order to add raspberry filling in his chocolate cake. I readily agreed knowing that would be easy as well. Soon, though, he was back home and sheepishly asking me if it would be possible to have raspberry cream cheese filling for his cake. I had never made a raspberry cream cheese filling, but being a bit of an adventurer in the culinary department, I was more than willing to accept the challenge.

I must say, the filling turned out spectacular, garnering raves from all who partook. By now, this ever-changing filling had turned into a joke between us, and to see Doug, laying in ICU grinning in response to the story, thrilled me to pieces.

Thank You, Father! How can I ever express my complete gratitude for what You have done for me? Please forgive me for the times I doubted that You would come through for us. Help us to shine Your glory for the world to see Your love through our lives. Jesus, help us steward this miracle well, never taking for granted this gift You have extravagantly bestowed upon us.

Transitions Ahead

Day 23

It was time for a transition once again, but the transition would not be to an LTAC facility. Instead, Doug was being transferred from ICU to a regular hospital room directly across from the nurse's station, where he would be closely monitored. Apparently, they had heard from the ICU team what a prankster he could be and that he would require close supervision!

Dave Murray spent four hours with Doug in his new room moving body parts while asking Doug to move what he could, which wasn't much. However, he smiled a lot in response to questions and even raised his eyebrows in response to a statement, which was made.

During the twenty-one days, Doug laid in a coma, his muscles were rapidly wasting away. This once Herculean man could not even lift his hand to scratch his nose. Doug had "bat wings" under his arms instead of the bulging biceps and triceps like he'd had only weeks before. The stubble of his unshaven face couldn't hide the obvious changes; it had become thin, gaunt, and pale. He had gone from weighing 236 to 186 pounds. It was heartbreaking to see my gallant white knight laid so low. I wanted to spend every minute possible helping him get back on his feet.

Now back at work part-time, I used my break periods to check on Doug. He was fairly alert and responding with his eyes. Fifteen minutes flew by. Before I left, I put lip balm on his dry, cracked lips. He waggled his eyebrows, winked at me, and puckered up for a kiss! I swooned.

What a flirt! And his sense of humor was very much back. I could see we were all going to be in for quite a ride as he got his bearings back.

> Give up the illusion that you deserve a problem-free life. Part of you is still hungering for the resolution of all difficulties. This is a false hope! As I told My disciples, in the world you will have trouble. Link your hope not to problem solving in this life but to the promise of an eternity of problem-free life in heaven. Instead of seeking perfection in this fallen world, pour your energy into seeking Me: The Perfect One.
> It is possible to enjoy Me in the midst of adverse circumstances. In fact, My Light shines most brightly through believers who trust Me in the dark. That kind of trust is supernatural: a production of My Indwelling Spirit. When things seem all wrong, trust Me anyway. I am much less interested in right circumstances that in right responses to whatever comes your way.
>
> Jesus Calling, January 26[24]

[/vc_row_inner]

Father, this is a lesson I am learning quickly. One would think having Doug in the hospital for twenty-four days fighting for his life would be enough. But no, I must also deal with the furnace not working and the alternator and battery dying in the suburb. I need to figure out how to go back to work, spend time at the hospital with Doug, and take care of the house, the animals, and myself. Yet, in all of this turmoil, You, Father, have given me the peace, "which surpasses all understanding" (Philippians 4:7 ESV).

I guess it is Your peace, which is enabling me to cope with these many distractions. I feel Your presence guiding me in every decision. Yes, I do have some uncertainty and frustrations as to how all this will work out, but I am not walking in fear. I am choosing to lean into You and Your promise to be there for me every step of the way. Looking at the situation with my limited understanding, I can tell I will need Your help every step of the way. Help me to magnify You. Holy Spirit, I ask You to direct me from this very moment. I pray once the drugs are completely reduced, Doug will be whole, or at least whole enough he will be content to live with what You chose to bless him with.

I kept a journal for Doug to read when he woke up, letting him know what was taking place each day. My journal for January 26 read:

Yes, you continue to get better. It is so encouraging to see the twinkle back in your eyes. They speak volumes, as do your smile and eyebrows. I am sure you have lots of questions like many of us. I can't wait until you can talk again or even write. As for now, we are thrilled to see your face react. You are starting to move your neck and shoulders more. You have moved your arms a bit. You even looked like you were trying to move your legs tonight.

I talked to your nurse before I left tonight, and she said she had something to show me. She brought me your medical chart to look at and told me the neurologist is so impressed by your progress that in your medical chart he wrote "Wow" across an entire page! She said pretty much anyone in the hospital who knows your story is totally blown away by the progress you are making. I am certain "Wow" is not in the medical dictionary; and yet, yay, God. You are going to be okay, just like God said.

I am not surprised by this. Rather I am thrilled and humbled by God's faithfulness. I felt from the beginning that God was going to do something big through this event. I am confident lives are being touched in ways we could never imagine. As I came into the hospital this afternoon, I was overwhelmed with emotion as I recognized what a privilege we have been given to be chosen by God to share His love and grace with others. You may not feel this way right now as you heal from this trauma to your body, but I believe that when you get to see the whole picture, you will agree.

My mom came in to see you for the first time in five days, and you puckered up for a kiss from her. She was so excited she practically crawled into bed with you to kiss you. She said she would kiss you as much as you wanted whether I was looking or not! We all had a great laugh!

When we got to your room earlier, two of the respiratory therapists were marveling at how far you had progressed in such a short time. One, in particular, was so excited. He said, "Dude, this is amazing!" He gave me high fives and hugged me. Corey Kaufmann, another respiratory therapist, told me ICU is abuzz with talk of your recovery. He himself was amazed at the miracle God is doing through you.

Today you seem tired and more emotional. I am guessing, as you become more alert and aware of how much strength and coordination you have lost, you are finding it overwhelming and terrifying. I can sense fear and discouragement in you today. I am so sorry I can't fix it for you. I am grieved as I watch you come to grips with the reality your body is no longer capable of doing what you were once accustomed to. The physical strength you have always counted on is not available right now. You are much like Sampson after Delilah cut his hair. Maybe we shouldn't have given you a haircut after all! I have faith you have what it takes to get back the muscle you used to have. You're more than a conqueror.

Having lost our dear friend and pastor, Steve Valentine, five years earlier, I knew I needed wisdom and counsel, which comes from seasoned warriors, to lean on and encourage me through this battle. Our friends Steve and Pam Jackson stepped up to fill the role. They had been pillars of strength for me during this time.

Knowing the Jacksons had done missionary work with Heidi and Roland Baker, who supernaturally feed hundreds of orphans and have seen the dead raised, I felt they would have the kind of faith I needed to tap into to see my dead man fully raised.

Recalling the story of Abraham's faith being tested by God as he was asked to sacrifice his long-awaited son, I felt compelled by faith to put Doug's life and our future on the proverbial altar. I bowed my head, holding my hands out in surrender. *Father, I am placing Doug on the altar and will accept Your will for our lives. By faith, I trust You for our outcome, and I am submitting to Your will.*

As Abraham was preparing to plunge the knife into his beloved son's body, he heard, "Don't touch him! Now I know how fearlessly you fear God; you didn't hesitate to place your son, your dear son, on the altar for me" (Genesis 22:12 MSG).

I shared with Steve and Pam how I put Doug on the altar, telling God I was prepared to do His will. Pam said, "Tammy, Doug is your Isaac. Just as God provided the sacrifice to take Isaac's place, if you trust God with Doug's life, He will provide a way out for you as well."

Lord, let it be so! Father, I pray I may pass this test as well as Abraham. Doug is making great progress so far. Father, help him stay strong in spirit and willing to persevere regardless of what challenges lie ahead. Even though he is waking up, interacting, and getting some movement back, we still don't know if there has been any brain damage or paralysis. I know in Your awesome power You may have preserved him. Yet in Your wisdom, You may limit him for Your glory. After all, You left Jacob with a limp after he wrestled with You as a reminder he had been touched by You. You also blessed Jacob and gave him a new identity reflected in the name Israel. "Your name will no longer be Jacob, but Israel, because you have struggled with God and with humans and have overcome" (Genesis 32:28 NIV). It would seem we both are wrestling with You now. Doug for his life and me to believe I can fully trust You and be willing to glorify You regardless of the outcome.

Unfiltered

Journal for Doug on February 1:

Yesterday was a huge day for you. Your spinal MRI came back normal! I have been so terrified ever since I took the cervical collar off to cut your hair. Irrespective of how careful I was with your neck after removing it, I worried I may have done some damage to your spinal cord. Even though I knew at the time the radiologist had cleared your neck for fractures, and you didn't need the collar for protection but rather support, I still had this nagging fear I had possibly damaged you in some way. Satan relentlessly and repeatedly whispered this accusation in my ear. I knew in my heart it would be my fault if you had any long-term consequences associated with a spinal cord injury. Thank you, Jesus, for the great news! What a relief.

You also got your trach out today. This was obviously terrifying for you. You were white as a sheet and sweating profusely as you struggled to figure out how to breathe without the opening in your throat. It was hard to watch you battle fear and not be able to do something to help relieve your distress. I couldn't even stay to provide emotional support because I had to go back to work. When I came back, you were sleeping hard. Who knew breathing normally would be so exhausting?

Sue Stanley and Carolyn Demin stopped by to see you. You were having a challenging time making your vocal cords work. You would move your mouth, but nothing would come out. Apparently, they got lazy during your twenty-one-day long nap. You could laugh fine, to which everyone was more than willing to contribute, but you couldn't get the words to come out.

I told you that you were going to have to figure out how to talk soon because I had been doing all the talking for the both of us for the last month and had used up all of my words telling everyone about the accident. Your response came in a forceful raspy whisper, "Bull$@%#!" You repeated it for emphasis, reminding everyone I never lack for words. Your vocabulary was a bit more colored than usual in the presence of the polite company. This initially concerned me a bit as I considered that your loss of "filter" may be indicative there could be some degree of brain injury that hadn't been originally detected prior to regaining your voice. But as colorful as your vocabulary was, it was music to our ears. It was just one more sign Doug Dove is alive and doing remarkably well.

Today when I came in at eight o'clock, you were awake and told me, "This is a weird place to be in, and I need to get out of here." Sometimes when I talk to you, you make perfect sense, and other times, you are way out there. But I have to remind myself that your body and brain have had a huge insult. You are still on mega-doses of medication too. We are so happy to have you alive and talking; we really don't care if you always make sense right now. It is rather funny anyways to listen to what you come up with.

One time when Dave Murray was in the room, you looked at him and said, "What's the protocol, Mr. Murray?" Dave looked puzzled, as was I. We were struggling to make sense of your question. Dave laughed it off and said, "The protocol is for you to get well, Douglas." Another time after Dave had been talking about a log chipper, you said, "Let's go cut some #$%*-ing trees!" You've never had a squeaky-clean vocabulary, but prior to the accident, you were always careful with your words. Dropping f-bombs is not something you normally do and again gives me a reason to be concerned about possible brain damage. You love to cut down trees more than just about anything else, but you've never been that enthusiastic before.

Speaking of enthusiasm, I am beyond overjoyed that you have been able to stay here in Missoula. It looked as though I was going to be dealing with mountain passes to visit you if you had been transferred to an LTAC. However, God had other plans, and instead, you will *be at Providence Rehab located at the foot of the mountain, with I-90 running west to Post Falls, ID, and east to Billings.*

Jesus Calling was on point once again:

> Follow Me one step at a time. That s all I require of you. In fact, that is the only way to move through this space/time world. You see huge mountains looming, and your start wondering how you're going to scale those heights. Meanwhile, because you're not looking where you are going, you stumble on the easy path where I am leading you now. As I help you get back on your feet, you tell Me how worried you are about those cliffs up ahead. But you don't know what will happen today, much less tomorrow. Our path may take an abrupt turn, leading you away from those mountains. There may be an easier way up the mountains than invisible from this distance. If I do lead you up the cliffs, I will equip you thoroughly for that strenuous climb. I will even give My angels charge over you, to preserve you in all your ways. Keep your mind on the present journey, enjoying My Presence. Walk by faith, not by sight, trusting Me to open up the way before you.[25]

[/vc_row_inner]

Day 30

Father, as I read the words from Jesus Calling yesterday, I was so encouraged. In some ways, I feel as though Doug and I have been scaling these same cliffs. Yet, when I look ahead at the rehab Doug will have to go through, I know there are going to be days of great frustration for both of us. I am not sure what is worse, waiting moment by moment for clues he might survive or watching him struggle to speak and move his body parts.

While waiting to see if he would survive, my brain was busy building different scenarios. One in which he would wake up like Sleeping Beauty, and life would be happy ever after. Another where he is limited in some capacity. And still another to the far extreme where he never wakes up but remains in a vegetative state for the rest of his life.

Watching him struggle to put words together and repeatedly ask the same question multiple times in the course of minutes makes it difficult to converse with him normally. As he works tirelessly to regain his physical strength, I wonder if he will ever be able to return to the things that brought him joy, like cutting firewood, taking long walks in the woods, or skiing. As his body twitches and jerks, I try not to give way to fear that the outcome will be less than desirable.

It really doesn't matter how enormous the mountains may seem or whether the outcome is not quite what we expect as long as we keep our eyes fixed on you. Holy Spirit, I need Your help today. I am not feeling as great as I could be. If I get sick, I won't be able to spend time with Doug or work this afternoon. Please infuse me with Your healing power that I may be well.

Journal to Doug on February 2:

When I got to your room, the nurse told me you would be moving to The Providence Center where you would begin rehabilitation because you are improving so quickly. You are truly improving by leaps and bounds. Your physical therapist, Tammy, came in today and was able to get you into a sitting position on the edge of your bed. You managed to sit with assistance for about ten minutes. It is so difficult to comprehend how simply sitting for such a short time could be so exhausting for you when you were able to work tirelessly for hours doing hard physical work before you got hurt. Nonetheless, we are blessed you were able to sit for ten minutes today.

I went to work the afternoon and had errands to run, so I had to leave. No matter where I go, there seems to be someone we know who asks how you are doing. It takes me much longer to get things done because I am spending so much time telling your story. However, I am so blessed to know how many people care about us and are praying for us. It also gives me the opportunity to give God the glory.

Day 32

Journal to Doug:

Yesterday was a milestone for you and all who have stood beside you on this journey. At 2:45 in the afternoon, you were transferred from St. Patrick's Hospital to The Providence Center to begin your rehab journey. Prior to the transfer, you had an EEG. When my mom and I got to the room, you seemed agitated and were twitching a lot. Apparently, the anticonvulsant levels were low enough your brain was agitated. Accordingly, they would need to be adjusted for you to get some relief.

It was so discouraging to see you like this. I know without trial and error, the doctors won't know how much medication you need, but I was concerned you may end up having a full-blown seizing episode as I watched you jerking, twitching, and agitated. You appeared to be absolutely miserable. My heart was aching as I watched you suffer. Finally, I couldn't take it any longer and had to leave. God, in His faithfulness, was quick to comfort me by reminding me to trust Him. I am trying to keep my eyes on the unseen while I watch you struggle to regain your mental and physical well-being.

"A new day will dawn on us from above because our God is loving and merciful. He will give light to those who live in the dark and in death's shadow. He will guide us into the way of peace" (Luke 1:78-79 GW).

Seek My face, and you will find not only My Presence but also My Peace. To receive My Peace, you must change your grasping, controlling stance to one of openness and trust. The only thing you can grasp without damaging your soul is My hand. Ask My Spirit within you to order your day and control your thoughts, for the mind controlled by the Spirit is Life and Peace.

You can have as much of Me and My Peace as you want, through thousands of correct choices each day. The most persistent choice you face is whether to trust Me or worry. You will never run out of things to worry about, but you can choose to trust Me no matter what. I am an ever-present help in trouble. Trust Me, though the earth give way and the mountains fall into the heart of the sea.

Jesus Calling, February 5[26]

[/vc_row_inner]

Journal to Doug:

On a brighter note, I took some things back to ICU today and spoke with one of your doctors and some other staff. They were quite pleased to hear of the continued progress you are making. Several of them teared up with joy. They said it was obvious to them how important it was for a patient to have such strong positive support when faced with a life and death situation as you were. They believe your mental and physical strength, the strength of my faith and positive attitude, as well as that of many others praying for us, is what pulled you through the impossible. I am learning quickly that knowing the God of the impossible certainly has its benefits!

Inch by inch, you are moving forward. You have been standing with assistance and transferring back and forth to a wheelchair. Now you are exhausted, and so am I!

Your occupational therapist, Bill, who was working with you, is also very impressed by your story and recovery. In his twenty-four years of neuro rehab, he felt your progress was far beyond normal recovery expectations. He sees great potential in you and for your future. Wow again!

You are making such great advancement with God's grace and excellent care. I am once again reminded that I must remember to care for myself. I feel guilty when I am not able to spend all my time with you because I can see how much my presence means to you. However, I can feel the toll beginning to wear on me as I have tried to be available for you as much as humanly possible while still caring for the animals and our home. Try as I might, it can be difficult to battle the anxious thoughts that assault me when I allow myself to slow down. Sleep has been difficult as I ponder our future. The nagging possibility of you having more seizures seems to delight in robbing me of sleep as well. My big girl panties might be sagging a bit as I attempt to fight this battle in my own strength instead of trusting in the One who contends for me. As has been the case so far, once again, *Jesus Calling* seems to have been written just for me.

Deadman Walking

Day 42

On day two of our journey, John, one of Doug's ICU nurses, handed me Doug's wedding band, which he had removed from Doug's swollen finger using dental floss to compress the tissue, allowing the ring to slide off before it became impossible to do as the swelling in his body would undoubtedly increase due to fluid retention. I had been wearing Doug's ring on a chain around my neck ever since. Doug would look at the ring as if he was trying to figure out why I had his ring, and he didn't. I would explain to him why I was wearing it; however, in his compromised state, the explanation didn't stick.

On Valentine's Day, I arrived with a gift. The nurses were busy in Doug's room, having just transferred him from the bed into a wheelchair. I walked in, got down on one knee in front of him, looked into his eyes while holding out his ring, and said, "Since we were married until 'death do us part' and you were technically dead, I wasn't sure if our marriage contract was null and void or not. But just in case it is null and void, I was wondering if you would marry me again?"

Doug's face split with a huge grin as he shoved his hand toward me with extended fingers, shouting, "Yes!" Tears trickled down both of our eyes as he pulled me toward him for a hug. The enormity of the blessing we received by his living was felt in every fiber of our beings.

"The way to love anything is to realize that
it may be lost." (Gilbert K. Chesterson).[27]

The hug was a bit awkward with him sitting in the wheelchair and his body twitching with excitement. But it felt so normal to have his arms around me once again, to feel the warmth of his body next to mine. To experience this closeness, this oneness, I could easily overlook the awkwardness. With great approval, the attending nurses clapped and cheered as they, too, shed tears of joy with us. There wasn't a dry eye in the room.

Day 47

How thrilling it was for me the day before to arrive at rehab and find Doug up and walking! Who would have thought a man who was dead for five to fifteen minutes, a man the medical community was certain would never live, let alone wake up from a vegetative state, was now up and walking? Doug was suspended in a harness from a lift on wheels (This is a type of device that is capable of providing lift and walking assistance for patients learning to walk again. It allows them to bear weight, but the harness prohibits them from falling. It is somewhat like a walker used for babies, but on a much larger scale.) He was able to walk 300 feet while being supported, while bearing 50 percent of his weight during this first walk. When I arrived, his physical therapist asked him to walk towards me while totally bearing his own weight. He was able to walk in the walking device, bearing all his weight another 100 feet. I was cheering him all the way. I was so proud of him and greatly encouraged.

Trying to simulate tasks that Doug would normally do in his job, his occupational therapist had him unbolt a wooden box that was designed specifically for this exercise and then bolt the box back together again. This exercise was to help redevelop dexterity and coordination in his hands and fingers. It also engaged the cognitive region in the brain. He was able to put wing nuts on a bolt. The PT and OT teams were very impressed by his dexterity and fine motor skill use. As his physical strength improved, he was able to get out of bed without lift assistance and started standing to transfer into a wheelchair. Slowly but steadily, he was regaining his robustness.

The nurse practitioner came by to take his PICC line out (the catheter, which provided prolonged intravenous access). She said his PEG (percutaneous endoscopic gastrostomy) feeding tube was scheduled to come out on March 9 or possibly sooner. He was cleared to eat and drink anything he wanted as he would no longer need nutritional support through the feeding tube, which was inserted directly into his stomach by cutting a small hole in the tissue in the abdominal wall. He couldn't wait to have real food once more. It was time for me to start cooking his favorite foods again.

Day 49

While we rejoiced at Doug's progress, we were quickly reminded of how far he had come when my mom ran into a nurse friend who saw Doug the night he was admitted to the hospital. After seeing the dire condition Doug was in, she told my mom she wouldn't have given two cents for his life that night. I must confess, much to my surprise, her comment made me furious. Was I being self-righteous in my faith? Had I not heard the audible voice telling me to trust? Was I really in denial?

Perhaps it was my fear that the more people who doubted his ability to survive created less and less chance that he would survive. It was as if I somehow thought the more people who believed he wouldn't live had the power to sway Almighty God. I had to wonder if I had enough faith myself to overcome all those who were doubting and to stand in faith against those whose experiences contradicted a more optimistic outcome, thereby threatening to sink my little dingy of faith. I believe this was God's way of reminding me who was in control. Perhaps in hindsight, it was a revelation showing me how much my faith had evolved as I spent time reading His word and in prayer drawing close to Him.

Abraham was considered a friend of God, and he petitioned God to spare the city of Sodom and Gomorrah for ten righteous people (Genesis 18:32). I don't know if I was considered a friend, but as a believer in Jesus, I knew I was considered a daughter of God. In my limited thinking, daughters usually hold more sway than friends do with their parents. I was willing to draw on my position as a daughter of God and believe He was more than capable of restoring Doug's life to whatever level He felt was appropriate.

In retrospect, no other opinion truly mattered. Doug had already far surpassed the expectations of those with years of medical wisdom. They were providing the best medical counsel in their experience. I am in no way discounting the integrity and experience of the medical staff caring for Doug, but it was obvious to me they had limited exposure to medicine, according to the Great Physician.

It became clear to me, my battle was not with flesh-and-blood enemies (not that the medical staff were truly my enemies, even though at times it didn't feel as though they were on my side), but it was "against evil rulers and authorities of the unseen world, against mighty powers in this dark world, and against evil spirits in the heavenly places" (Ephesians 6:12 NLT). I recognized these little barbs were a distraction meant to create division—a key tactic of the enemy to divide and conquer. I held no animosity toward her or any other medical person's opinion. They had years of medical experience and spoke directly from what they knew to be true. The nurse who once wouldn't have given two cents for Doug's life then, now marveled at his progress, reminding me how very faithful and trustworthy God is. I do not have to understand or agree with His ways to know the Creator will always do what is best for His creation.

> Faith is more than a belief in God. It is also a way of life. Faith is the belief that God is real, and that God is good. It is a choice to believe that the One who made it all hasn't left it all and He still sends light into the shadows and responds to questions of faith. Faith is the belief that God will do what is right.
>
> Max Lucado[28]

[/vc_row_inner]

Days 50-51

Doug was expending mass amounts of energy while working to regain his strength. His brain and body were healing from the trauma and required lots of rest. He quickly realized how much he took for granted physically. Merely chewing food took effort! Never having been one to sit or lay around much, he was surprised by the great need his body had for sleep at this time. Despite this, his spirit was excellent, as was his humor. He was keeping the nurses and staff on their toes, and he continued to be the guy with the largest number of visitors!

Doug progressed from walking in a harness with lift support to using a standard walker (the kind older folks tend to use when necessary). He was now able to walk 164 feet. When he wobbled a bit, he was able to right himself with only 40 percent assistance from his physical therapist. He even climbed stairs for the first time since his accident.

His physical therapist told me he had been working in this field for a long time and therefore was usually able to calculate a patient's progress closely. Doug, however, exceeded his expectations. He continued to thrill the rehab team with his exceptional progress and positive "can do" attitude. Upon hearing the PT's assessment, Doug's response was, "All I know how to do is put one foot in front of the other."

I am so grateful and relieved Doug was blessed with the opportunity to live and exceed the expectations of the medical community. I believe even in our modern-day lives, we all need these kinds of miracles to encourage us and cause us to think outside of the box and color outside of the lines from time to time.

In reading the Bible, we are shown God's omnipotent power as He performed miracles time and time again. How quickly we forget God's great deliverances in our lives. How easily we take for granted the miracles He performed in our past.

David Wilkerson [29]

[/vc_row_inner]

Through modernization and the industrial revolution, as humankind, we have become rather self-sufficient and independent. We no longer need to be delivered from plagues or towering giants in our first-world living.

But even today, we still have sudden inopportune deaths, illnesses, financial crises, and a myriad of other circumstances that would benefit from a miracle. For many, it seems they have forgotten that God is still in the miracle-working business and therefore do not ask for one at all. Or they have such little faith believing God is no longer able to provide a miracle. They must have forgotten or not read the promise in Malachi 3:6 (NLT), which says, "I am the Lord, and I do not change." We would be wise to remember this today. We have the God who never changes, who knows every hair on our head, and who is aware of a single sparrow falling to the ground and clothes the lilies of the field. Will He not grant us everything in His power necessary for our well-being?

Sometimes our well-being requires suffering. Yes, I say "suffering." I know you are probably thinking that facing suffering and enjoying well-being seem to be contradictions. However, if He sees that suffering will cause us to draw closer to Him, He will allow it in our lives. He will allow a loved one to die what seems an untimely death or some other form of devastation take place in our lives.

Lysa Terkeurst sums this up perfectly in her book, *It's Not Supposed to Be This Way*:

> But here's the craziest thing of all. God doesn't want you or me to suffer. But He will allow it in doses to increase our trust. Our pain and suffering isn't to hurt us. It's to save us. To save us from a life where we are self-reliant, self-satisfied, self-absorbed, and set up for the greatest pain of all...separation from God.[30]

[/vc_row_inner]

Out of His abundant, extravagant love, this gracious God of ours wants us to know (to be intimate with) the miracle-working power of His love. He desires to exceed our expectations and empowers us to do the same while transforming us in the process.

Jeffery Tacklind explains in his book, *The Winding Path of Transformation*, "It is a sobering realization that new growth only comes at great cost. It is out of seasons of suffering that new life begins. Only when we've weathered storms do we see more clearly."[31]

It ages us, this cycle of growth. It steals away our naiveté, and yet it need not be replaced with hardened callouses. When we've suffered well, we grow. When we die to ourselves, we are reborn. When we give up the need to be right, the truth is resurrected. This is the pattern of transformation. Death and resurrection. The need for rebirth. In that process of death and rebirth comes something new and greater. It is transformation.

In Doug's transformation, he had an unexplained capacity to overcome all odds to utter amazement of his medical team. I am guessing his natural report card may have read, "Exceeds Expectations." However, I am convinced his supernatural one reads, "Well done, good and faithful servant." With grit, sweat, tears, faith, and grace, Doug took what was left of his life and his body and began the work of reformation. Crushed but not destroyed, his body, mind, and spirit were being meticulously restored in the perfect timing of the One who created him from the beginning.

Due to his exceptional improvement, we were optimistically planning an outing for the four hours he got to escape Rehab. He was very excited to come home for the first time since the accident, and the plan was to have a celebratory meal with the Murrays and Vander Zwaggs. I hoped he wouldn't be so exhausted from the excitement that he would fall asleep in his garlic mashed potatoes. Not having had children, I imagined this must have been what it felt like to bring home a new baby!

I was reviewing his hospital menu with him and asking what he thought he might want for lunch that day. His response was a sarcastic, "Remind me what I am having for dinner tonight." I was assuming he wanted to make sure he wasn't going to pick something for lunch that he would be choosing for dinner, so I began reiterating the dinner menu, but he stopped me, saying, "Why then would I care what I eat for lunch?" He obviously preferred my cooking to what he was being served at the hospital, and he had little interest in lunch. Dinner had fully captured his attention, and his sense of humor was sharper than ever.

Doug was in for a big surprise on the ride home. Several of our neighbors took it upon themselves to organize a "Welcome Home Brigade." That evening on the drive home, Doug was greeted for several miles by many friends and neighbors who were standing along the roadside with brightly colored, hand-lettered signs declaring their love and encouragement. Some even rang cowbells with great enthusiasm. Others cheered while waving to welcome him home! He was moved to tears by all the warmth and support. I wasn't sure who got more out of the experience, Doug and I, or those who were able to see a miracle produced through their participation in prayer.

As we made the long drive home, he tried to choke back the tears rolling down his hollow cheeks and onto his jacket. "I am just a guy, nobody special. Yet they all turned out to welcome me home. Tammy, why would all these people come out to see me? I am just a guy. I am just a guy."

As the miles went by and the people continued to greet us, Doug was even more overwhelmed. "Why would all these people come out to see *me*? Who am I? Why would they want to see me?" I tenderly explained to Doug that he had somehow impacted their lives in ways he didn't understand. He may not have believed he was a person of significance, but these folks and God obviously thought differently and wanted him to know it.

Dinner was a tremendous success. Apparently, my cooking still agreed with him as he ate more that night than he usually ate in two days at the hospital. He said rather woefully, "Having a wonderful meal tonight makes the dry hash browns and overcooked eggs I'll receive tomorrow morning even less appealing."

Someone then asked if he would rather stay home than go back to rehab. Understanding what was best for him and necessary for recovery, his immediate response, "The only way I am going to get stronger is to go back." I was grateful and relieved he recognized his need for continued therapy. At the rate he was improving along with his determined attitude, I was fairly certain he would soon be 100 percent Doug. It was so remarkable to see more of him come back day by day. This confirmed to me, once again, that Matthew 19:26 (TPT) is true when it says, "But what seems impossible to you is never impossible to God!"

Day 59

Given the success of Doug's first trip home, he was quickly granted another get-out-of-jail-free card. We learned quickly that normalcy is a critical component in recovery. The more normal we could make his life, the quicker he would most likely respond. Doug soon made another trip home. Not knowing how frequently this would happen, we were quick to jump at the opportunity. Apparently, he wanted to spice things up a bit this time and ordered a hot pepper cheeseburger. He was looking forward to some peace and quiet. He greatly appreciated the little things like the cat snuggled on his lap and burgers hot off the grill.

The sun was shining on the trip home, glistening on the freshly fallen snow. It was breathtaking, particularly when compared to the sterile surroundings of the rehab center. The water ouzels, otherwise known as the American dipper birds, were standing on the rocks in the creek. They were singing their mellifluous song as they enthusiastically bobbed up and down. I have always marveled at this drab grey-brown nondescript bird who was gifted with such a magnificent song. Its song brought tears to my eyes and joy to my soul as I listened with wonder at the beauty created by such an unseeingly source. And a bald eagle soared next to us as if it was ushering us along. Doug's spirit seemed to be soaring right along with the eagle. He was grinning from ear to ear, and I could see the mischief dancing in his eyes once again.

Twenty-nine years of marriage gave me time to know Doug much more intimately than anyone else. Some of you may have heard the term "intimacy" defined as "in-to-me-see." Intimacy grants us the privilege to know another person in ways not afforded to others. I knew him as a man who was fiercely passionate about the things he believed in. He was extremely dedicated and disciplined, but he also loved to laugh. And being relatively young, healthy, and exceptionally strong, he was quite confident in his own ability to overcome most adversity. In fact, there were moments he lived with a somewhat cavalier attitude as though he was invincible. However, I was now seeing a very serious side of him, which wasn't there before the accident. Having conquered death, he appeared to have gained much greater appreciation and respect for life. It was as if he realized he may never be given another second comeback chance, so he needed to live each moment for all it had to offer. He had always had a "glass half full" attitude, but it continued to increase as he continued to get stronger.

Doug was quick to express his appreciation to all who had helped him in his recovery. He was looking forward to a physical therapy field trip back to ICU. His PT helped him walk into the unit using his walker to greet all those who had a hand in saving his life. He was a bit shaky at first due to what I believed to be stage fright because he wanted to make his PT proud, as well as show off to the staff.

He was also rather apprehensive because he knew the visit would be very emotional for him. As expected, there were lots of tears and hugs. Despite their former reservations and lack of hope for Doug's survival, the doctors, nurses, and medical staff worked tirelessly in caring for Doug. And now they were receiving a huge pay off for their efforts. So often, for many patients, their story doesn't turn out this well. Others simply don't think or have the time to return to thank those help as they are anxious to return to "normal." The medical staff said Doug's recovery had helped renew their faith to believe others could live despite the odds.

The next stop was to visit the staff who took care of him in a regular room on the fourth floor. This, too, was so encouraging. The general response was, "Wow! You look like a million bucks!" And I have to say he was looking quite dapper, partly because I trimmed his hair and his bushy eyebrows and gave him a good shave.

His jeans were also two sizes smaller, and he was down a shirt size. I suppose a fifty-pound weight loss will do that. In my opinion, all that could have made his look complete was a little sunshine to bring the color back into his face. I offered him a little bronzer, but he didn't appreciate my suggestion.

In addition to this wonderful day, Doug was given notice that his days in rehab would come to an end on March 15, barring any unforeseen obstacles. This meant I would need to prepare the house, and there would cease to be medical assistance a holler away!

Even though Doug hadn't had any seizures in two months, the thought of him having one at home lingered around in the back of my mind. Our house was miles from medical help, and all the what-ifs began to play out in my imagination. As well as he was doing and for as strong as he had gotten, he was still a long way from where he had been before the accident. He would have to make it up two steps into the house without a handrail for assistance.

In addition to caring for him, I would still have firewood to pack, snow to shovel, dogs to walk, and other miscellaneous chores. I also realized my sleep would be compromised at times to be available for his needs. I would have the additional responsibility of his care once he was home. He would be participating in outpatient therapies, which would mean multiple trips into town each week. I could no longer come home and relax as I had been when I knew he was well cared for at the hospital. His homecoming, as monumental as it would be, would create further testing of my faith and ability to walk in grace.

The Last Two Weeks of Rehab

Doug made his first visit to our church since the accident. This was an incredibly emotional time for all as Doug was face-to-face for the first time since returning from the dead, with numerous friends and fellow churchgoers who had prayed for him. Many had not been able to get to the hospital to visit and were eager to see him. Everyone was absolutely amazed at how remarkable Doug was doing, all because of God's grace and faithfulness. Once again, there were tears of joy.

Doug assured all who would listen, "As hard as this journey has been, I wouldn't trade it for all I have learned in the process and the impact it has had on the lives of those touched by it." He went on to explain how even though he perceived he was a relatively humble person prior to the accident, he now understood he wasn't even close to understanding humility until he had to rely on others to meet his every need after waking from a coma.

My heart swelled with pride to hear him honor God instead of spewing forth anger and bitterness, which could have easily been the case as the significance of his limitations became more obvious. We both were humbled by God's favor in choosing him to be the recipient of a life-restoring miracle and the grace to walk the journey to healing.

> "My grace is always more than enough for you, and My power finds its full expression through your weakness." So I will celebrate my weaknesses, for when I'm weak I sense more deeply the mighty power of Christ living in me. So I'm not defeated by my weakness, but delighted!

For when I feel my weakness and endure mis-
treatment—when I'm surrounded with troubles
on every side and face persecution because of my
love for Christ—I am made yet stronger. For my
weakness becomes a portal to God's power.

2 Corinthians 12:9-11 TPT

[/vc_row_inner]

Dead seemed to be about as weak as one could get. It was
through death God chose to demonstrate His power once again. No,
Doug did not die on a cross, but it was because of the One who did
that Doug was made to be a portal for God's unlimited power and
was raised to life again. In restoring Doug's life, the faith and hope of
both of us and many others were revived and quite possibly enlarged.
Individuals came to us exclaiming how they had been ready to give
up on their faith because their prayers had gone unanswered. But
after seeing Doug's life restored, they decided to put their faith back
in God, trusting His will for their lives. In the moments like these, I
could hear him whisper a gentle reminder, *Remember when I told you
this was for My glory?*

"For everything comes from Him and exists
by His power and is intended for His glory. All
glory to Him forever! Amen" (Romans 11:36
NLT).

God was indeed getting the glory.

After church, Doug wanted to go out to lunch. It was our first
date since his accident and a most welcome return to a somewhat
normal existence. While he was enjoying the change of scenery and
socialization, he continued to reiterate the need for him to be in
rehab for as long as necessary for him to get stronger. I am certain
I let out a sigh of relief. Yes, he had come a long way in regaining

strength, but he was, in my opinion, in no way ready to be home. His brain may have suffered damage, but it wasn't a total loss, he was very high-functioning. He refused to be a victim, which was of great comfort to me. He was a victor—the new poster boy for overcoming adversity—according to his medical team.

Day 66

A week after his last trip home, Doug fell in the rehab. With so much progress and increased confidence, he apparently took it upon himself to go to the bathroom without calling for nursing assistance. He said, "I was walking along, and before I knew what was going on, I was about a foot from the floor."

Fortunately, he did not hit his head as he fell into the wall and onto the floor.

As he laid on the floor and eventually crawled to a chair, he had plenty of time to think about how foolish he had been. This fall put a good and needed scare into him. He was now thinking twice about what he was doing. He said, "It is hard to have been as independent as I was and now have to rely on others to care for me all the time."

Obviously, he was getting better since he felt the need to be independent!

Doug had a meeting scheduled with a neuropsychiatrist to evaluate, as Doug put it, "How scrambled my eggs are!"

Personally, I didn't think much scrambling happened—I thought maybe he was a bit over easy, but definitely not scrambled! Actually, I was still hopeful that once all the drugs were out of his system, he was going to be perfectly fine. Again, I had to trust God with Doug's outcome and my ability to navigate our future.

Trust in the Lord completely, and do not
rely on your own opinions. With all your heart
rely on him to guide you, and He will lead you in
every decision you make. Become intimate with

him in whatever you do, and he will lead you
wherever you go.

Proverbs 3:5-6 TPT

[/vc_row_inner]

I had to remember that God sustained me those first several
months, and He would continue to do so if I let Him. I am still awed
by the fact that our all-powerful God has given me free will regarding
the decisions in my life. However, sometimes I don't make the best
decision. My ego thinks it knows best. Independence wants to do it
my way! The sluggard in me usually wants to take the path of least
resistance instead of the one, which will produce the better results.
Impatience always seems to be in a hurry to get to the finish line
rather than slowing down and enjoying the journey. This little dove
needs to take a lesson from the sparrows and allow Him to guide and
watch over me.

> I sing because I'm happy.
> I sing because I'm free.
> His eye is on the sparrow,
> And I know He watches me.

Civilla D. Martin and Charles H. Gabriel[32]

[/vc_row_inner]

Knowing Doug would soon be coming home, I was very concerned with how I would be able to schedule work around Doug's
needs. As I was racking my mind or rather (ahem) praying for solutions on how to solve this dilemma, I was reminded by the Holy
Spirit my work schedule had been very slow, and I had to take advantage of the situation and take some time off. This all seemed to be
divinely orchestrated and came together perfectly as I would get to

spend the first two weeks of Doug's return home caring for him and adjusting to our new "normal."

Day 70

Doug got his neuropsychological report back and was blessed to learn his eggs were not scrambled. Quite possibly, the shell wasn't even broken! His neuropsychologist said cognitively Doug was 100 percent. The testing showed some motor skill challenges and some short-term memory loss. Still, considering the extent of Doug's accident, it was absolutely amazing to have such minimal loss. However, the doctor believed those losses were most likely related to the drugs Doug was still taking. Doug's response was, "It doesn't seem fair to say I have problems if they are drug-related." Obviously, he was not willing to accept a diagnosis, which could limit his future. In his typically positive way, he would push for the very best outcome possible.

He was scheduled to start outpatient rehab three days a week starting the next week. And he was even able to go outside to walk during physical therapy, where he found the uneven ground and sidewalks to be challenging. I was sure there would be something challenging every day for a while, but in time his walking ability would all come together.

Home Sweet Home at Last

Day 74

"I haven't heard a bed alarm go off, and I haven't had to listen to the old guy next door cough up a lung or the TV two doors down," Doug said the first morning home. And he continued to relish the sound of silence since he got home two weeks before.

Having him home was wonderful, but it was rather stressful getting him there. I had to get the last of his prescriptions filled before we left town. Leaving him alone in the car was not exactly what felt right, but he didn't want to come inside with me. "I just want to go home," he said. Believing I would be in and out in no time, I agreed to leave him in the car to wait.

And he did wait. Somehow in the confusion of the extraordinary number of pills and unheard-of milligrams he was taking, his prescription was not ready. When he was discharged, he was taking twenty-eight pills a day, which amounted to 13,500 milligrams of anticonvulsant medication. We were later told a horse couldn't function with that many milligrams of an anticonvulsant on board. The pharmacy scrambled to fill his ginormous order. Forty-five minutes later, we were finally on the road headed home.

Moments prior to arriving at the house, it dawned on me we had missed the time he was supposed to have taken a dose of medication. Not wanting to alarm Doug, I didn't say anything. I managed to get him inside and seated comfortably in his recliner. Frantically, I dumped out the bag containing the many bottles searching for the medication he was late getting. One by one, I examined each bottle, reading the labels trying to find the right one. No luck! Certain I had missed what I was looking for in my panicked state, I went back to each bottle, reading labels one more time. Strike two.

My stomach sank as I realized the medication he needed to have taken an hour ago had not been included in this huge sack of pill bottles. As calm as I could be, I explained to Doug what was going on. On the inside, I was struggling to breathe. Sweat beaded on my brow as I prayed feverishly that he would not have a seizure because he was not getting the dose of medication he needed on time. It felt as though my worst nightmare was about to come true. I was an X-ray tech, not a nurse or doctor! I didn't know seizures, I knew bones! I think I came close to having a meltdown as my blood pressure rose.

Several phone calls later, we ended up going to a nearby town to secure enough pills to get us through a few days. When we made it back home, we were both exhausted and slept ten hours that night!

After that first night, we were able to resume normal family nights with the cats and dogs curled up with us on the couch watching TV. My stress meter was no longer completely maxed out. I still had concerns that were greatly relieved when his medications were on track. It was also nice not to have any interruptions for temperature and blood pressure checks, no drab rehab walls to stare at, and no nasty hospital smells. Slowly, we were getting the hang of life back at the "ranch." We both needed this.

My confidence in my ability to care for Doug was growing, however, I was concerned about how long I could provide the care he required without some help before I crashed from exhaustion. Life was quite busy since Doug arrived home. Of course, I cooked all his favorite foods and tried to meet his every need. Most of the time, I did well, but every now and then, everything happened at once, and life got a bit challenging. My Spidey senses were on full alert as I tried to stay ahead of his needs and anticipate what he may want.

We were learning to just go with the flow, but at times he did have to wait for my time and attention. The pot of pasta almost boiling over was more important than whatever he just dropped on the floor. His sudden need to use the restroom when my hands were covered with raw hamburger created a bit of a conflict. And we had several stops along the roadside to pee because when asked if he needed to when it was convenient, he said he didn't need to go.

I didn't fully trust him to wait for me to finish a task because it seemed like he thought I had to come at his beck and call. This made going outside to chop and pack firewood a bit nerve-wracking, as did trying to spend a few moments playing outside with the dogs. The dogs were used to daily exercise, and I could feel the tension building in me as I was somewhat torn in my desire to care for both Doug and them.

Years ago, before having dogs, Doug told me I couldn't have them until I had the time to care for them. As a result, I made every effort to ensure my dogs were exercised regularly. Now it was creating conflict for me—as was Doug's growing self-sufficiency. I sensed his desire for independence was going to challenge my instinct to keep him safe and, thereby, my need for control. I prayed again for grace, wisdom, and strength.

I was blessed to be physically strong for a woman, but it soon became obvious my strength wasn't sufficient to get Doug out of the pickles he seemed to get himself into. One day he was feeling so strong he decided to ride the recumbent bike a quarter-mile longer than the day before. Then, against my advice, he decided also to do his floor exercises. After he completed his floor exercises, he didn't have the strength to get up from the floor. He started twitching like a fish out of water. The harder he tried to get up, the worse the twitching got.

I attempted to help him up but wasn't successful. I used every lift technique I could remember to no avail. It was like wrestling with a 187 pounds fish flopping around. He had no control over his muscles and was unable to aid in the uprighting process. As a result, I was attempting to lift the dead weight while he was pitching to and fro. I was being jerked around in sync with each twitch of his body.

After several minutes of trying to get him off the floor, we were both exhausted and gave up. We finally both laid back on the floor and laughed and laughed as tears streamed down our faces. Though we could have cried, laughing felt significantly better. It seemed ridiculous not to be able to get up off the floor, particularly for

Mr. Strong-as-an-Ox. While lying on the floor, Doug's body finally relaxed. After some creative thinking and fifteen or so minutes of rest, I had him crawl over to the couch rather than try to stand and walk over to it, and we were able to get his 187 pounds on the couch.

I believe God was reminding us we were exactly where he wanted us to be, on our faces before Him, weak and helpless without His divine guidance. He was none too gently reminding us, "Surely the Lord's power is enough to save you. He can hear you when you ask Him for help" (Isaiah 59:1 NCV).

Just because Doug was home, it didn't mean we no longer needed divine help. In fact, as we entered a new phase of our life, we need all the help we could get.

Doug was totally dependent on me for almost his every need, and he was worried about me getting hurt. He said he didn't understand how, when working in Alaska, he had not been too concerned about me taking care of myself, but now that he could do absolutely nothing for me, it bothered him.

Upon further questioning, he said, "While I was away working in Alaska, I thought it was just me making the sacrifice to be away from home and earn a living. Now that I am not able to earn a living and am here to see all that you have to do to maintain our lifestyle and not be able to help, I realize how much of a sacrifice you are making as well. I don't like the fact that I am incapable of helping you in any way at this time." I don't believe Doug fully understood the severity of his injury or the time and process necessary for recovery.

He believed it was his ego causing his feelings of insecurity, as he didn't like the reality that he couldn't do all his therapists were asking of him either. After all, how hard could it be to simply walk without falling or to put his medications in the small organizational boxes? Especially since he had been walking most of his life and easily accomplishing tasks requiring fine motor skills. In time it was recognized the falling was because of acquired ataxia.[33]

He was a bit downcast after rehab because he was unable to balance on his left leg; some of the memory testing challenged him as well. He told the therapist his memory issues, such as recalling a person's name, had always been an issue. It wasn't something he believed was associated with his traumatic brain injury (TBI), so he didn't think it was fair for him to be judged on something, which had always been an issue for him. However, there were many things he was not able to recall, which pointed to the oxygen deprivation, not just a challenge with recalling names.

Like most of us, we want to be encouraged as we journey through life. We never want to believe we aren't measuring up to the world's standards. Since waking up, Doug was accustomed to hearing how well he was doing. Now that he wasn't getting continuous praise, his ego was indeed screaming for attention. I tried to be an encourager but was finding it exhausting to build him up continually. It was apparent he didn't fully understand the miracle he had been given in having his life restored and the limitations ensuing.

Reiterating what the doctors repeatedly said, I reminded him, "You should be grateful you are doing as well as you are. Medically, you shouldn't even be alive. I know this is difficult. It must be devastating to have been alive and high-functioning and now to be alive and struggling to accomplish the basics. But this is where you are right now. I know you have what it takes to get your strength back. Your brain has been highly traumatized and needs time to heal. This is not an overnight process. In fact, the healing process could take months or, heaven forbid, years. I know patience is not a word you like to hear, but you are going to have to embrace it for the time being."

I must confess, however, that I was discouraged too. I wanted him to recover quickly for both our sake. I wanted this nightmare to be over. I wanted to resume life as "normal." In the moment when I agreed to trust God for Doug's life, this was not exactly what I was expecting. I knew there would be a recovery process, but once he finally woke up and at the rate he was exponentially progressing, I wasn't expecting the rocket to take a nosedive. The optimist in me was getting a reality check as well; my expectations were sputtering like a dirty carburetor. I had to wrestle to keep my attitude in check. The reality was, I wasn't enjoying this process any better than Doug was embracing his constraint. As a result, my role as his primary cheerleader was being challenged as my pompoms got soggy with self-pity and discouragement.

It all made me look forward to returning to work in the upcoming week. I would be there Monday, Wednesday, and Friday afternoons while he would be at rehab. Work was sure to be a welcome distraction where I could focus on something besides our current circumstances for a few hours. My co-workers were such a strong support network for me, and I was ready for an infusion. Filling my four-hour shift required dropping him off at rehab an hour early, but this was the only way I could accommodate both of our schedules.

Fortunately, my work schedule remained slow, and my job-share partner was able to pick up the hours I was not able to cover. I was so blessed to have a very understanding employer and co-workers. Many co-workers donated their vacation time to me, ensuring I didn't have to worry about the money I would be losing by not working. In the end, they were able to donate enough time to me I barely missed a single paycheck.

"Grateful" is inadequate to express my feelings about their generosity. I was humbled by their sacrifice and expression of compassion. It was evident God was mindful of our years of sacrificing to share our resources with others. I know He will bless each one copiously in return for their selflessness on our behalf.

> Given generously and generous gifts will be given back to you, shaken down to make room for more. Abundant gifts will pour out upon you with such an overflowing measure that it will run over the top! Your measurement of generosity becomes the measurement of your return.
>
> Luke 6:38 TPT

[/vc_row_inner]

Once we got somewhat settled in at home, it was time to reach out to others who had a hand in the making of our miracle. Doug and I wanted to visit his co-workers and the crew at the fire department who were responsible for rescuing him. We wanted to express our gratitude and let them see firsthand how well he was doing. Doug chatted exuberantly on the drive, fueled with anticipation and excitement at the prospect of meeting those who saved his life and reconnecting with the work crew who sent cards, money, and prayers.

Our first stop was at the paper mill. I barely had the car in park before Doug tried to open the door to get out. Knowing he would be twitchy with excitement, I said, "Doug, you need to wait for me to help you before you try to get out of the car, please." I scrambled, frantically trying to get out of my seat to retrieve the wheelchair from the back of the car and back around to his side of the car to assist him before he had a chance to get out on his own. Just as I expected, he was so excited to go into the lunchroom, he wouldn't wait for me to help him. In his haste, he managed to step one foot on the toes of the other, crashing to the ground just as I was coming from the back of the car with the wheelchair.

I turned around in time to see the car door swinging toward his head as his body was falling toward the ground. The door missed his head, hitting him in the midback instead. He landed in a heap in the mud as his body let out an involuntary grunt. I raced toward him to determine how badly he was hurt. Fortunately, nothing was hurt but his pride. His pants were muddy, where they connected with the ground. In agitation, his limbs were really twitchy now because of the fall, but otherwise, he was fine.

I, on the other hand, was furious with him for not waiting for me to help. He was acting exactly like my disabled, hard-headed, ninety-one-year-old grandfather, who seldom would ask for assistance as nerve dystrophy slowly stole his abilities, muscle coordination, and balance. My grandfather had several falls due to his unwillingness to humble himself and allow others to help. Prior to his accident, Doug often lamented over my grandfather's impatience. "If he would only wait for help!" Now Doug was in my grandfather's proverbial shoes.

I asked Doug later if he got hurt, and he said no. In my frustration, I said with obvious irritation, "Too bad you didn't!" I got the stink eye in response as he looked at me like a belligerent child. He said, "Well, I thought I would be fine this time. It's not like I meant to fall."

We would later learn TBI-sufferers struggle with impulsivity issues. The cognitive portion of their brain does not have a chance to rationalize the decision. Instead, as soon as the thought occurs, the impulse to accomplish the action gets put into motion. I don't think Doug understands every time he hurts himself or puts himself in a dangerous situation, it creates huge stress and anxiety for me while potentially creating increased hardship for both of us.

> The best way to handle unwanted situations is to thank Me for them. This act of faith frees you from resentment and frees Me to work My ways into situations, so that good emerges from it.

> Jesus Calling, April 11[34]

[/vc_row_inner]

Through gritted teeth, I muttered, "Thank you, Jesus, Doug didn't get hurt," as I pushed Doug in his wheelchair through the muddy gravel parking lot toward the building. The Murrays wanted to know if we needed help as they were taking the celebratory pizza to the lunchroom. Trying to brush off my irritation, I assured them we were fine and were looking forward to seeing everyone.

Despite a rough start to the day, we had a wonderful lunch with his crew. They were totally shocked to see him in the lunchroom. It was fun to see their reactions when they walked in one by one and saw him sitting in his old chair. The first response was a look of confusion, which rapidly turned into a face-splitting grin as their brains registered it really was Doug sitting there. Most of them had not seen him for quite some time and had no idea how much he had improved. I believe they all were greatly relieved from the grins, tears, hugs, and words expressed. Several guys said, "Buddy, we thought we had lost you. We are so glad to see you doing so well."

Grinning from ear to ear, Doug took great joy in reassuring these fellas he was doing just fine. Promising everyone he would back to work as soon as he was able, he reminded them to save his spot at the table. Too soon, it was time for the crew to head back to work. We exchanged hugs and goodbyes with everyone as they headed out.

We then took the opportunity to look at the piece of metal that fell on him, aspiring to figure out what went wrong. Doug was hoping that by looking at the scene, he might be able to piece together what happened since he was unable to recall a single event from that night. It was with apprehension we drove out to the location of the deadly metal. PTSD is an unpredictable animal. Who knew what memories seeing the metal might stir up in Doug? Would they be ones of terror as he laid on the frozen ground gasping while every last bit of oxygen was squeezed from his lungs? Would he even recall anything at all?

This time Doug waited for me to help him out of the car. He used the walker for assistance as he walked around the massive hunk of metal, looking from all angles for any clue that may provide an answer. I was anxious with every step we took. It felt like we could be walking through a minefield. I held my breath as I anticipated an explosion as Doug's memory was jolted through a recall of that deadly night. But there was no explosion; the ground didn't shake. Instead, the atmosphere was eerily quiet. The metal was not going to give up the secret. The mystery would remain. Doug shook his head in disappointment and confusion, saying, "I can't recall a single thing."

Even though we were a bit disheartened by a lack of answers as to how the metal fell on Doug, our spirits were quickly lifted as we drove to the Frenchtown Fire Department. As a small token of our gratitude for their challenging work in rescuing Doug, I made snickerdoodles, butterscotch-chip-chocolate chip-coconut-oatmeal cookies, and Mostaccioli for them. I haven't met a man who didn't appreciate good food, and I could think of no better way to say thank you than to fill their stomachs with some homemade food. (A little lovin' from the oven!)

135

But I knew home cooking could never express how grateful we were for their help. When they last saw Doug, they didn't expect him to survive. Once again, we were told how little hope they had of Doug's survival. Yet there he was smiling and laughing right before their very eyes.

When they took stock of how much he had improved in such a brief time, they called him a walking miracle. Assuming these EMTs and firefighters had seen more than their fair share of trauma and death, I could only imagine what was going through their minds as they watched what had been the cold dead body of Doug standing before them.

He was warm to the touch as they shook hands with him. His voice communicated clearly, and his belly shook with laughter, and they joked with one another. His eyes twinkled with gratitude as he thanked them for their part in restoring his life or perhaps it was tears of humility glistening as an expression that words couldn't communicate.

It seemed to me that God was in the process of restoring hope to those who had perhaps grown battle-weary. Being on the front lines of battle isn't for the faint of heart. First responders may not know each person they care for intimately, but they still grieve and are adversely affected by what they witness. They need time to heal and be encouraged too.

It was important to me to meet those responsible for saving Doug's life, and look them in the eyes and convey my gratitude for their sacrifice and effort. This was the night shift. They had sacrificed time with their families to provide trauma care to those requiring it. I wanted them to know their sacrifice was more than appreciated. Whether Doug lived or died, it was important to me to acknowledge their efforts.

"We must find time to stop and thank the people who make a difference in our lives" (John F. Kennedy).[35]

By the time we were getting ready to leave, it seemed their shoulders were a tad more upright and their heads a bit higher than when we first arrived. Although the cookies they were eating with gusto may be to credit for the smiles, I couldn't agree more; Doug was a walking miracle. Perhaps, the greatest miracle of all was how many lives were being changed by one man's death and resurrection.

> On the contrary, everything happening to me in this jail only serves to make Christ more accurately known, regardless of whether I live or die. They didn't shut me up; they gave me a pulpit! Alive, I'm Christ's messenger; dead, I'm his bounty.
>
> Philippians 1:21 MSG

[/vc_row_inner]

Heading to Denver

April 14

Doug had his first evaluation with Providence Rehabilitation and Workers' Compensation (Work Comp). Despite how well he was doing, the general feeling was the sooner he could reduce or eliminate the humongous amounts of anticonvulsants he was taking, the faster he was likely to improve.

The nurse from Work Comp told me if it was her or me on this magnitude of medication, we would be flat on our faces. A horse couldn't even function on that amount of medication. She suggested Doug be sent to the Craig Hospital in Denver, Colorado, to go through a titration[36] protocol where he would be weaned off the anticonvulsants under medical supervision. They specialized in neurorehab and dealt with serious brain trauma on a daily basis. Medical professionals I had been consulting with confirmed that Craig is one of the best neuro rehab facilities in the nation. And knowing that the neurologist had to consult with Mayo Clinic to determine the best course of anticonvulsant treatment, the thumbs up I was getting for Craig Hospital reassured me that was where Doug needed to go to continue his medical therapy. I would have been foolish to disregard the signs God seemed to be using to answer my prayers regarding our next step.

In the meantime, their director reviewed Doug's case and determined the best course of action to decrease Doug's meds while we were still home. However, it appeared very likely Doug would be admitted to their facility to be closely monitored as he detoxed. Given the severity of Doug's seizures, it required a significantly higher than normal dosage of anticonvulsants to finally stop the seizing. The doctors in Missoula were not accustomed to prescribing or monitoring such high doses. Now that Doug was stable as far as seizures were considered, there was some reluctance to reduce the anticonvulsant for fear of him seizing again. Ongoing seizures caused brain damage, and the doctors wanted to avoid any possibility of seizures. The hospitals in Missoula did not have the brain-monitoring devices, which would allow them to closely monitor Doug's brain as the anticonvulsants were slowly reduced. Essentially, now that the baby was asleep, no one wanted to do anything to disturb the peace.

We were in favor of going to Denver. Knowing Doug would be closely supervised as the medications were reduced brought me great comfort. I was terrified of him having a seizure at home forty long miles from medical care. I didn't want Doug to be at home if we had an emergency with his weaning process.

Having said that, I was quite confident that nothing would be amiss. God, in His infinite wisdom, knew if He was going to upgrade Doug's "hard drive," he would need to be out of commission for some time so God could have his full attention. Knowing Doug, he would either resist or press on with God's plans with all he has. God's timing is always perfect.

> "When the time was right, I answered you;
> on the day you were delivered, I was your help"
> (Isaiah 49:8 VOICE).

And His timing really messes our lives up when we don't cooperate with Him, just as Moses found out:

> Moses knew he was a Jew, and he was aware
> of God's call on his life to lead the children of
> Israel out of Egypt, but it's not enough to know
> what God wants you to do. You have to know

God's plan and timing for accomplishing His will. Moses missed it on both of these counts.[37]

[/vc_row_inner]

***

The sky was the perfect shade of sky blue, and the sun seemed to be giving Old Man Winter a run for his money as its brilliant rays warmed the world. It was an absolutely perfect day to get out of the house and work on Doug's walking. We got him all set up to use walking sticks while I followed behind with the wheelchair. He had only walked a short way when I noticed he was getting tired.

"Doug, do you want to take a break?" I asked.

"No," he replied. "I want to go just a little farther."

"Are you sure?" I countered.

"I am fine, just let me go a little more," he said.

I could tell he really needed to sit, but I didn't want to argue with him, so I placed the wheelchair right behind him so he could easily sit back when needed. But I watched in horror as he began to fall forward toward the gravel road. My short arms couldn't reach past the wheelchair to grab him, so I rushed around it to help him but couldn't reach him in time. He had already crashed his face into the grit and grime of the road.

He pushed himself up to his knees. Blood was running profusely down his forehead into his eyes. His sunglasses were broken into several pieces. The skin on his face showed gashes where the sunglasses cut into it. The gravel had ripped the skin and embedded bits of rock and dirt into his face as well.

"Oh, Doug, are you okay?" I asked in despair and frustration. I was supposed to be protecting him and had failed.

"No!" came his terse response.

"Why wouldn't you listen to me when I asked you to sit down?" I asked, knowing I was helpless to protect him if he wasn't going to listen to me.

"I thought I could make it," he replied.

We got him into the wheelchair, so I could further access the damage. He was a bloody, dirty mess. Neither one of us had anything to wipe up the blood, and I knew I needed something to use as a compress to reduce the blood flow. I racked my brain for a solution. I was wearing a T-shirt and shorts and didn't want to take off either one of them and risk indecent exposure. Then it dawned on me that my sock would be absorbent. Bending over and untying my shoe while holding on to the wheelchair for balance, I took off my sock. Hoping it wouldn't be too germy or stinky, I pressed it against his face to stop the blood from running down his face.

As we made our way back to the car, a nice man stopped and asked if we needed help. I responded, "Thank you, but we've got this." But after he got a good look at Doug's head and face, he was really concerned and thought he had to do something. We assured him the damage was not as bad as it looked, and we could get back to the car safely.

We did get back okay, but Doug was pretty shaken up. The rehab team once told me he would test the boundaries and that he may act like a toddler learning to walk. And boy, did he ever. But, as with any toddler, Doug merrily went along until he suddenly found himself knocked down on his butt. Then he got up, dusted himself off, and had another go at it until he finally got it figured out. Slowly we were getting this new life figured out. Some days were easier than others, but we pressed on.

> "For I am confident of this very thing, that He who began a good work among you will complete it by the day of Christ Jesus" (Philippians 1:6 NASB).

April 21

Apparently, after reviewing Doug's case and seeing how far he had progressed, Craig decided he was not acute enough to warrant their services. Wanting to bring some levity to the situation, thereby making a play on the word "acute," I told Doug's doctors I thought he was pretty cute too, but that didn't change our outcome.

In some ways, this news was discouraging, but it was also good knowing he had progressed so far that Craig didn't feel they could do much for him and suggested another facility in Omaha called Quality Living, Inc. (QLI).

In the midst of these decisions, I had a dream that we were driving a familiar road, and suddenly there were lots of S-turns where they shouldn't have been, and we were going way too fast. We managed to get through all the corners and suddenly we came upon a bridge that was under construction, so the last section was missing. I couldn't stop in time and woke up as we were falling over the end of the bridge.

Apparently, this dream was confirmation that I was feeling like I was losing control. I was very familiar with our local hospital. I didn't want to learn about a new hospital. Being close to home, family and friends felt reassuring. I didn't want to be far from them. We thought we were heading to Craig Hospital in Denver. Now we were not. We thought we had answers. Now we didn't. Everything was spiraling out of my control, and I didn't like it one bit.

We had experienced many turns in the road of life lately and were in a transition as Doug was weaned off the anticonvulsants; but it was uncertain whether we were at the place of reducing medications or if there was something else, which needed to be done before the medications could be reduced. Perhaps there was more healing, which needed to take place first. We certainly didn't want to get in the way of what needed to be done.

I was reminded of *Jesus Calling* from April 15:

> Trust Me, and don't be afraid. Many things feel out of control. Your routines are not running smoothly. You tend to feel more secure when your life is predictable. Let Me lead you to the rock that is higher than you and your circumstances. Take refuge in the shelter of my wings, where you are absolutely secure.

When you are shaken out of your comfortable routines, grip My hand tightly and look for growth opportunities. Instead of bemoaning the loss of your comfort, accept the challenge of something new. I lead you from glory to glory, making you fit for My Kingdom. Say yes to the ways I work in your life. Trust Me, and don't be afraid.[38]

[/vc_row_inner]

After having my dream and reading this *Jesus Calling* passage, it seemed like God was reminding me that He had been faithful this entire journey. I simply needed to trust Him again, knowing He would always be there for me.

Now it was my turn for walking lessons. He was right there to catch me if necessary, but I knew sometimes falling is necessary for growth. Step by step, holding tightly to His hand, I knew I would prevail.

Doug's point person at Missoula Community Bridges Rehabilitation sent a letter to his neurologist, asking what the next step was. We hoped that sometime in the next week we would have some answers. In the meantime, he was attaining celebrity status. He had an interview with a local news station, and he made the front page of the *Missoulian* newspaper.

Then, we were at Costco, and I noticed a young man in a blue uniform who kept pointing to and looking at us while talking to another fella in the same uniform. He and I were looking at each other trying to figure out who each of us were while trying not to be obvious. He must have connected the dots before me because he soon came over and bashfully introduced himself as one of the EMTs who rode in the ambulance with Doug and then introduced us to his partner.

"Oh man, it is so good to see you alive," he said while choking back the tears. "We all thought for sure you were a goner. You were seizing so hard, and we couldn't keep your airway open."

His partner nodded in agreement as he struggled to keep his emotions in check too. He explained to us that he operated the Ambu bag used to push oxygen into Doug's lungs until they got him intubated. It was clear he was beside himself with joy as he observed Doug in his present condition.

"Wow, you look so good. It is amazing to see you alive and well," he exclaimed. As if on cue, Doug stood up from his wheelchair to show them he could actually walk. They both gasped as tears filled their eyes, seeing the full impact of the miracle of Doug's life being restored. This was confirmed as this young man said, "It is so good to see firsthand you survived against such dire odds. Despite our best efforts, not all we care for make it. It is so amazing to meet someone who has beat the odds."

To God be the glory!

Father, as I look at the uncertainty of our future, I find myself succumbing to fear. Yet, I know You are fully able to meet our every need. At times I am overwhelmed by the many responsibilities I have right now. Again, I know You will carry me and enable me to get through each day. I look to You now and ask for wisdom, discernment, and discipline to get through today.

I have little left to give. Holy Spirit, will you fill me up? Father, forgive me for my selfishness and forgive me for wanting my needs met when Doug has so many more. Why can't I just get over myself and merely be grateful he is alive? In the hospital, while he was in his coma, I prayed, "Let it be done according to Your will, Lord." Now that I am walking in Your will, I don't seem to be as willing. Does this make me a hypocrite?

My pot is cracked and leaking. Perhaps You should throw this flawed pot to the ground so it may shatter, grind the pieces up, and form into something more useful. God, I am failing Doug and therefore failing You. Yet, I do know, in You all is good—not easy, but good. Can Your goodness restore me? I feel as though I am in transition, ready to give birth to something. I want to push so hard and scream to bring this thing forth, but I don't even know what this thing is. How can I birth what I don't know?

"You can never become who you have been destined to become until you lose who you used to be" (Rex Crain).[39]

Faceplant: Goals Reevaluated

April 28

I was in the middle of fixing dinner when I saw Doug get up from his recliner by himself instead of asking for help. Frantically, I tried to clean off my hands, which were covered with raw hamburger. I hesitated to say anything to him, fearing he would fall due to his exacerbated startle response. Ever since waking up from his coma, his startle response was hair-trigger. The littlest noises or movements would cause him to jump violently. Simply, his brain was now overreacting to anything it perceived as a threat, essentially overcompensating for Doug's untimely fatality prior to his resuscitation.

As I watched him fall, it was as if his legs were sawed off at the ankles, and he keeled over like a tree falling. Face first, he slammed into the hardwood floor. *Boom!*

"Doug!" I screamed, running toward him. Terror gripped my heart as my brain rapidly went through the list of possible casualties I would see when I rounded the corner to him.

He was groaning and writhing in pain when I reached him. Slowly, he rolled over while holding his head. There was blood all over his face and a pool of blood on the floor. As I examined him, I noticed the cartilage had broken away from the nasal bone, creating a horizontal gash halfway down his nose. The bony protrusion behind the eyebrows on his skull poked through the skin on impact.

I was petrified as I contemplated the ramifications of this fall. *How much more damage can his brain take and still function?* I didn't allow myself to dwell on outcomes. It was time to be practical. The stove needed to be turned off. Dinner would have to wait.

Doug needed to get off the floor and back to his chair. Nurse Nellie reported for duty.

Doug crawled back to his chair, where I assisted him up and to sitting. Once he was safe in his chair, I went to the bathroom to gather up first aid supplies. Carefully, with trembling hands, I wiped the blood away as best as I could. I made a compress to hold on his nose where the cartilage was split open, hoping to stop the profusion of blood. Once the bleeding stopped, I put a bandage across his nose.

Concerned he may have a concussion, I frequently asked throughout the evening, "Do you have a headache?" His reply of "No" did little to reassure me he was internally okay. Knowing he could be evaluated in rehab the following day brought some comfort to me.

Rehab did a great job of spanking him. He came home with his tail between his legs, feeling quite sorry for himself because his goal to be walker-free by the end of the month may not be realized. His physical therapist told him goals were wonderful but then compared his efforts to a trip to the moon without the right tools. "If you don't have everything you need, you most likely shouldn't try."

As a result, his chart now read in bright red letters: "Fall risk." He didn't like the label one bit. He became very good about waiting for me to assist or supervise his walking. However, there were times he went a bit overboard with the dramatics when asking for assistance. His inner pouty little boy came out. Even so, I believe God had him exactly where he was supposed to be, and in God's perfect timing, he would get to move forward.

In fact, despite all the setbacks, he was moving forward every day. And some steps were noticeably bigger than others. One big step was reducing his Klonopin (anticonvulsant) by two-thirds.

Welcome problems as perspective-lifters. My children tend to sleepwalk through their days until they bump into an obstacle that stymies them. If you encounter a problem with no immediate solution, your response to that situation will take you either up or down. You can lash out at the difficulty, resenting it and feeling sorry for yourself. This will take you down into a pit of self-pity. Alternatively, the problem can be a ladder, enabling you to climb up and see your life from My perspective. Viewed from above, the obstacle that frustrated you is only a light and momentary trouble. Once your perspective has been heightened, you can look away from the problem altogether. Turn toward Me, and see the Light of My Presence shining upon you.

Jesus Calling, April 26[40]

[/vc_row_inner]

These words so fit our current circumstances. Doug's rehab was not advancing as quickly as we had hoped. He needed 24/7 supervision, which I had been able to provide by reducing my normal nine-hour workday to four hours while dropping him off at rehab. I couldn't resume my regular work schedule and leave him home alone. The therapists determined he was impulsive and therefore not safe to leave unsupervised for extended periods of time—especially given his tendency to fall.

I wondered if it was possible if he could do full-day therapy or even live in an apartment at Bridges during the week where he would have supervision while I was at work. Both of these options would enable me to return to work on my regular three-days-a-week schedule and allow me to get some things done at home without having to be concerned with his needs all the time. I felt so selfish thinking this way, but I was not able to continue to care for him full-time, stay employed, and keep up with the home and the animals.

I found myself trusting God for divine guidance again. In as much as we wanted to get back to life as we used to know it, it was now our responsibility to submit to Him. I was hoping to get back to work soon, but because Doug was not ready to be left on his own for very long, I guessed I would have to wait unless I could figure out one of those alternatives.

Given our current circumstances, I felt compelled to sell my horses and horse trailer. In as much as they brought me great joy and it was painful to let them go, it would be worse feeling guilty that I was not able to utilize their full potential or potentially afford their upkeep. I also had a strong sense I was not going to have much time, if any, to ride or care for them. By selling them, I could put all the money toward a more functional mode of transportation (four-legged versus four-wheeled), which would better suit us as well. We were in far greater need of a dependable vehicle than we were of three horses and a trailer.

I knew God was more than capable of meeting our needs. However, sometimes He asks us to sacrificially participate in having that need met.

> When some basic need is lacking—time, energy, money—consider yourself blessed. Your very lack is an opportunity to latch onto Me in unashamed dependence. When you begin a day with inadequate resources, you must concentrate your efforts on the present moment. This is where you are meant to live—in the present; it is the place where I always await you. Awareness of your inadequacy is a rich blessing, training you to rely wholeheartedly on Me.
>
> The truth is that self-sufficiency is a myth perpetuated by pride and temporary success. Health and wealth can disappear instantly, as can life itself. Rejoice in your insufficiency, knowing that My Power is made perfect in weakness.
>
> Jesus Calling, April 30[41]

[/vc_row_inner]

With God, all things are possible. He is our provider. Instead of fully trusting him, I was getting stressed out trying to figure out how we were going to make life work, and then He simply opened some doors and closed others. And as Doug found out, when you bang on those He has closed, you end up with a bloody nose.

Trust and patience were the big lessons here. In this fast-paced world we live in, slowing down is difficult at best. However, there is a time for everything (Ecclesiastes 3).

I was reminded of a documentary I had seen on PBS about a caterpillar in the Artic. It couldn't get enough nourishment to fully transform from a larva into a butterfly during the short summer season, so the caterpillar had to wait nine years to complete the transformation process. The butterfly life cycle is approximately three weeks. Females lay eggs five to seven days after emerging from the chrysalis. The eggs hatch after three days. Adult butterflies emerge from the chrysalides in seven to ten days.[42] Perhaps this is what we were experiencing as we waited for Doug's brain and body to transform!

And likewise, I felt like I, too, was being transformed as I waited and trusted for Doug to "be okay." I was constantly reminding myself to trust the process. I needed to be patient like the Arctic butterfly. I had to surrender all that wasn't serving me, knowing in time, I would be equipped with all I needed to succeed in this journey.

As Doug and I chatted during the prior several months, one day he said, "You know, Tam, as I have been forced to slow down, giving me time to stop to consider how God orchestrated the events of my accident by having the Fire Department immediately available to bring me back to life, I realized what a precious gift I have been given in having my life restored. For me to be careless with this gift is foolish. I don't want to cause more damage to my body or brain by my stubborn independence. I want to take the best care of my body as possible. I want to regain my strength and freedom sooner than later, and perhaps in the process, I get carried away and push myself too hard sometimes."

It appeared to me he was finally recognizing the harm his impulsive decisions created. This was another glimmer of a gem of hope for me. I took this as a sign his brain was healing, and he was starting to discern the ramifications of his poor choices. Treasures are usually found through careful searching and exploration, not racing along as we had spent most of our lives doing.

A song by *Love & the Outcome* says, "How can You be my treasure / If I am digging for gold."[43] We spent much of our lives prior to the accident working tirelessly, trying to get ahead. We had been seduced by the American dream, where success is portrayed by a substantial bank account, a beautiful house (or two, maybe three), nice cars, clothes, and vacations.

We thought we had surrendered to God's plan for our lives, but in hindsight, it seems we were still living under the curse of the almighty dollar. There were moments we would sit at the feet of Jesus like Mary did. But soon, the Martha in us was urging us to our feet, saying there was work to be done (Luke 10:41-42).

Now that we were sidelined by our circumstances, we were reaping the treasures of heaven as we found ourselves once again at the feet of Jesus. We were discovering we were richly blessed. We were uncovering jewels we didn't even know existed.

When we slow down, we can finally enjoy the flowers and discover our personal treasures.

Off to Omaha

You are on the path of My choosing. There is no randomness about your life. Here and Now comprise the coordinates of your daily life. Most people let their moments slip through their fingers, half-lived. They avoid the present by worrying about the future or longing for a better time and place. They forget that they are creatures who are subject to the limitations of time and space… As you give yourself more and more to a life of constant communion with Me, you will find that you simply have no time for worry. Thus, you are freed to let My Spirit direct your steps, enabling you to walk along the path of Peace.

Jesus Calling, May 1[44]

[/vc_row_inner]

I could see the Father's hand busy at work in Doug's heart. After being at home these last several months and seeing how difficult life was for us to live remotely in the middle of the forest, forty miles from the hospital—eleven of which is a gravel road, particularly during the winter months—he was now pondering the idea of moving somewhere where the winters are warmer. While it did seem like a good idea in some respects, it would be another major change in our lives, and he has deep roots in this valley. His grandfather homesteaded here, and that original land borders our property.

Before the accident, Doug was always adamant he would never leave, even though at times I thought it would make our lives easier even before the accident. After hearing stories from my elderly patients about how difficult it was for them to get around, I could see how we would benefit from living smarter, not harder, as we had done most of our lives. In the meantime, we continued to wait here at home to hear what the next step might be for Doug regarding the possibility of reducing his medications under medical supervision.

May 10

We were informed by Workers' Compensation that Doug would be heading to Omaha, Nebraska, to attend Quality Living Institute (QLI) for approximately eight weeks to manage his medication reduction. They are a state-of-the-art rehab center for brain and spine injuries. I planned to fly out with him and stay a few days until he was settled into his routine there. I would then return home and try to resume a somewhat normal work schedule. As needed, I planned to fly back and forth to spend some time with him on weekends.

I knew this was an answer to prayer as it would allow Doug to get the care and rehab he needed. I was also looking forward to having a bit of a respite and a chance to take care of myself for a while. Thankfully, I wasn't always aware of how intense our situation really was until moments like this when I knew I could let my guard down instead of functioning on high alert all the time.

At the same time, I was trying to wrap my head around the idea of being home alone for the first time in months. It felt like what I imagined a mother must feel like sending her child off to school for the first time. I was so excited for the improvement Doug would experience by being in full-time rehab, but I was simultaneously concerned about not being readily available if something happened. I had officially become a helicopter wife!

Before Doug left, we had decided to make a visit to see the staff at the Providence Rehab Center. When the elevator doors opened, there stood Nurse Judy looking all professional in her white lab coat and a stethoscope around her neck. She was the physician's assistant who cared for Doug regularly. Judy obviously was deep in thought by the look on her face. However, she startled in recognition of us, her head jerked up, bouncing her reddish-blond hair as a smile spread across her face. "Doug," she exclaimed excitedly, "I was literally just talking to a patient about you and what you have overcome, hoping to encourage him with your story. I was wishing you could be here to inspire this man on his road to recovery. And suddenly, like magic, you show up a minute later."

After explaining how discouraged this fella was after rolling an ATV and suffering vertebral fractures, she asked if Doug would mind visiting him to share our hope with him because he was very discouraged at the speed or lack thereof in his progress. We readily agreed, and the young man lit up like a 1000-watt light bulb when he was introduced to Doug. He said, "I have read and reread the newspaper story and the *St. Patrick's Hospital Life Flight* magazine story about you, and I watched your interview on TV. Your story has motivated me to push hard to overcome the pain and limitations when I would rather just lay here in bed and feel sorry for myself."

We were delighted to be of help, and Doug was glowing with the same wattage as he felt the impact of words of hope hit the mark. I could see the twinkle in Doug's eyes as he was able to use his suffering to benefit another soul. He was adding value to another human being and was feeling valued in turn.

It was truly a joy to help this young man and to reconnect with the staff who had become like family and took such great care of Doug. They were all equally excited to see him and were impressed by how far he had come and how good he looked. Once again, good comes out of bad situations.

So we are convinced that every detail of
our lives is continually woven together to fit into
God's perfect plan of bringing good into our

lives, for we are His lovers who have been called to fulfill His designed purpose.

Romans 8:28 TPT

[/vc_row_inner]

May 28

QLI was even better than we expected. The facility was set up like a college campus. Doug lived in a house, which had ten bedrooms, a kitchen, and a laundry room. The bedrooms had private toilets and sinks, but the handicapped shower was down the hall for communal use. There was no institutional feel about the facility, and the staff wore street clothes without name tags. It was explained to us that they didn't want the patients to feel set apart.

This was a bit of a challenge for me after working in professional environments where I was taught to dress to certain standards, and the failure to wear a name tag could be grounds for a firm reprimand. However, I have to admit that the team there was the most welcoming and friendly staff I had ever had the pleasure of meeting. I now knew why this place was the top-ranked place in Omaha to work.

QLI's campus was both very relaxed and beautiful, and the compassion the staff had for their patients was outstanding. And to boot, most of the food was quite tasty! Even Doug remarked that this was the best decision we had made yet. I was greatly relieved to hear him say this because I had been concerned with how well he would do if he found the campus less than desirable.

We met with the psychologist, who was confident that Doug most likely would come out of his accident processing information better than before. Apparently, the brain would find other more efficient routes to use if the old ones didn't work any longer. He believed Doug was an exceptionally brilliant fellow and would be able to function very well mentally after some needed therapy.

Doug was quite shocked to find he was being regarded as brilliant. After all, he is just a kid from the sticks who barely graduated from high school. Doug wasn't interested in school, and his grades revealed that. He would have much rather been in the woods working than at school. His test scores significantly improved once he began his Pipefitter and Welding Apprenticeship in 2004. Highly interested in the trade, Doug applied himself to his studies scoring well on his tests and completing the apprenticeship in record time. I had always known that Doug was nobody's fool, and he was incredibly capable of whatever he set his mind to do. Proving, motivation, and interest determined the outcome.

However, I was dismayed when the psychologist said he felt the ataxia (lack of muscle control/coordination) might have to do more with the anoxia (lack of oxygen to the brain) than the medications. This meant simply reducing medication would not be a cure for ataxia. Now that it was essentially linked to brain damage, who knew if he would ever be free of the symptoms, making the likelihood of returning to a "normal" life less than likely. This also meant it was possible he may never return to the work he so enjoyed.

I had held out for the best possible outcome for Doug by leaning into my faith and taking the words of the naysayers with a grain of salt, but to hear this challenged my thinking. I am in no way Pollyanna, but neither am I someone who focuses on the worst possible outcomes. I knew from the beginning that Doug had little if any chance of arriving at the place where he currently was medically. After hearing stories of the miracles, I was willing to take a chance and ask for one.

> "And all the time you don't obtain what you
> want because you won't ask God for it" (James
> 4:2 TPT).

However, when I looked around campus and saw the degree of injuries and limitations other patients had, I had to remind myself the seemingly small degree of limitations Doug was dealing with was nothing when compared to what many others were living with—perhaps permanently.

Once again, I had to remind myself that "with God everything is possible" (Matthew 19:26 NLT), and therefore, I was not wrong to continue believing for the best possible outcome for Doug.

I had to believe that if Doug continued to have ataxia, it was perhaps God's way of reminding him who is really in control.

> "For this is why a thorn in my flesh was given to me, the Adversary's messenger sent to harass me, keeping me from becoming arrogant" (2 Corinthians 12:7 TPT).

When you totally surrender to God's plans, His blessings come your way—even if they don't always look as you expected. However, the Giver of Life always reveals His best for you when the timing is right.

As humans, we tend to believe perfection is the only acceptable completion. If the results don't meet a certain standard we have in mind, they simply won't make the cut. Yet God, in His divine wisdom, seems to take great joy in taking broken vessels and remodeling them to fit *His* standards.

Eve ate the apple, yet she was the mother of all living things. Moses stuttered and was a murderer-turned-into-deliverer. Noah got drunk but crafted the ark to house the animals to repopulate the earth after the flood. Abraham lied, yet God considered him a friend and a man of faith. Rahab was a prostitute and, eventually, the great grandmother of King David. King David committed adultery and murder, yet God called him a man after his own heart.

And the list goes on and on from failure to fame. Despite these seemingly detrimental, flawed, and corrupt souls, God used each one of them to create history.

Doug would come out as God's intended vessel!

Not Walking on Water Yet

June 10

Doug had been pushing himself quite hard and found himself on the ground more often than he would care to. Last Tuesday, he fell twice and was very discouraged. However, last Saturday, he was able to go kayaking and had a marvelous time. QLI provided excellent recreational therapy with their program, which was a significant motivator in the drive to increase his physical ability to participate in those activities. Being able to engage in "normal" fun activities created an enjoyable and stimulating environment for Doug.

But with his ups and downs came mine as well. The workers' compensation insurance company, his employer, used informed me they would not be paying for a monthly plane ticket for me to visit Doug unless traveling was medically necessary. After being told by one case manager I would receive airline tickets to visit, I was feeling confused and frustrated. I would think his mental and emotional state was deemed a medical necessity, but apparently, it was not. Most likely, their reluctance to finance my travel had to do with their bottom line. I guessed Doug was becoming a million-dollar man and was depleting their bank account, so they were trying to save money.

In my state of discouragement, I had to remind myself not to grumble at the discouraging news from the insurance company. Instead, I consoled myself with the knowledge my Heavenly Father was my provider as well as my "travel agent."

"For it was I, the Lord your God, who rescued you from the land of Egypt. Open your

mouth wide, and I will fill it with good things"
(Psalms 81:10 NLT).

He could turn this around for His glory. Time after time, I had
seen His hand of provision—like the time I prayed for a Chevrolet
Suburban. I made a list of exactly what I wanted in this vehicle:
year, interior and exterior colors, price range, and mileage range.
Sometime after I had been praying specifically for my new ride,
Doug and I were on I-90 driving into Missoula, and a Suburban
passed us matching the year and color criteria. I was astonished to
see it had dealer license plates on it. As it drove out of sight, I said to
Doug, "That's it! That is my new Suburban!" I was filled with awe
and optimism as I watched this red Suburban exit the freeway. *Is it
really possible it will be mine soon?*

"You could be right, Tam," Doug said in agreement.

The following week Doug insisted I check out some cake decorating supplies I had seen posted for sale. This would require driving
almost one hundred miles one way. I didn't want to give up half a
day, but I consented at Doug's urging. Two-thirds of the way to my
destination, I was approaching a small auto dealership when, to my
utter amazement, I saw a red Suburban that looked identical to the
one that passed us days earlier. I checked my watch and determined I
did indeed have enough time to stop in to inquire about it. I pulled
into the lot with anticipation dancing expectantly around in my
heart. I forced myself to walk and not run as I approached the office.

I introduced myself to the salesman and asked about the
Suburban. Yes, it was the one that passed us on the freeway. Yes, it was
within my desired mileage range. Yes, it was within our price range.
I was giddy with joy as I realized God was answering my prayer. The
cake decorating supplies were simply the bait to initiate my treasure
hunt. Answers may come in ways you would never expect, or they
may come down to the very last minute, but He never fails.

I also reminded myself the devil delights in bringing discouragement, and I was allowing him to get the best of me, so once
again, I put the nasty ole devil back in his place! I turned on the CD
player, cranked up the volume, and sang at the top of my lungs. I

worshiped and danced to a rousing round of the *Enemy's Camp* by Lindell Cooley. I belted out, "He is under my feet, / Satan is under my feet,"[45] while dancing on the enemy's proverbial head. It was just the antidote I needed to reassure myself of where I stood and to refresh the devil's memory of it too.

June 18

Last Wednesday, during breakfast, Doug scooted his wheelchair over to the counter to pour his coffee. When he went to put the pot back into the coffee maker, he had a spasm and hit the glass pot against the countertop, breaking the pot and spilling the hot contents into his lap. The scalding hot coffee immediately soaked through his sweatpants and pooled in his seat, burning him enough to blister.

Due to his newly acquired burns, he was unable to go to the climbing wall on Friday as the therapists had scheduled. Having never rock-climbed before, he was looking forward to the experience and was greatly disappointed by the missed opportunity.

I would be flying to Omaha soon after, and, I must confess, I was looking forward to seeing him and getting a "Doughug." Even though we usually talked on the phone for hours every day, it didn't replace the physical element. I now understood why babies die if they don't get enough physical contact. I missed his physical touch. When friends gave me hugs at church on Sunday, I wanted to hold on to them for dear life and get my tank filled back up. Doug must have been feeling the same way because he said the four days I was going to be with him were not going to be nearly enough time together.

But short of quitting my job and moving to Omaha, we had no other option of spending time together. But just as we had for the last few months, we would persevere.

July 1

Funny how life seems to be driven by waiting for the next big event to occur. When one looks back at them all strung together, the bigger picture becomes a bit clearer. Experience has taught me that this is the mysterious way of God. He seldom reveals the big picture. Instead, it seems He leaves clues in the shape of puzzle pieces, providing us with an ample opportunity to test each piece for placement until we finally discover the perfect fit. And in His quintessential timing, He drops another puzzle piece right where we are sure to find it. Eventually, clarity is gained with every piece acquired. This arduous task brings with it a gratifying sense of accomplishment once completed.

Who would have thought six months before we would be able to witness a miracle and pull together a community in a life and death battle—all for the encouragement of so many other people?

I often had the opportunity share our story with strangers at work, in the marketplace, and when I traveled to and from Omaha. I was having so much fun with the opportunity to partner with God to encourage others as they endured their own battles.

Everyone needs to be encouraged, whether they have had a life-altering event or are simply dealing with the daily grind of life. A bit of motivation may be just the push someone needs to make a life or world-changing decision. It was the uplifting of others and their stories of overcoming, which empowered me to believe we could prevail through our trial too. I believe that God comforts us through the words of His people. I wanted to reciprocate with words of inspiration, not to tear down and discourage, but rather to build up and speak life into others.

Much like the puzzle and words of encouragement, I believe we have a blank canvas before us, and we are patiently waiting for God to show us where to put the color and whom to encourage. I shared this thought with Rhonda, one of Doug's ICU nurses, several months after the accident. She got teary-eyed and reiterated to me what a miracle it was he was alive and doing so well. Then she said, "God has put the pots of color before us and is custom-mixing the colors. The colors He has given us will be far richer than any we would have had to paint with if we not gone through this trial in our lives."

Needless to say, her response caused both Doug and I to tear up at the profundity of her discernment. And as I continued to ponder her words, I was blessed that God had spoken to me through Rhonda. I am a person who absolutely loves color. The more colorful, the better in my book.

Speaking of color, there was a painting at work I loved. It hung in the hallway outside of the patient exam rooms near the employee lounge. I had multiple opportunities to pause and contemplate its complexity and vibrancy as I delivered reports to the nurses' stations during the early morning hours before the arrival of most of the employees. This painting was so rich in color and texture. I am assuming that it was heavily applied with a spatula and then sculpted to create an intensely colorful 3-D effect. I couldn't help but think of this creative work of art and how it seems to apply to our life journey, varying layers of overlapping events cumulating into a beautiful masterpiece.

God offers us such rich abundance in a life filled with color, texture, and minute detail. And yet we settle for so little, all while He offers the world to us. I think one of the reasons we reject His offer of abundance is because we don't want to leave our comfortable nest. The nest we currently occupy may not be as spacious as we would prefer, and it may even have some sharp sticks protruding here and there, making it less than optimal, but it is what we know. It is our proverbial comfort zone. Discomfort can be more tolerable than attempting the unknown, which will most likely present us with challenges and obstacles to overcome. We don't take the risk and put ourselves out there because we don't want to suffer. We want our Christianity to be comfortable.

However, Jesus suffered for our salvation and restoration. Each whipping lash He endured inflicted tremendous pain as it buried itself deep into His skin, ripping the tissue of His body as it pulled chunks of flesh in its upward retreat. The process was repeated over and over again until Jesus' body was consumed in torturous affliction. Once His body was whipped and beaten beyond recognition, He was made to carry a cross through the streets and up the hill where He would make the ultimate sacrifice of His life for us. He endured far greater pain than any of us will know. Paul invites us to suffer as Christ suffered, allowing His likeness to manifest in us (2 Corinthians 3:18).

According to Ann Voskamp, "Suffering which does not break us away from more of this world and break us into more of God is wasted suffering."[46] As Doug and I suffered, we discovered what we were truly capable of even in the midst of our pain. Doug's brain continued to heal and find new neural pathways to overcome the damaged areas. Slowly, he was gaining his independence, and in an oxymoronic way had become more dependent and submitted to God's plans and timing.

Being someone who has always preferred to be part of the pit crew rather than the driver of the race car, I quickly realized I was now behind the wheel with the Holy Spirit as my copilot. As I careened around blind corners, only to be thrown into a deep descent or possibly having to dodge a falling boulder, I was driving through life in blind faith. It was this harrowing ride where I discovered the depths of my faith as I stood believing against all odds for the miracle of Doug's recovery. I learned how deeply God cared for me as He revealed Himself in so many ways most every day through a timely word or unexpected blessing. His provision came despite our job losses. Our suffering was noticed and noted by others providing us the opportunity to share our faith with them. Our suffering became an opportunity for encouragement as others inquired as to how we were managing so well.

As for me, I plan on living in Technicolor, filled with rich detail and texture and if I bleed red from drawing closer to Christ, so be it. In as much as I liked my creature comforts, our journey taught me that to truly live is to experience both the depth of pain and joy. Pain and joy seem to be in balance. The more you experience one, the greater the ability you have to experience the other. In an attempt to self-protect oneself from suffering, one also limits their capacity to encounter joy.

"The walls we build around us to keep sadness out also keeps out the joy" (Jim Rohn).[47]

As I chose to be thankful for the challenges and painful circumstances, I was seeing life with new eyes and was given the opportunity to reevaluate what is truly important. In doing so, I gained a far greater appreciation for the little intricacies of life and the blessings in disguise.

Doug and I could have easily felt sorry for ourselves as we seemed to have taken one hit after another, barely catching our breath before the next crisis presented itself. Many times, friends and loved ones said, "You have already been through so much. I don't know how you guys are surviving this onslaught of misfortune. It's like you can't even catch a break."

Yes, it seemed like we had experienced a loss of quality of life over six months' time and that we would possibly be facing many more as Doug continued to battle to get back on his feet. Yes, our finances took a huge hit. Yet, life is not always what it seems to be. Life becomes what you choose to focus on. Therefore, it is imperative you focus on the outcome you desire, not what you are currently experiencing.

I am motivated to hit the gym when I focus on the strength and endurance I am achieving rather than the exertion, pain, and sweat I am experiencing during the growth process. Your perspective will determine your outcome. As Andy Andrews says, "A grateful perspective brings happiness and abundance into a person's life."[48]

I may find it difficult to be grateful for Doug's accident, but I was ever so grateful the outcome revealed such lavish love, compassion, support, and encouragement from so many individuals, many of whom we would have never encountered had it not been for tragedy.

And just as some of the most ingenious inventions have come about by pure accident, I believe some of our greatest opportunities to become the best possible versions of ourselves are developed through adversity. A disaster may save us from destruction. We may also discover what we thought was urgent was keeping us from something greater and significantly more important. Therefore, I will take the rain coming down as an indication I should clean the house instead of working outside!

July 6

Just as Peter sank after walking on water because he allowed fear to convince him that what he was doing was impossible, Doug struggled to stay afloat as well. Up until this point, he had been making such huge steps forward, but since he was not progressing as quickly as before, his spirit was sinking. Knowing he was discouraged, I called him several times, and I could hear the defeat in his voice.

"What's going on?" I asked.

"I went out for a walk before lunch today and fell again."

"Are you okay?" I asked, feeling concerned about injuries.

"No," he said with Eeyore-sounding despondency in his tone. "I hit my head on the sidewalk again. There was blood everywhere. Both my knees are scraped up. The Physical Therapy Aide fell on top of me, and she got hurt too. I was doing so good," he sobbed. "I don't know what is wrong with me right now. All I know is that I am sick and tired of falling. I am tired of getting hurt and hurting others. Why do they send the smallest woman out with a big guy like me?" he asked me in frustration.

I hadn't recalled ever hearing him sound so helpless, broken, and defeated. My heart ached for him. I, too, felt helpless being so far away and unable to be there in person to comfort him.

His tone changed from self-pity to anger as he went on to say, "The QLI therapist told me the quickest way to come home is to get better. I am working so hard to get stronger, and now therapists are telling me to slow down and that I'm working too hard. They can't seem to make up their mind, and this really pisses me off. I am doing what I was told only to be told I am doing it wrong."

"Doug, most people with injuries are not as determined as you to recover, and they require massive amounts of encouragement to gain the slightest improvement. You need to understand the PT's perspective. They are only trying to keep you from overdoing it and injuring yourself further."

What the PT failed to understand was telling Doug to slow down was equivalent to asking a bull not to charge the red flag. I could envision the tension in his jaw and the steely glint in his hazel eyes as the emotion in his voice conveyed his frustration loud and clear. "Slow down" is simply not in his vocabulary. Those closest to him know if you want him to do something, tell him he can't. He really needed a good dose of patience, but I knew better than to tell him to be patient or that I would pray for patience for him. In his words, "I was foolish enough to ask for patience years ago. I suffered the consequences as everything I undertook for a year fell apart as equipment broke down and decisions backfired. I was the best student in an apprenticeship in the development of patience."

I had a hunch that a bigger part of his problem was loneliness. I asked him if he could have anything besides his physical strength to make his life better at QLI, what would he desire? He responded by saying me being there for him physically would be helpful. In a later conversation, he said it was a selfish request for him to ask me to be there to be as his support system. He decided he needed to pull up his big girl panties and deal with it. Perhaps he is wearing the wrong panties!

I read Romans 8:17, which says just as we get to share in all the blessings and gifts of Christ, we also get to share equally in the suffering. In an attempt to encourage Doug, I told him after having gone through what he has, he must have some exceptionally huge blessings coming.

"Remember those He bruises, He uses. Those He blesses, He breaks. And ofttimes His tactics baffle the very best of us" (Timothy Paul Green)[49].

A Step Backwards

July 12

QLI staff called to tell me Doug had fallen many times in the last week. As a result, he had an excruciating headache and was confused. Considering his history, he had an MRI today. I didn't have all the details yet, but the doctors believed he had a brain bleed, but that it may have been from an earlier fall. If I had to guess, I'd have said it was from when he faceplanted on the hardwood floor.

The following day one of the QLI nurses called to give me an update on Doug's condition and suggested I take the next available flight to Omaha, given the dire circumstances Doug was in. She felt my presence would be calming for him. In addition to the MRI, testing indicated his platelets were very low, and the doctors were suspicious his brain was still bleeding. He was admitted to the Methodist Hospital for more extensive testing. The nurse told me when patients have an active bleed, there is a simple procedure, which can be done to stop the bleeding, and they are usually back on campus in two days. Hopefully, this would be the case for Doug.

After getting off the phone with the nurse from QLI, I immediately called Work Comp to get authorization to fly to Omaha. This was indeed a medical necessity. They were very gracious and told me to pack my bag, and they would get me on the next available flight to Omaha. By now, it was late afternoon, and I knew I wouldn't be able to get a flight out of Missoula until the next morning. I had mixed feelings about this, I wanted to be there for Doug as well as for my own peace of mind, but I needed to make arrangements for pet care and possibly time off work once again. I would now have time to get myself and my home organized before flying out.

I called our families and support crew and explained what was happening, knowing they would be once again going to prayer for us. I was grateful beyond words to know I was not alone, but rather steadfastly held up and encouraged by our faithful family and intercessional friends.

> "If one of them falls, the other can help him up. But who will help the pitiful person who falls down alone?" (Ecclesiastes 4:10 VOICE).

I was able to quickly organize the details necessary for me to leave on such a short notice. It would seem I was becoming a pro at crisis management.

Once I had my travel arrangement taken care of, I called Doug to let him know I would be arriving the following day. He seemed relieved to know I was on my way, but it was obvious he was not functioning well. The conversation was very scattered as his compromised brain tried to assimilate all the information. Knowing that rest was more important than talking to me, I said, "Doug, I need to pack and get things ready before I come and see you. We will talk as long as you want when I get there. Right now, why don't you take a nap and rest up for my visit?" He conceded easily. It may have been in part to a sedative or simply the effort it was taking to try and understand what was going on.

Now that I had checked in with Doug, it was time to check in with God. I called the dogs and headed out the door to walk along the banks of the 9-Mile creek to pray. It was a beautiful evening. The sunlight filtered through the evergreens, dappling the forest floor. I could smell the warm scent of pine and fir needles as I wandered through the trees toward the creek bottom. Leaving the forest, I stopped at the edge of the meadow to watch a doe and fawn scamper into the alders. I loved this spot. It was a place of transition and tranquility. The dense forest gave way to the open meadow. The view was expansive as I gazed across the valley. McCormick Peak punctuated the horizon standing proudly as a landmark on the 9-Mile Divide Trail. For a moment in time, I could forget my troubles as I lost myself in the beauty that surrounded me. It was as though the peace of God was distracting me from the potential worry and fear poised to wreak havoc at the first opportunity.

The forest offered a form of protection, while the meadow required a sort of vulnerability to fully appreciate all it offered in flora and fauna. The deer often grazed on the lush forage while keeping an eye out for predators. Ground squirrels were at risk of being picked off by birds of prey, an agile fox, or a cunning coyote. What a paradox life seems to be as it is held in a tenuous balance. To fully experience is to risk safety. Such are the mysteries of God and His creation. I am constantly in awe and wonder as to how He manages to hold all of it together, but because He does, I knew I could trust Him with Doug's outcome.

Nearing the creek, it was as though I was breathing in His heady perfume as the sweet scent of fresh creek water delighted my nostrils. The dogs raced off like a lightning bolt at the sound of a ground squirrel squeaking nearby, threatening to interrupt my time of reflection. Once again, I was left to ponder how quickly life changes. I would be returning to Omaha much sooner than anticipated, and without the birthday cake I had planned to make and take with me to surprise Doug.

Yes, it was the chocolate cake with the raspberry cream cheese filling. His birthday is on July 15, and it was just three short days away. Originally, my plan was to arrive the week after his birthday. We decided to stretch out the time between visits because while my work schedule provided the flexibility to make frequent trips, my budget was not as accommodating. I knew he was in very capable hands between QLI and hospital staff, and there was little I could do to change the circumstances. Taking care of myself and our home was the best choice, but I sure felt better knowing I would be flying at six o'clock in the morning.

I was met at the Omaha airport by QLI staff. After receiving a welcome hug, I was quickly updated on Doug's condition as we walked to baggage claim. The doctors wanted to do surgery to fix the brain bleeds. However, this would necessitate the elimination of his blood thinner, Coumadin. In the meantime, the doctors would be putting in an IVC filter to prevent possible further clots from migrating to his heart and lungs.

I was able to make it to the Methodist Hospital prior to the IVC placement. Once again, I found myself being ushered down the gloomy halls of a hospital, my sandals were slapping against my feet as I walked with purpose. I was intent on seeing Doug as soon as possible, not knowing exactly what to expect despite my briefing. However, the fact he was in ICU once again was a telltale of the severity of the situation.

I knocked quietly on his door to announce my presence, yet not wanting to cause any noise or disturb Doug if he was sleeping. His nurse from QLI was the one who invited me in, much to my surprise. When I expressed my shock and delight at seeing her, she reassured me it was their policy not to leave patients alone until the family was able to be present. Initially, I was also surprised to discover his room was almost dark, but I immediately understood the light was exacerbating his headache. Despite the lack of light in the room, it was obvious at first glance that all was not well. His eyes had dark circles around them and seemed sunken into his ashen face. His usually twinkling eyes were dark. He attempted to smile in recognition, but I could tell he was in pain. His voice crackled a raspy, "Hello." After I said my hello while reaching for his hand, the nurse gave me the latest update. The IVC procedure was scheduled to take place in the next half hour. I arrived just in time to review the procedure with the doctor who would be performing the surgery.

The doctor went on to explain that after several tests, it was determined the Depakote, one of his anticonvulsants, was interfering with the formation of platelets in his blood and would need to be discontinued immediately. I could feel fear coiling its tentacles around me as images of Doug seizing flashed back in my mind. I calculated what removing 6,000 milligrams of anticonvulsant would do to his brain.

With as much calm as I could muster, I asked, "What if he seizes?" The doctor responded, "At this point, we have no choice. We either eliminate the Depakote and risk seizures or chance him bleeding to death." I understood perfectly well; it was time to batten down the hatches and prepare for the worst while hoping and praying for the best. Doug's situation was the perfect storm as his thin blood meant any small bump would cause his body to bruise—and that meant in his brain as well. It appeared he had bruising on both sides of his brain, which provoked the headaches and confusion—thus causing more falls.

The surgery went off without a hitch. He didn't have any seizures, much to my relief. Doug was transferred out of ICU to a regular hospital room and was recovering. Hopefully, he could get back on the road to healing if we could keep him in his hospital bed. In his confusion, he tried to walk unaided to the bathroom and fell on the floor, hitting his head once again while losing control of his bladder. The nurse found him thrashing in his own urine, unable to comprehend what was going on. It took several minutes and several nurses and aides to get him to calm down so they could get him up and back to bed.

Doug's supposedly short stay in the hospital turned into five days as he continued his attempts to climb out of bed without assistance. Each attempt resulted in additional falls—worsening the bruising on his backside, which had taken a beating during the many falls he incurred. It looked like someone took a 2×4 to him. His arms and legs were also covered in dark bruises. Consequently, the hospital nurses had to use restraints to keep Doug safe in bed.

Needless to say, Doug was not happy about being restrained. Hoping to help him see he would be stronger and more capable if he would be patient and wait for God's timing, I reminded him of the verse Isaiah 40:31 (NKJV), "But those who wait on the Lord shall renew their strength." His reply came in the form of a scowl. Despite him scowling at me, I noticed a clarity in his eyes that I hadn't seen since before the accident. Even though the Depakote was immediately stopped, it took several days for it to be flushed from his body. I was delighted to see more of the Doug I knew emerge from behind the veil of medication. In the end, this turned out to be a blessing in disguise. He couldn't ask for a much better birthday gift.

The staff at QLI had a special birthday cake made for Doug after I told them about the surprise cake, I had planned on bringing but didn't have time to make before I left. They knew we were sad we were not to be able to celebrate as we normally would have for his fifty-third birthday. He took great joy in telling them about what he was accustomed to having. Knowing how spoiled he was and his standards, they said they couldn't make him a box cake or buy one from the grocery store. His nurse from QLI arranged for a cake to be brought to his room and had the floor nurses sing to him. Doug was blessed by such a kind and thoughtful gesture. However, he took two bites of the cake, pushed it away, and said, "This isn't your cake!" What a spoiled guy! The cake was beautiful, but I hadn't tasted it yet. Hopefully, we would try eating more of it tomorrow, and it would be more to his liking.

July 17

Doug appeared to have turned the corner.

A CT indicated that his hematomas appeared stable. And while the neurologists wanted to keep him overnight for continued observation, I could already see a difference in his mental clarity and physical function. We hoped he would be able to return to QLI the next day.

It was interesting to see how this puzzle was fitting together. I was extremely grateful he was where he was. The Lord, in His wisdom, knew what He was doing, and we would trust Him once again. He was so very faithful thus far!

Regarding life's trials, 1 Peter 1:7 (NIV) states:

> These have come so that the proven genuineness of your faith—of greater worth than gold, which perishes even though refined by fire—may result in praise, glory and honor when Jesus Christ is revealed.

[/vc_row_inner]

I was struck with awe by these words. My faith *is* of greater worth than gold.

Apparently, we were making a sizeable investment in our faith portfolio. When you think about the streets in heaven being paved with gold, this makes more sense. Gold only has real value here on earth; in heaven, it's asphalt, common everyday sand, gravel, and tar. While gold is the standard of currency here on earth, in heaven, faith is what is of supreme value.

Faith, however, has natural and supernatural value. Jesus said we would do even greater things than He did (John 14:12 NIV), and if we had faith as small as a mustard seed, we could move mountains (Matthew 17:20 NIV). Well, I was beginning to understand this concept more fully. The more we exercise and develop our faith muscles, the more mountains begin to turn into molehills.

This was happening before our very eyes, and we were overcoming the many mountains in our path.

Faith doesn't make it easy, but it does make it possible!

Back at QLI

July 19

Doug was released from the hospital and was back at QLI. He was welcomed with lots of hugs and love. He finally got to eat his birthday cake, and I will admit I thought the cake was pretty darn tasty even if I wasn't the baker! What's not to love about a chocolate fudge raspberry cake?

He rested most of the time, although he did spend some time catching up on his email. I found this to be strange because Doug never showed any interest in computers before the accident, but whenever I came to Omaha, he proudly showed me all the new skills he acquired since my last visit. His computer skills prior to the accident were specific to work at the paper mill. He did not have an email account, nor did he know how to google, but he was eager to demonstrate his newfound abilities with pride. For a guy who should not have been alive, he was not only getting back what the devil attempted to steal from him; he was evolving in ways, which were boggling my mind.

I was also noticing mental clarity in him, which was not evident since before the accident. I believe this was directly related to the continued reduction of the anticonvulsants. He seemed to be much more like the old Doug we knew and loved. He didn't miss an opportunity to take a shot at someone or situation in a humorous and teasing way or spout off a funny comeback like he used to before the accident. In fact, he had the staff in stitches much of the time. His hilarity was a welcome contrast to the anger and misery many of the other patients suffered from. I missed his quick sense of humor and was thrilled to see it being restored. The twinkle in his eyes got brighter every day. He even said he felt like a million bucks. He was hard at work in PT and excited to finally get a chance to combat the climbing wall.

I was truly grateful for our Heavenly Father's arms. He is always willing to catch us when we fall or help us up when we stumble, just as in the story of the prodigal son. Despite the son having turned his back on his father, the father waited patiently for the son to come to his senses and return home. When he did, the son found the father waiting expectantly for him. The son was welcomed warmly into the father's arms. He was even restored back into the family (Luke 15:11-32). However, in as much as He restores us, He will push us hard for improvement like any great coach would do.

I read a terrific book called *The Circle Maker* by Mark Batterson. He says manna was a daily reminder of the Israelites' dependence on God for daily provision and that nothing about this expectation has changed for us today. Jesus taught us to pray through the pattern of the Lord's Prayer, which reads, "Give us this day our daily bread." He goes on to say:

> We want a one-week or one-month or one-year supply of God's provision, but God wants us to drop to our knees every day in raw dependence on Him. And God knows that if He provided too much too soon, we'd lose our spiritual hunger. He knows we'd stop trusting in our Provider and start trusting in the provision... One reason many people get frustrated spiritually is that they feel like it should get easier to do the will of God... But the will of God doesn't get easier. The will of God gets harder. Here's why: the harder it gets the harder you have to pray.
>
> God will keep putting you in situations that stretch your faith, and as your faith stretches, so do your dreams. If you pass the test, you graduate to bigger and bigger dreams. And it won't get eas-

ier; it'll get harder. It won't get less complicated
it'll get more complicated. But the complications
are evidence of God's blessings. And if it's from
God, then it's a holy complication.[50]

[/vc_row_inner]

I believed Doug and I were truly blessed! Despite all he had
been through, Doug was doing amazingly well. His voice and reactions were so normal and so Doug. It's hard to explain the change I
saw in him after the reduction of anticonvulsants, but I was encouraged by what I saw. Other people were not, though.

Doug's neurologist met with us to go over an evaluation he
had taken of Doug's progress. "In my opinion, you will never return
to work as a pipefitter or to any other job, which requires lots of
strength and agility. You need to figure out what you can do from a
desk for the rest of your working life."

I am fairly certain I could see smoke coming from Doug's
ears. I watched as his body stiffened and his nostrils flared in anger.
Unsuccessfully struggling to keep the irritation out of his voice, he
asked the doctor, "What makes you say I won't be able to work as a
pipefitter and welder?"

With carefully measured words, the neurologist responded,
"Given the severity of your injury and ataxia, you will never be capable of doing work, which puts you in a high-risk situation. No one
will be willing to hire you in your current condition."

Doug, somewhat deflated but not to be deterred, said, "But I
am so much better than anyone ever expected, who's to say that I
won't recover enough to do what I want?"

I watched this battle of wills play out as the neurologist snuffed
out Doug's flame of hope with his response. "I have been in this business for a long time, and I have never seen anyone with your level of
injury recover beyond where you currently are."

Later, when we were alone, I could tell Doug needed a pep talk.
"Listen, if your life was based on the opinions of others, you wouldn't
even be alive, let alone mostly in your right mind excelling at Excel.

Are you going to let this doctor derail you from your hopes and dreams? Are you going to let the devil win this round, or are you going to do what you do best and prove everyone wrong? Remember, this is one person's opinion."

It has been my experience that if you tell Doug he can't do something, you better get out of his way as he shows you he can and he will. But this news really developed into a disappointment he didn't recover from as quickly. He did however, finally calm down after much discussion. He decided to explore all options while he regained strength and agility all the while intending to return to work as a pipefitter or welder. We both understood, however, if God shuts one door, He always opens a better one. Unfortunately, sometimes our vision is clouded, making the better door tough to see in the moment of frustration. Sometimes it requires wrestling with God and surrendering our wills before we can come into synch with His. It was too soon to tell for sure, but I was beginning to wonder if the neurologist was right. His time at QLI was definitely making a difference, but not nearly as much as I had hoped for.

While Doug did not enjoy being away from home, he had so many opportunities he would never have otherwise had. The quality of care was far superior to what he would have gotten at home. In addition, the weekly fishing trips, kayaking, climbing wall, and bike riding provided normalcy to his recovery process. He was also able to meet people from several different states as QLI serviced a large territory. It was easy to become a family of sorts with other patients and their loved ones who were also dealing with their life-changing circumstances.

I was finally able to bring Doug's birthday cake with me when I visited next. I made a huge cake, knowing how disappointed he had been with the bakery cake and how fun it would be to share its fourteen and a half pounds of goodness with as many as possible. It was the chocolate one with the raspberry cream cheese filling. I have never flown a cake before, but it was worth all the effort to make it happen. The cake was a huge hit! I now had had several requests for wedding and birthday cakes. I also packed four quarts of pickles in my suitcase for him as well. The staff pretty much thought he was spoiled rotten. I sacrificed several articles of clothing to make the weight limit, but he was worth all the effort.

Birthday parties seemed to be a theme for me. After returning home, I went to a birthday party for our grandnephew, Sawyer, who was turning one. When I arrived at the party, Roper, Sawyer's six-year-old brother, asked me where Uncle Doug was. I explained to him Uncle Doug was in Omaha. Roper matter-of-factly asked me if Doug was working there, so I said, "No, Uncle Doug is doing rehab."

Roper asked, "What's rehab?"

"It's a place where they do special types of exercises after an accident to help you get better and stronger."

Roper contemplated this information for a while, and confidently replied, "Yep, Christmas will be just right because by then Uncle Doug will be all muscled up!"

Oh, the wisdom of a five-year-old! He seemed to think August to Christmas was enough time for Doug to regain his strength. I was trying not to laugh at his innocent deduction.

When I told Doug later, he got a good laugh out of Roper's statement. He also said, "I better workout a little harder to meet Roper's expectations. I am going to have to hulk out to impress that boy!"

Calm Seas, Gentle Waves

September 1

Finally, we were informed Doug would be given the opportunity to discontinue all the anticonvulsants he was taking. This would be undertaken in the hospital with close supervision to monitor for potential seizures. The side effects of the medications were of concern since when he first had to take them, particularly in the quantity he had been using.

I recall the looks of concern from the medical team as they calculated how much of the paralytic drug Doug had been given, knowing they were about to administer more to control the relentless seizures. I inquired about the risk of using that amount and was informed that it could potentially cause kidney and liver damage in addition to multiple other side effects and that it may be the reason for his ataxia. We definitely didn't want him to seize again, and God willing, he wouldn't. The very thought of him seizing made me ill because watching his body contort into unnatural positions was devastating to watch. I in no way wanted to have to revisit such a traumatic experience ever again. All I could do was pray he would be able to remain off the anticonvulsants indefinitely.

Not only was Doug concerned about his kidneys and liver, but he was also a bit concerned about all the radiation he had been getting. I then explained to him he had been having MRIs, not X-Rays, therefore, there wasn't any radiation involved. Unfortunately, he did have to have a CT scan, which *is* X-ray, because he tripped and fell a few days before. He was able to get his hands out to help break the fall, but his cheek managed to plow up the fibers in the carpet, leaving nasty carpet burn on his face. Fortunately, though, the CT came back normal; the wounds were only on the surface. After seeing the nasty scab forming on his cheek, Doug said he hoped I hadn't planned on taking pictures for our anniversary. However, if I was insistent, he said he could "turn the other cheek," and they might come out okay. What a funny boy!

Knowing Doug was going to be taken off the medication, I spent quite a bit of time talking to God about how this would all turn out. *Papa, ever since I heard Your voice in the beginning, I have trusted You to the best of my ability. I have believed Doug could come through this accident and be completely fine, contrary to my medical experience and the advice and experience of highly trained doctors and medical staff. But lately, I find myself doubting he will ever be his old self. I hate that I am wavering in my faith. I want to fight this fight well and not allow doubt and fear to get the better of me. Please assure me once again that all will turn out as You have said.*

Reassurance was slow in coming testing my faith yet again. As I watched Doug's rehabilitation, it became obvious to me that he was not progressing as quickly as he once was. He still required so much assistance. He needed help getting in and out of the shower. He was still very twitchy and dropped things, which frustrated him greatly. I could see the despair in his eyes when he struggled to complete basic tasks. I knew his progress would naturally slow down at some point., but I kept expecting him to wake up one day, and everything would be as it was before the accident. However, I realized I needed to prepare myself that Doug may end up with some limitations once the dust finally settled.

After looking around QLI and seeing the challenges and limitations other patients had, what Doug was dealing with seemed like very small potatoes. I should have been incredibly grateful Doug was doing as well as he was. And while I was indeed grateful, I struggled to reconcile the evidence before me to my hope that he would be okay. I am a realist and understand life happens, and you must deal with the consequences in the best way you are able to with the resources available.

As much as I still believed God could bring Doug through this whole ordeal, I won't pretend I wasn't disappointed and a bit discouraged he was not progressing faster, especially when I considered what this could mean for my future. After all, he was still falling, had ataxia, and short-term memory loss. It seemed likely we may not return to life as we knew it.

However, as I recall, there are many Bible stories of others like Abraham and Moses, who didn't get the results they wanted *when* they wanted either. But in the end, guess who always managed to come through in His perfect timing? God. In fact, I heard a teaching on Daniel and was reminded of how God showed up in the darkest hour through the story of Shadrach, Meshach, and Abednego. They were thrown into the fire, and not only did they not burn up, but not a hair on their heads was singed, and their clothing was not scorched. They didn't even smell like smoke! (Daniel 3:26-27).

If Daniel and his buddies could go through the fire and not burn, couldn't Doug go without oxygen and have a brain that was fully intact? I was willing to hear no, but I also knew God can't tell you no if you don't ask. Everyone thought I was a fool to believe Doug could even live, and I was still willing to risk looking like a zealous nut holding on to my belief that Doug's brain could be fully functioning in time.

Perhaps I was a fool. Doug was certainly providing plenty of evidence he wasn't progressing but rather floundering. When I got in on September 13, I thought he was going to cry. This was not how I anticipated celebrating our thirtieth anniversary.

Before I arrived, he decided he was doing so well walking he no longer needed assistance and attempted to walk to the bathroom by himself. His walk did not go as well as he imagined, and he fell on his face again. Due to his failure to comply with QLI instruction, he was locked in his wheelchair, which was a huge mental challenge for him.

QLI also installed a laser beam alarm next to his bed. Essentially, if he broke the beam, an alarm went off to alert the staff he was up. This added insult to injury, and he couldn't understand the nurses' concern for his safety or the liability he was creating. "How can I get better if they don't let me do things for myself," he muttered when I asked him what was going on.

"Doug, don't you realize every time you fall, you risk damaging your brain further? If you continue to damage your brain, it could be irreparable. You will never get the opportunity to do the things you love to do then. You could break your bones," I said, trying to reason with him. "If you won't cooperate with the staff, they have no choice but to restrain you to keep you from damaging your brain and body further. You have become a liability to them when you fail to comply with their safety requirement. They may ask you to leave if you won't cooperate, and you will be sent home without further possibilities of rehab. The sooner you comply, the sooner you will get to come home stronger and whole."

When God really wants to get your attention, He has a way of taking you to the place where He can reveal His power and your lack thereof. Hoping to encourage Doug, I reminded him of when Joseph was unfairly sold into slavery by his brothers and put in prison as a result of being betrayed by Potiphar's wife as God's way of preparing him for an opportunity of a lifetime. As a second-in-command over all of Egypt, whereby he was able to later reconcile with his brothers, Joseph found that despite the hardship he endured, everything worked out quite well in the end. I assured Doug it was quite possible he would find it would all work out better than expected too. But I was not the one locked in my wheelchair undergoing a life lesson in humility and submission.

In the end, our anniversary weekend turned out perfect. The Murrays flew in to join us in our celebration, treating us to a fine dinner, riverboat ride, and a trip to the Omaha Zoo. Doug was given a reprieve and thoroughly enjoyed getting out of the house and off the campus. He struggled some being around lots of people, particularly the children with poor behavior we encountered at the zoo. He never tolerated screaming kids, but knowing he was being blatantly gawked at by them as he sat in his wheelchair was more than he could cope with. I think he had sensory overload from the break in routine and all the stimuli. By the end of each day, he was exhausted but happy. It was a whirlwind weekend for all of us. It wasn't going to slow down for a while. Even though I flew home with the Murrays that Sunday, I knew in less than two weeks' time, I would be returning again for another one of Doug's medical procedures.

Doug was scheduled to undergo a video EEG to monitor his brain as he was going to be taken off all his medications on October 1, 2012. As we approached that date, I had a dream in which Doug was trapped in a similar accident to the one he had experienced. Five days into the dream, and Doug had not yet been rescued. I was told to let Doug go. I was angry and drove out to the mill to look for Doug myself. As I got out of the car, Doug came staggering out of the building exhausted, dirty, wet, carrying a bag of personal belongings, and completely in his right mind, and fully functional. Then I woke up.

Knowing God spoke regularly to people through dreams in the Bible and that He speaks to me from time to time in that way as well, I found the timing of this dream to be interesting. It was as though God was reassuring me Doug would be okay despite my fears and despite what others were saying. It was just going to take more time than I had expected it to take. Doug was essentially trapped by medications and the limitations of his injured brain. I chose to believe this dream was confirmation Doug would come through this totally intact.

October 2

It was finally the day! We were at the Nebraska Medical Center through the recommendation of Doug's epileptologist to begin the reduction of anticonvulsants. It is one of the top five nationally ranked hospitals for neurological treatment, and it was only fifteen minutes away from QLI. Doug would be a recipient of some of the best medical care in the nation. We must have had divine intervention to have a place in the schedule open up because we were told it would take months before they would be able to fit Doug in for a video EEG. Somehow, though, months turned into weeks, and there we were preparing for one more procedure.

Truly our Father knows every hair on our head (Luke 12:7) and provides for all our needs. Doug would be greatly blessed and benefit from being able to reduce, if not completely eliminate, the anticonvulsants.

In preparation for the procedure, the leads for the EEG and heart monitors were literally glued to Doug's head, chest, and back. He kind of looked like he had multicolored dreadlocks or was, perhaps, an electric version of Medusa. The heart monitor patches had to be changed daily, which meant hair loss each time over a four-day period. Suddenly, our sunny skies got a bit cloudy, and I was certain I heard the roar of thunder as the tech pulled the patches of hair, and possibly skin, off his head and chest. His aide, trying to bring us a little levity, said there was no extra charge for the waxing.

Once Doug was hooked up to the EEG, he was monitored continuously for seizure activity as the anticonvulsants were reduced over a forty-eight-hour window. As the reduction in meds occurred, there was some mild seizure-like activity on Doug's EEG. The epileptologist described the mild seizures to be equivalent to sparks rather than fires. He believed it would be in Doug's best interest to use a modest amount of medication to ensure the sparks were not able to manifest into raging fires.

The doctors also indicated that I should expect to see improvements for the next five years. But while the brain continued to heal, it was best to give it some help to ensure the best recovery possible. Doug was able to reduce Keppra he was on by 2,000 milligrams, which was significant. However, he still required 4,000 milligrams to hold the seizures at bay.

In addition, the epileptologist added a small dose of a new anticonvulsant called Vimpat. He felt it would complement Keppra and keep the brain stable. Even though Doug wasn't able to get completely off the anticonvulsants, he was a long way from the 13,500 milligrams he had been on originally. Clearly, when God updates a hard drive, the rebooting process can take some time!

Nevertheless, that time of darkness will not
go on forever... The people who walk in dark-

ness will see a great light. For those who live in a
land of deep darkness, a light will shine.

Isaiah 9:1-2 NLT

[/vc_row_inner]

Despite what seemed to be a dark beginning, Doug was slowly
seeing more light coming into his life as the imprisonment of his limitations were reduced. We rejoiced at the good news of his continued
healing.

From all indications, we were prepared to dock there for a few
days after the prodecure as Doug continued to be monitored to see
how he responded to the new anticonvulsant. If all went well, we
would lift anchor and cruise back to QLI until Doug was cleared to
go home. Time would tell if ataxia and tremors reduced. As much as
I wanted Doug to be whole immediately, I learned a great lesson in
patience, hope, and faith.

In *Relentless* by John Bevere, he describes much of the journey
we were undergoing. He starts the book with a verse from Ecclesiastes
7:8, which states that finishing is better than starting. He then goes
on to say:

> To finish life well requires that we live life
> well… To finish life well we must be relent-
> less-persistent, resolute and unyielding…
> Completing our course is crucial not only for us
> but also for those we are called to influence. It's
> important not to turn back on or veer from the
> path that God has put before us. If you are a child
> of God, you have what it takes! God has placed
> His enabling power, the Holy Spirit, within you.
> Remain steadfast, you will be able to declare with
> the apostle Paul, "I have finished the race, and I
> have remained faithful" (2 Timothy 4:7).[51]

Despite the many challenges we endured as we journeyed to that point, we chose to remain relentless as we embraced our destiny. We knew our future may not look exactly like what we thought it would; but we discovered when you take the scenic route, the ride tends to be longer but definitely more meaningful and beautiful.

October 3

Doug was back on course after the many setbacks and as he adapted to the new anticonvulsant. Yesterday he was grinning like a Cheshire Cat! He was punctuating his words with the black licorice stick he had been eating by tapping it on the table or in the air as he spoke with enthusiasm. Later, he stuck out his licorice-covered tongue at me! He even did a *Happy Feet* dance on the footboard of his bed. My heart was warmed to recognize these quirks manifesting in him after not seeing them since he had gotten hurt. I didn't know if the staff at QLI was ready for this much of Doug! He was always funny, but I was seeing childlike silliness emerging from the likes even I had yet to experience.

Just before releasing Doug from the hospital, the epileptologist stopped by for a final assessment, and he also remarked how much more alert and engaging Doug was. I asked if the medications could be adjusted to get rid of the obnoxious tongue behavior, and the epileptologist laughed and said he didn't think so.

Prior to discharging from the hospital, one of the male techs was unhooking the compression wraps around Doug's calves to keep the blood moving when he noticed the stoutness of Doug's legs. "Wow, you have logger's legs!"

I asked, "How would you know what logger's legs look like?"

"I worked in the industry several years ago," his reply was.

We had a great laugh as we explained Doug had done a lot of logging in his day. But for now, he would have to settle for another round of PT to maintain such manly specimens. This was perfect as he was anxious to get back to therapy because, God forbid, he should lose any of the muscle he worked so hard to rebuild.

Pressing On

October 7

When I returned home safe and sound from my most recent trip to visit Doug, the air was crisp, and the warm autumn colors preceded the dark starkness of winter. Each time I returned home without Doug, I thought the separation got harder for both of us, particularly since he was doing so much better. Accordingly, before I left, I spoke with his team at QLI and told them our hearts' desire was to have Doug home by Thanksgiving if at all possible.

They said Thanksgiving was a great goal to shoot for, and they would meet that week to determine what would be required to make it happen. His house supervisor, Jill, asked me if Doug would need to be able to walk 100 percent of the time to make this happen.

I thought about it for a moment before replying, "I don't think so, but he would need to be capable of staying home alone safely, getting himself to the bathroom, and fixing easy meals. If that is realistic, we can work around any remaining limitations. However, if you don't think he is ready to be safe on his own, we understand and will be patient until he is."

As much as he desperately wanted to be home, I wondered if renting a house closer to my work and his continued treatment facilities in town would be a more reasonable solution until we knew his needs. In addition, not having to deal with the long drive and snow removal would certainly make getting through the winter months a bit easier. Perhaps we could have a townhouse *and* a country house!

I chose to cast this care upon the Lord, for He alone knew our destiny and would direct our steps. As much as I wanted security and to have all the answers, I continued to learn through this journey that all things work themselves out according to His plans, purposes, and timing, just as God's promises in Romans 8:28.

John Bevere says:

> Casting all our cares on God gives us the ability to remain relentless in our mission. In order to press on we cannot carry cumbersome weights... Our very heavy weight that hinders our progress is our care and concerns. At various times in our lives, each of us has to choose between security and destiny. Will we choose the path leading to significance, or will we attempt to secure our comfort and wellbeing? If you choose self-preservation, its end will not be your divine destiny. You may succeed in maintaining your sense of security, but you'll eventually discover, at the judgment seat of Christ, the abundant fullness of life that you forsook for the sake of maintaining your temporary comfort zone.
>
> It's a fact, verified again and again throughout God's Word: if you are going to fulfill your God planned journey, you'll need to leave the weight of your cares and concerns with Him. His path is one of adventure and faith, and the reward is always far greater than your sense of security and comfort. Strip off the weight that slows you down by casting your cares on Him.[52]

[/vc_row_inner]

I can truly say this was certainly an adventure, and I believed with all my heart the best was yet to come! I may not have been able to see into the future, but I knew, "...faith brings our hopes into reality and becomes the foundation needed to acquire the things we long for. It is all the evidence required to prove what is still unseen"

(Hebrews 11:1 TPT). We had a solid foundation under us, our identity was rooted in Christ, and the strength of our faith seemingly received a steroid injection over the months leading up to that point (Colossians 2:7).

Jesus was filled with power after He had been filled with the Holy Spirit upon His baptism. The Spirit then led Him into the wilderness to be tested. It was in the wilderness He stepped into His full identity, never letting Satan defeat Him, but instead using the Word of God to prevail over Him.

I certainly learned how to use the power of the Word and prayer to keep myself built up in my faith. Doug and I were given the opportunity to learn what was truly important in life. Our faith, family, and relationships are our most valuable treasures. We were stripped down and could move into this new chapter of our lives, or should I say sequel, with a clearer understanding of what was important. We could stop wasting time on mundane activities and use our story to enrich the lives of others.

> Yet I totally trust You to rescue me one more time, so that I can see once again how good You are while I'm still alive! Here's what I've learned through it all: don't give up; don't be impatient; be entwined as one with the Lord. Be brave and courageous, and never lose hope. Yes, keep on waiting—for He will never disappoint you!
>
> Psalm 27:13-14 TPT

October 12

After discussing the realities of trying to bring Doug home at Thanksgiving, I realized there would be an influx of travelers, making it a terrible week to travel. He made great improvements in his recovery, but anything out of the ordinary would still cause him great anxiety. We learned how important routine is for individuals recovering from a brain injury. Consistency is of utmost importance to their sense of security and stability, so when an individual with a TBI is removed from their familiar environment, their anxiety tends to increase.

Our brain is always trying to protect us and bring us pleasure with the least amount of effort possible. The brain resists change in order to protect the individual. For those of us with "normal" brains, traveling during a holiday season usually tends to create anxiety. I could only imagine how much anxiety it could have potentially created for Doug in his compromised state. Pressing questions were always swirling in the back of my mind, *What will it take to cause him to seize again? Are we truly out of the woods as far as seizures are concerned?* If something was to go wrong that could potentially cause a seizure, it would likely happen in a moment of anxiety.

God was totally capable of granting Doug special travel considerations to enable him to fly home successfully, but perhaps this time, he was giving us the wisdom to exercise a little common sense instead. Wisdom prevailed, and we came to the conclusion Doug had to travel at the end of November, believing it would most likely be less stressful than traveling at Thanksgiving.

In the meantime, I called Work Comp to see what they were thinking regarding Doug's return and so I could be proactive in setting up his ongoing therapy. I quickly came to the realization we were not exactly on the same page. In response to my question, the nurse said, "Once Doug is home, there will be no more therapy. If he has improved enough to leave QLI, he should no longer need continued therapy."

I replied, "He is still in need of therapy, but our thinking was we could continue it back in Montana as an outpatient." The nurse said, "Doug has already received far more therapy than we are accustomed to providing, and there will be none available once he returns home."

I argued, "But it will save you so much money to have him living at home instead of paying the daily fee to keep him at QLI. You would be saving thousands of dollars if he was home. He is homesick. He desperately wants to come home. It makes sense to have him in an environment where he can thrive, surrounded by family and friends now that he has improved to the degree he has. As you know from the reports from QLI, Doug is not yet able to be totally independent, particularly given his impulsivity, he is going to require supervision for some time."

The nurse countered, "Once Doug is released from QLI, we feel he should be independent and will not provide for therapy beyond QLI. He could be set up with a home exercise program, which he could do on his own. If he qualifies for any home care, the most he could get would be eight hours a day. But since he can dress himself and walk some, he would most likely not be eligible for any home care. He is eligible for vocational rehabilitation, and Work Comp will set it up."

She also clearly stated the likelihood of Work Comp renting us a house in town to allow Doug to be closer to health care, vocational rehabilitation, and a gym, would not be forthcoming as we had hoped it would.

The Work Comp nurse said, "If Doug was back in Montana at a rehab facility, he would have been discharged some time ago because he was doing so well. QLI sets a very high bar for their patients—far above and beyond the normal standard. Doug should take advantage of their program as long as they feel he needs their service."

If I understood all this information correctly, they were willing to pay $1,250 a day for Doug to be at QLI, but $0 for him to be back in Montana doing limited rehab. I was dumbfounded. In what seemed an attempt at compassion, knowing how important it is to our well-being to have family involved in recovery, she also said if there was any way I could move to Omaha while he continued at QLI, my presence would be beneficial to him. I sure do wish moving was as easy as thinking about it.

She also suggested we could sell our house or house-sit for someone else traveling south for the winter so we could move to town for the sake of convenience. This definitely would have allowed Doug to be in Missoula to do his vocational rehabilitation, go to the gym, and be close to help if it was needed. However, I was confident Doug wouldn't agree. Imagine that!

I tried to explain why none of that would work either, "I will need to work to pay the bills. Once he does get to move home, he will be alone almost twelve hours a day, three days a week." As we continued to discuss the pros and cons of him coming home, I tried to appeal to the fact that if he continued to have ataxia, he would still be considered a fall risk, figuring that would require some kind of understanding and assistance. She rebutted, stating they would provide a lifeline device so that if he did fall, he could push a button to call for help. I could feel the burn of anger and frustration ignite within me. *What part of "we live in the middle of the woods an hour away from medical assistance" don't they seem to understand? A lifeline device would alert someone, yes, but would it get someone to him in time to give him the help he needed? Probably not!*

I hung up the phone feeling frustrated, discouraged and irritated that Doug's well-being was being sacrificed in the name of bureaucracy. I was beginning to understand why so many had warned us early on to expect the generosity of Work Comp to be revoked before the needs were completely met.

I knew we had overcome all of the hurdles thus far, and this one would also be overcome for God declares, "So it is when I declare something. My word will go out and not return to Me empty, but it will do what I wanted; it will accomplish what I determined" (Isaiah 55:11 VOICE).

Doug was going to be okay. We were going to be okay. If God said it, I was willing to believe it even if it didn't look exactly like I thought it would. If God could miraculously raise Doug from the dead, ironing out the details with Work Comp would be an easy task for Him. I recognized I was not exercising patience! In fact, I was being impatient. I wanted answers, and I wanted them right then. It was time to take a deep breath and remind myself that while I may not have had the answers, I knew the One who did. He had been faithful so far, and I knew He would be to the end.

October 18

Go gently through this day, keeping your eyes on Me. I will open up the way before you, as you take steps of trust along your path. Sometimes the way before you appears to be blocked. If you focus on the obstacle or search for a way around it, you will probably go off course. Instead, focus on Me, the Shepherd who is leading you on your life-journey. Before you know it, the "obstacle" will be behind you and you will hardly know how you passed through it.

That is the secret of success in My kingdom. Although you remain aware of the visible world around you, your primary awareness is of Me. When the road before you looks rocky, you can trust Me to get you through that rough patch. My presence enables you to face each day with confidence.

Jesus Calling, October 18[53]

[/vc_row_inner]

After reading these words, I let out a huge sigh as the words brought clarity and relieved tension in my body. The conversation with Work Comp was not at all encouraging, and then there had been evidence to suggest a coyote killed my cat, Spanky.

He was so sweet, innocent, and fearless. He lived his short life to the fullest. He was glued to me whenever I was home and had been such a comfort to me since Doug's accident. I felt as though my heart had been ripped out of my chest, and hot, angry tears rolled when I discovered his white hair spread across the field in the creek bottom.

How many other things I love will be taken from me, God?

When I told Doug what had happened to Spanky, he said, "The devil knew where he could hurt you the most, and he may have won this victory, but he will lose in the end."

Everything I was currently reading or hearing spoke of over-coming trials in our lives. The story of Joseph in the Bible tells of the many ways he suffered after being thrown in prison twice through no fault of his own. John Bevere stated, "Joseph was learning to exercise his obedience muscles through suffering."[54] God was preparing Joseph for a future far greater than he could have imagined. A future his dreams had alluded to, but now his circumstances were grooming him for, as he went from a favorite son to being sold into slavery, to being in charge of Potiphar's house, to being sent to prison, to being in charge of the prisoners, and finally to becoming the second most influential person in Egypt in his position under Pharaoh.

With every high and low on his rollercoaster ride of life, Joseph experienced character development. He did not allow his circumstances to make him bitter, and as a result, God continued to pour out His favor on Joseph until he was eventually reunited with his family. Joseph was indeed elevated in position above his brothers and even his father. As the dream indicated, they all bowed to him as a second-in-command of Egypt, not knowing it was Joseph they were bowing to (Genesis 42:6).

In the end, Joseph's trials developed a life surrendered to God's will, a deeper faith, and a greater revelation of God's faithfulness, integrity, discipline, patience, and self-control. Joseph had the fortitude to trust God despite the seeming hopelessness of the circumstance in which he found himself.

Like Joseph, I, too, was learning about character development. I kept thinking at some point things must get better. I would finally have a chance to relax. But no, it felt like the load I was carrying just kept getting heavier and heavier. Spanky's death felt like such a cruel blow after all the trauma I had already endured in the ten months prior. All the while, I had no idea if Doug would survive, how intact his brain would be, or that I would have to manage a long separation from him while he lived in Omaha. This last affliction was a bitter pill to swallow, especially when I had absolutely no doubt God was fully capable of preventing the coyotes from choosing sweet Spanky for dinner.

I could no longer hold back the grief I had been squelching for ten months. Spanky's death was the tipping point for my capacity to contain my heartache and the agony I had been experiencing. I hadn't realized how much I needed to surrender my suffering to His care.

> God loves you so much that He won't take away the pain if it serves a greater purpose in your life. Instead, He will walk the path of pain with you, and in the person of the Comforter (see John 14:16) will sustain you each step of the way.
>
> Steve McVey[55]

[/vc_row_inner]

As I opened my heart to let the pain and agony out, the healing balm of God's love found its way in, replacing torment with peace.

The Dove Comes Home to Roost

In preparation for Doug's return home, Work Comp arranged for a wheelchair ramp to be installed outside the house. The contractor and I could not meet at the house at the same time to discuss the installation options, so I explained to him over the phone what I believed would be the best layout based on our lifestyle and space constraints. He seemed confident in my instructions and said he would get right on it. Knowing this was one more step to getting Doug home, I was eager to see the finished product, confident it was going to be just what we needed.

Unfortunately, though, I arrived home from work to find he had designed the ramp to run under the eaves of the roof, parallel to the house and dumping out into the middle of the lawn instead of the gravel parking area as I had instructed.

This is never gonna work! Extreme irritation threatened to ignite into an inferno of anger. I recognized my patience had worn thin as I noted how easily anger sparked within me. I reminded myself this was just another attempt by the devil to get me off balance. Even though I tried to find the good in the situation, I envisioned the snow sliding off the roof onto the ramp. And when it did, I would have even more shoveling work to do, not to mention the potential for ice to form on the snow-laden path was very likely. This would be a hazard as well. And if you live in the northwest long enough, you know grass doesn't dry out from all the snow we get until late spring. Rolling a wheelchair through soggy, muddy grass would be difficult at best, and most likely impossible.

Why didn't he think about this? I thought I was so clear about what we needed.

At this point, my stress meter had pegged out and blown a gasket. Grace was nowhere to be found.

I stomped into the house to call the contractor. It may have been in both of our best interests he didn't answer the phone. I am certain smoke was billowing from my ears as I spoke angrily into the telephone, "Joe, we seem to have a problem with the way the ramp is laid out. I am not sure where the communication failed, but the way you have set it up is not acceptable, it will need to be fixed ASAP."

When he finally called me back, he said, "I set it up how it seemed best to me. If we did what you wanted, it would cost more money and require more material."

I responded, "What part of 'the snow will fall on the ramp from the roof, and we will have to wheel the chair through the muddy grass' don't you understand? What you have created is a hazard to both my husband and me. If he must get out of the house in case of a fire, he will be stuck on the lawn with no way but to crawl to get away from the house. I want you to fix it exactly how I instructed you to the first time. As a service provider, you should be able to find time to meet with me to go over the details. I believe this is called 'customer service.' I will be calling Work Comp to inform them of my experience with you and my extreme dissatisfaction."

After hanging up the phone, I was ashamed of my poor behavior. This was not at all how I wanted to act. Nor was it an exemplary representation of Christ. I did not enjoy speaking to him this way, but I was really past my limit of understanding. Eventually, the ramp situation did get straightened out, but with much grumbling by the contractor.

Doug was scheduled to come home on December 21 at nine o'clock in the evening, seven months to the day since he left for QLI. Once we decided Thanksgiving was not a good idea, we jokingly said 12-12-12 would be a great time for him to come home. I guess I had my numbers transposed. Instead of 12-12-12, the date turned out to be 12-21-12! In my mind, I did a happy dance because after flying Doug to QLI on May 21 and returning home, I inquired of the Lord how long Doug would be there, and I was given the verse Jeremiah 29:10 (NLT). "You will be in Babylon for seventy years. But then I will come and do for you all the good things I have promised, and I will bring you home again."

I knew seventy years was not appropriate, but I believed seven months was, and apparently it was. Yes, indeed, He is a good, good Father.

However, my celebration was short-lived because QLI called to tell me Doug's new custom wheelchair would not be ready for him until at least December 22, and more than likely, not until sometime after Christmas.

You have got to be kidding me. I could feel my blood pressure rising rapidly to a very unhealthy level.

I said to the bearer of bad news, "What you are telling me now is Doug will most likely not be home for Christmas?"

"I'm sorry, but a return home for Christmas is very unlikely at this point."

With my anger mostly in check, I tried to be as polite as possible. "I am trying very hard not to be upset about this and am having difficulty restraining my frustration. We were told everything was in order, and it's Christmas! We can't not be together at Christmas after all we have been through. Isn't there anything you can do? I can't believe this is happening."

In my disappointment and fury, I wanted to reach through the cell towers to grab her by the throat and let her feel my frustration. Suddenly, God whispered to me, *Satan uses very good and wonderful people to bring fear and discouragement into our lives.*

I took a deep breath, and a calm washed over me. Apparently I was still in the process of learning patience and trust in the Almighty.

I had to be the one to break the bad news to Doug later. "I got a call from QLI today. They gave me some distressing news. It appears your new wheelchair won't be ready in time for you to come home on the twenty-first."

Doug responded in frustration, "How can that be? They promised to have it done in time for me to come home on the twenty-first!"

I replied, "I am not sure what went wrong, but at this point, we will be lucky to have it on the twenty-second, but I was told to be prepared to not have it until after Christmas, which means you won't be home until sometime after Christmas."

I could hear the grief in Doug's voice as he said, "They promised me I would be home for Christmas. How can they not let me come home? I am so sick of this place! I miss you, and I want to be home." His voice was cracking with emotion as he struggled to keep from crying. I could feel the warm wet tears edging over my eyelids, easing down my cheeks. My throat ached with emotion as I thought how unfair it was to have been to be given the promise of Doug being home for Christmas; then, suddenly, the promise seemed to be callously revoked. We continued commiserating together over our disappointment, all the while still trusting and submitting to God's will for our lives.

I know the team at QLI dreaded having to relay that disagreeable news to us. They truly were a caring and compassionate crew. This circumstance was completely out of their control.

It was as though a light bulb went off, and I said to Doug, "You flew to Omaha without a wheelchair because the airline provided one for you. You don't need a fancy chair to come home. We will find a way to get a different chair, and your new chair can be sent later. I will talk to the staff tomorrow morning about this option." A glimmer of hope brought a bit of comfort to what had been a disheartening conversation.

After I got off the phone, I opened the devotional *Jesus Today* by Sara Young. It read:

> I will fight for you; you need only to be still. I know how weary you are My child. You have been struggling just to keep your head above water, and your strength is running low. Now is the time to stop striving and let Me fight for you.[56]

[/vc_row_inner]

This pretty much summed up where we were. Nothing seemed to be working. We had been so frustrated and discouraged, but we continued to remind ourselves God knew exactly what was going on, and there must be something we needed to learn from all those delays.

What was comical, yet extremely frustrating, in all of this was we had been working diligently to have all the handicapped devices put in place so he could come home and be safe. Yet none of the devices would be fully completed or put in place when he finally arrived. Essentially, I felt as though he spent the last two months in Omaha playing a waiting game.

> Waiting on the Lord happens after you have done all that you know how to do, and nothing happens. It's after we have exhausted our efforts that God can step in and take care of our needs.
>
> Unknown

[/vc_row_inner]

December 23

Much to our relief, Doug was able to return home on the twenty-first as originally promised. And much to my surprise, he was in a shiny Christmas red wheelchair. Somehow all the details came together just in time for Doug to have it for the trip home. Due to holiday air traffic and delays, Doug's plane didn't arrive as scheduled, but I was so relieved he had finally made it home without having a seizure or other major incident. I could tell he was happy to be home and in familiar surroundings. However, I could see the exhaustion in his eyes as well. I, too, was exhausted, having been up since 4 a.m. I worked a full day and spent the rest of the evening in the hospital with my dying grandfather as I anxiously waited for Doug's plane to land.

We were not exactly like two long-lost lovers swooning over one another. This was in no way a romantic reunion one typically sees in the movies or reads in a novel. We both just wanted to be home safe and sound at that point without making the commute to get there.

Home would be a couple of hours away yet. We had to wait to grab his bags and then take Ashely, his caregiver, to her hotel before we could begin the fifty-minute commute home. While we waited for his bags, friends and family enthusiastically greeted Doug.

I am not sure who organized the welcome-home party, but fifty or so friends from church, in addition to family members, were gathered at the airport with welcome-home signs to greet Doug at nine o'clock when he was scheduled to arrive only to discover his flight was delayed. Unfortunately, with the delayed arrival time, some were not able to return at eleven o'clock that night to greet him. I certainly didn't blame them for not coming back, especially those who needed to get up early for work. Despite the confusion with the delayed flight, there was still a strong contingent of well-wishers numbering thirty or so. Doug was extremely blessed and humbled by the warm welcome he received from the many folks who returned a second time to express their love and to greet him at the airport.

By the time we got home, it was after one o'clock in the morning. Doug was one exhausted fella. After the energy-consuming events of my day, I was running on adrenaline once again, of which I was going to need another dose, as I soon discovered.

No sooner than we pulled into the driveway, Doug said, "I need to pee really bad and have had since we arrived at the airport."

I replied, "Why didn't you say something then?"

"I didn't want to be a bother," he replied.

Exasperated, I failed to consider that we were home in the driveway, and it was dark. No one was around for miles, so he could have peed in the driveway. Instead, I frantically got him into the house to use the bathroom.

Then, knowing he would want to go right to bed, I figured the master bathroom would be the logical one to use. My exasperation transformed into frustration when I realized I couldn't get the fancy new wheelchair through the bedroom door.

"Tam," he said, "I can't wait any longer, I gotta go now."

I said, "The only other option is for me to assist you into the guest bathroom." Abandoning any further notion he would be using the master bathroom, I immediately helped him get from his wheelchair into the guest bathroom to take care of business.

"I am confused as to why the chair won't fit through the doorway," I remarked. "QLI called and asked for specific measurements for the doors, which I supplied. Someone must have transposed the measurement."

Doug spoke up and said, "Oh, the guy who custom-fit the chair to me widened out the chair a bit so it would be more comfortable for me." Much to my chagrin, I realized his chair would not fit through any of the interior doorways. At that point, I knew the only other option was to take the doors off the hinges and pray there would be enough room to get through once the doors were removed.

I left Doug sitting on the toilet while I went to find the tools necessary to remove the pins holding the door in the hinges. The hammer and screwdriver worked like a charm. Violà! I was now able to get Doug and the wheelchair into the bedroom. I knew I could remove the master bath door after some shuteye. Sleep was more important to me in that moment than removing doors.

Practically asleep on my feet, I crawled into bed. It was the first time being there next to him in seven months. It felt good to listen to him snore. As exhausted as I was, I thought I would fall asleep immediately, but sleep was elusive. It wasn't so much his snoring keeping me awake. Instead, it was my brain trying to figure how we were going to make this transition work. Doug obviously was going to need more care than I had anticipated. He wouldn't be able to manage on his own from the little I had observed that night.

Have we jumped the gun in having him come home? How will I be able to work if he requires care? Who can I find to sit with him while I am at work? My brain was gaining momentum with each thought. At some point, I finally succumbed to the bliss of sleep.

***

Now that Doug had officially made it home, I could finalize our Christmas plans. But first, there was the unpacking of all his bags, adjusting to having him home, meeting his needs, and keeping up with the daily chores. In an attempt to regain a sense of normal, I asked Doug to help me peel apples for a pie since he loves to run the apple peeler. Once the apples were peeled, he zested and juiced lemons for lemon curd. Helping me wasn't as easy for him as he was used to due to ataxia, yet it felt so normal working together as a team as we had done for years. What a blessing it was to have him home!

My plan for your life is unfolding before you. Sometimes the road you are traveling seems blocked, or it opens up so painfully slow that you must hold yourself back. Then, when time is right, the way before you suddenly clears—through no effort of your own. What you have longed for and worked for I present to you freely, as pure gift. You feel awed by the ease with which I operate in the world, and you glimpse My Power and My Glory.

Do not fear your weakness, for it is the stage on which My Power and Glory perform most brilliantly. As you persevere along the path I have prepared for you, depending on My strength to sustain you, expect to see miracles—and you will. Miracles are not always visible to the naked eye, but those who live by faith can see them clearly. Living by faith, rather than sight, enables you to see My glory.

Jesus Calling, December 21[57]

A New Year, A New Lifestyle

January 18

What a happy new year we were experiencing. I was very glad to get 2012 behind us. Doug was also glad to be home, but it had its challenges. The peace and quiet were enabling him to rest, but exercise equipment here at the house was limited. He had lost a significant amount of his physical strength as a result of not exercising at the level he had been accustomed to while in Omaha. He was quite discouraged, and justifiably so. He didn't realize how convenient it was to have a full gym available any time he was inclined to use it. We had talked early on about the possibility of joining a gym once he returned home and were able to find a place in town to live. Since the "townhouse" idea didn't work out, the closest gym was about a forty-minute drive away. It was certainly not convenient and required more of my time to drive to the gym and assist him with his workout.

It was quickly becoming obvious Doug was not able to be independent at home alone. He still was struggling with impulsivity. Not being able to think about the outcome of his actions clearly put him at risk of injury when his body did not comply with his thinking. His decision to go outside and bring in firewood resulted in yet another nasty fall. I understood he just wanted to help but having to get him upright and back inside wasn't exactly helpful. I kept wondering how I could possibly leave him home alone and feel it was an acceptable and wise decision? I knew we had to have help even though Work Comp said they wouldn't provide any.

Once Doug was able to meet with and be assessed by Valerie Chyle, NP, his Work Comp advocate, she was able to convince them of the necessity of a caregiver for Doug. This resulted in the blessing of finding someone who was willing to travel to our remote location to care for Doug. I was greatly relieved knowing I was starting back to work Monday through Wednesday. However, my first day back got off to a rough start when the caregiver failed to show up. We found out later she was afraid to make the drive. She didn't bother to tell anyone or answer my call. The company providing the caregiver apologized and promised to find a replacement immediately. Fortunately, my mom was available at the last minute and willing to come to stay with Doug until I could return home.

The caregiving dilemma got sorted out, and a new caregiver was sent out the next day. Knowing he had someone to assist him was a huge relief. His safety was absolutely critical to his continued improvement and progression to independence. I still believed someday he would be independent enough to stay by himself, but this was the best option for the time being.

Work Comp was leaning towards declaring Doug permanently disabled. In some ways, this was a bummer. Permanently disabled and "he is going to be okay" didn't reconcile in my brain. This was not the vision I had for him, nor the one he had for himself. When I told him of Work Comp's consideration, he asked, "How do they know I won't continue to get better?" He still believed that in time he would be able to return to the work he loved and was very disappointed and discouraged by their assessment.

The lack of ability for his body to cooperate with his desire certainly revealed evidence of a disability. Not being able to stand and walk consistently or keep his body from twitching and jerking would make finding employment highly unlikely. Without further improvement, Doug would be less of an asset and more of a liability for an employer. However, being permanently disabled would allow him to have the time to share his story and encourage others without having to be concerned about earning an income. Perhaps this could be a blessing in the end since there didn't seem to be much call for pipefitters and welders around here anymore.

After the paper mill shut down, the local market for these trades was flooded with twenty-five or more of his former co-workers. Missoula is not highly industrialized, so there was not a significant demand for welders or pipefitters. In addition, the few positions available in our area did not pay at the higher scale he was accustomed to earning. Instead, he was using his time voraciously reading a new book every one to two days, depending on topic and length. He flew through mystery novels but had to slow down and chew his way through the meatier books on brain rewiring and rehabilitation. Doug and I had always been avid readers, but he had never had the opportunity to devote this much time to it before.

January 22

We had been praying for an open door to share Doug's testimony and hopefully help others when we got a call from the Montana Brain Injury Alliance. Our name had been given to them by one of the social workers at St. Patrick's Hospital. They invited us to go to the Capitol building in Helena to testify on behalf of a bill that would add a $1 fee to vehicle license registration/renewal to help educate and support Montana families of those who had had a brain injury. The funds generated by this bill would allow the Montana Brain Injury Alliance to qualify and apply for $3 million in grants.

After Doug's accident, we learned Montana has the second highest rate of TBI's in the nation. Now knowing this statistic and after his experience at QLI, Doug had a vision for a care facility similar to QLI in Montana, which this type of funding could support. During the drive to Helena, Doug said, "You know, Tam, I believe it is a crime to send our people with brain injuries and their money out of state. If we had a QLI in Montana, it would be a fantastic way to generate good jobs for the people of Montana."

I replied, "Yes, I can see what a great opportunity it would provide for everyone. However, I don't believe Missoula has the neurology support it would take to care for the number of patients it would potentially house. It is a struggle to schedule an appointment with the neurologists serving the greater Missoula area right now." Doug enthusiastically replied, "Build it, and they will come." I didn't want to discourage him, so I redirected the conversation to our impending speaking opportunity. We were excited to participate in this event because when God opens a door, one would be foolish not to run through it!

Exodus 9:16 (NLT) was resonating in my spirit. "I have spared you for a purpose—to show you My power and to spread My fame throughout the earth." From the moment of Doug's accident on January 3, 2012, and throughout that year, I still heard God telling me, *This is for My glory!*

What Satan meant for evil God was going to use for good, just as he did for Joseph.

Over the course of Doug's recovery, we witnessed several people who were not able to get the quality of care, which Doug had been blessed to receive. His heart broke many times as he watched residents at QLI leave long before they should have due to lack of funding.

A week after our meeting in Helena, we received a phone call telling us that, unfortunately, the bill did not pass. Despite it not passing and feeling discouraged it didn't, Doug said he finally felt like he was making a difference in the world each time he was able to share his story with someone. While we were at the Capitol Building in Helena, Doug connected with a couple of people he had met years earlier while lobbying for the pulp and paper industry. He was able to update them on his accident and miraculous recovery while giving the glory to God.

Several weeks later, when I got home from work, Doug was practically glowing. I asked him what had happened to create such a state of euphoria, and he said, "Nothing. I just feel good!" But I knew this glow was more than just a good feeling. As any wife would, I continued to interrogate, or rather, probe him. He finally admitted that he had come to the realization that getting frustrated and angry about things he couldn't control was a waste of his time and energy. For the Herculean man he had been prior to the accident, struggling to do the most menial task like buttoning his shirt, tying shoelaces, or writing was now challenging. The lack of motor control while eating and drinking often left food and beverage down the front of his shirts. Not only did this make a mess, but it also brought significant shame and humiliation with it, especially when others were present. The lack of control often resulted in an angry, frustrated, and raging Doug. He would, as I say, hulk out, as he bellowed in exasperation with his uncooperative body.

He was soon able to test his new revelation when, as he stood up from the toilet, he quit thinking about his legs or rather their mobility. They gave out on him. I couldn't break his fall in time. He fell backward onto the toilet, scraping his backside down the lid and slamming his butt on the seat. My heart sank in despair as I watched his face flush and contort with pain once again. "Lean forward. I want to see your back." As he complied with my request, I saw the peeling skin, which had been scraped away. Blood was running in rivulets down his backside. The purplish marks indicated bruising, which in the days to come would turn a ghastly shade of yellow.

After collecting his wits and getting dressed, he went to transfer from the wheelchair into his recliner and did the same thing. He went from standing to dead weight. Again, I was caught off guard and couldn't prevent his fall. This time he slammed his elbow into the corner of the end table, knocking coffee all over the floor. Fortunately, he was able to fall back into the wheelchair instead of on the floor. Instead of crying, even though he looked like he wanted to, he said through gritted teeth, "God, I thank You for the trials, which You are allowing to make me a stronger man!"

I was impressed by his ability to control his frustration. "Well done, Mr. Dove," I said. "It seems God did indeed get through to you." I was so relieved he didn't swear or yell in frustration. I found the emotional impact on myself was difficult enough as I watched him injure himself, but when he verbally erupted, my psyche was assaulted. I knew he was not yelling at me, but somehow my brain registered that he was. I found myself holding my breath every time I even thought he may have an accident. Therefore, his ability to restrain his verbiage was a blessing to me. It also indicated healing in the cognitive area of his brain. It is the cognitive area where our emotions are controlled. Even though I knew he was not angry at me, I still took it so personally when he was angry. It hurt my heart and caused me to pull back from him when his negative emotions threatened to drown me.

I was not the only one suffering from overload. We discovered Doug was easily overwhelmed by large crowds. Therefore, on Easter Sunday, we chose to stay home from church and have a quiet day with only the two of us. We made it outside for a walk, and while doing so, we decided to set up our firepit and roast bratwursts. I had already started the fire with newspaper, pitch, and kindling before I realized I didn't have enough kindling to sustain the fire. I raced to the woodshed for more kindling, hoping to salvage my fire. As I was hurrying back, I heard a loud crash. I looked over to see Doug face down on the ground with the chair stuck to his butt.

Wanting to save the fire from going out before I returned with the extra wood, he scooted his chair toward the firepit so he could stoke it. As he did, the gravel around the pit built up in front of the legs of the chair, and he tipped face-first into the crushed gravel. Fortunately, he did not fall into the embers of the dwindling fire.

We had recently had a conversation with Doug's psychologist about his impulsive decisions, such as going outside without asking me for assistance or even to let me know he was going outside or pushing himself harder to exercise and later not having the strength to move from the bike to his chair. The doctor assessed that yes, Doug was behaving impulsively. However, he wasn't surprised since impulsivity is quite common with TBIs. He was optimistic that in time, once Doug's brain healed, the impulsivity would be greatly reduced if not resolved. Lack of insight is common for those with a TBI; often they do not recognize the consequences of their actions or understand what others may be feeling. Medications can help reduce incidences, but otherwise impulsivity is managed one incident at a time. As a family member and caregiver, it would be important for me not to react negatively as it only exacerbates the problem, even though it is a natural reaction to do so.

Well, I didn't need to say a word at this point; the evidence was all over his face. I got him upright in his chair and ran to the house to get a towel to clean up the blood, which was running profusely down his face onto his clothing.

His face was imbedded with dirt and hunks of gravel. I removed what was left of his sunglasses while noting where the glass had gashed his eyebrow. Then I carefully picked the gravel out from his face, jerking my fingers back every time he winced in pain while saying, "I am sorry, I am so sorry." I wiped away as much of the dirt and blood as possible, revealing multiple gashes on his face and nose. His upper lip was split in the middle and torn to the outside edge of his nose. It was obvious this was going to require much more than a simple Band-Aid, so I loaded him into the car, and we headed to the ER.

Seven hours and thirty stitches later, we were back home. It was now midnight. I was supposed to get up at four o'clock in the morning and go to work. After several hours in the ER, I realized we would be very late into the night getting home. Sleep was going to be minimal at best. As a result, I knew I would have a difficult time making the early morning drive safely; nor would I be highly functional at work. Wanting to give my supervisor as much notice as possible, I made the call from the ER to let her know I would not be at work as scheduled. I was mentally and physically exhausted.

Crawling into bed, I pondered briefly how Doug managed to come through the "original" accident without any physical scars. I would have never imagined after having overcome death, his road to recovery would be so tortuous.

***

For a day that had started out so well with our first walk on the Frenchtown Bike Path, it literally came to a crashing halt. Knowing how desperately Doug wanted to resume walking, I set him up with a four-wheeled walker. It had a seat built into the frame, which allowed Doug to sit and rest when necessary. On our first walk, I managed to hold him back as I recognized the signs of fatigue at four-tenths of a mile. Wanting to know what his intentions were, I asked, "How far do you think you want to go for your first attempt?"

"As far as I can," he replied.

I responded, "Remember, you have to walk all the way back. You can't just go until you get tired and are done."

"Yes, I know that," he said. I could see his body was getting twitchy, and he grunted several times as his body tried to quit on him.

Concerned that he was pushing himself too far, I had to negotiate prudently to convince him to turn around. I was also trying to minimize the assault on my own body. Every time his knees buckled, it was up to me to break his fall. I was holding on to a gait belt, a fabric belt around his waist intended for such assistance. His sudden collapses were jerking me off balance and straining my muscles as I fought to keep both of us upright and not sprawled out on the asphalt. He finally conceded to turning around after another massive twitch nearly put us on our faces. In the following two weeks, we continued to increase our walking distance, achieving an amazing 3.6 miles! No, I did not make a typo, 3.6 miles it was! Mr. Doesn't-Know-When-to-Quit-or-Comprehend-Moderation pushed us as far and fast as he could.

A few days later, we managed to walk 5.2 miles in one hour and fifty-five minutes. I jokingly said to Doug after achieving the three-mile walk so swiftly, "Maybe we should walk the half-marathon in the upcoming Run Wild Missoula Marathon in July." Doug actually liked the idea and mentioned it to his health care providers on his next visit. They were completely on board, saying it was an excellent goal. Now the joke was on me! I wasn't sure where I would find the time to train for thirteen miles of walking, but somehow, I would find a way. Barring any unforeseen circumstances, we would be walking the Run Wild Half-Marathon.

In addition to finding time to train for a marathon, I needed to find time to get our house ready to sell. After much prayer and discussion, we both felt it was in our best interest to be closer to Missoula. As optimistic as we had been, we understood he may never be able to drive again. And for as capable as I was, I didn't believe I could run the road grader to plow the mile of the driveway through the winter season. We hoped someday he would achieve greater healing in his brain and be able to drive, but until then, we had to live with what we had that day.

We were trying to figure out how to pack up thirty years of life and move forward. I believed the right home or building spot was out there for us and that there would be a buyer for our place. We needed a home, which was wheelchair-accessible with all the necessary living quarters on the main floor.

We had been blessed with God's favor to this point, and I believed we would be in the days ahead.

Test Driving, New Meds, and a Marathon

"Start by doing what's necessary; then do what's possible; and suddenly you are doing the impossible" (St. Francis of Assisi).[58]

June 5

We were seeing positive results since Doug had been taking a new anti-anxiety medication. He was able to control the jerks much better. He even walked a quarter mile on the dirt road successfully without assistance as the Murrays and I filled the potholes with gravel. However, upon encountering our neighbor, who created much conflict for him in the past, he did fall due to increased anxiety of being in her presence. Fortunately, nothing was hurt but his pride.

This encounter demonstrated how anxiety affected him so adversely. After getting back on his feet and dusting himself off, he chose to lean against our SUV while the rest of our crew continued down the road filling potholes. We got about 1,500 feet away from him, and he apparently decided we were too far away, so he got in the SUV and drove to catch up with us. This was his first time driving since the accident.

It was nerve-wracking as I kept wondering, "what if..." On the one hand, I was thrilled he was doing so well. On the other hand, I could imagine all the things that could go wrong. With Dave Murray riding shotgun, he later drove the three-fourths mile back to the house, turned the car around, and backed up the driveway like an old pro! Dave complimented Doug on his ability, and not wanting to dampen the mood; I chose to keep my concerns to myself. Despite how well Doug performed, I was not yet confident he could handle the stress of driving in traffic and dealing with fast-moving situations.

After undergoing another neuropsychological evaluation, the doctor stated he was not sure if Doug was able to respond quickly enough to sudden events, which would be required to safely drive in traffic. Due to Doug's expressed desire to return to driving, the doctor agreed to have a driving simulator test administered once again. Doug had had a driving test administered early on in his assessments.

Overall, the driving test results were great. In comparison with the test the year before, he improved from a C- to and A-. His major deficits were delayed response time and trouble retaining lots of information quickly. Already knowing this, I was not surprised in the least when he was told he would not be permitted to drive.

Doug, however, argued the reason he struggled was the driving test was in the afternoon, right after lunch, which is when he usually naps for one to two hours. This reasoning didn't work with me or the examiner, and I'm fairly confident it wouldn't work with law enforcement if he were to get in an accident. Regardless of the driving test results, the doctor commented several times about Doug's remarkable recovery.

July 3

After months of juggling my schedule to accommodate the marathon training, I came up with creative ways to get in the necessary miles. Often, I would have the caregiver bring Doug from home and meet me at the bike path in Frenchtown on my way home from work. It seemed like Doug was the baton being passed for the next leg of the race. There was no time for chit-chat. I needed to make sure we got our miles in before returning home to fix dinner and prep meals for the next day. By the time I was finally able to go to bed each night, I was exhausted. On the upside of all this exercise, I slept well and was in great shape. My brain also appreciated the endorphins the exercise was creating. Every week, we increased our miles. The week before the big day, we walked the full thirteen miles in a little over four hours. We knew we could do it, now we could coast for a few days.

Our marathon morning started out with fireworks and cop cars with flashing lights. As we were driving, right before we got to the starting place of the half-marathon, fireworks began to erupt in the early morning dawn.

Unfortunately, the car in front of me decided to stop on the highway to enjoy the light show. I pulled around the stopped car and stomped on the gas, but the suburban's driver hit the gas, and the next thing I knew, I looked up to see the flashing lights on a cop car. He was kind enough not to ticket me.

The marathon committee was also kind enough to excuse us from having to ride the shuttle bus with the other participants from town to the starting point at Blue Mountain due to Doug's anxiety, so I followed behind the shuttle busses. Unfortunately, more "pretty lights" flipped on behind me as I pulled off the main highway into the bus-only lane as I had been instructed by the marathon representative.

A stern voice erupted from the police officer's bullhorn, telling me to pull over. To which I immediately complied, trying to ignore the pounding heart in my chest. The bullhorn yelled at me, "You can't go in there." I politely replied, "Sir, my husband has a disability and isn't able to ride the shuttle. We were given permission by the marathon committee to drop him off early and were told to use the bus-only lane."

Needless to say, the man with the badge increased his volume as he explained to us, "We were not notified of any exceptions, so you can't go in there!" Once again, I politely tried to explain we had been granted favor, but when one has reached such a high of a level of authority, it seemed he had great difficulty in his ability to hear from way up there.

Fortunately, a marathon representative came running over and explained to the policeman, "Yes, sir, they do have special permission." To which the "nice" policeman bellowed, "No, we did not!" Because no one from the marathon committee had informed anyone in law enforcement authority of our *privilege*. The marathon representative confidently replied to the "nice" policeman, "I'm informing you of their privilege now."

I bit my lip to keep from letting out the "well, he certainly told him" giggle, threatening to stir up more irritation for our nice policeman. As he muttered under his breath and backed away, the marathon representative leaned into our window and said, "Sorry about that. You're all set. Go ahead and follow the shuttles and have a great race." At last, we were free to proceed to the drop-off point.

Because this was our first marathon and Doug's anxiety could be a little unpredictable, we decided to exercise caution and hang back from the starting line, letting the "hares" get the jump-start they wanted. For us "turtles," or turtledoves as we have fondly been called, the road before us was a sight to behold. For as far as we could see, there was a multicolored ribbon of bodies ahead of us.

As we got about a mile down the road, articles of clothing were strewn along the side of the road. The farther we went, the more clothes were discarded. Never having participated in a marathon before, this was all new to me. I began to get a little concerned but mostly perplexed by the amount of clothing I saw. "At the rate, the clothes are coming off these people. I wouldn't be surprised if everyone was naked by the time we reach town!" We both laughed. "I didn't know we were actually signing up for a Run Wild *Naked* marathon." At this, we both guffawed, and it took some of the edge off our nerves and the distance yet to accomplish.

We sure got lots of funny looks as people wondered what was up with the guy wearing a bike helmet and using a wheeled walker. As we walked, though, we were able to share our story with many and encourage others along the 13.1 miles. We were mutually encouraged by the stories of others and by the twenty-six-milers, who, upon realizing Doug had a disability, told him, "Way to go, dude! Keep up the good work!" Many of them high-fived him as they passed.

The Missoula community was out in full force to encourage marathoners. There was lots of signage, music, cowbells, snacks, hydration, and plenty of sprinklers to run through. One family was even concerned with our bowel health. Their yard sign inquired, "Have you pooped yet?" Another said, "Don't trust the fart!" Never having competed in a marathon before, we had no idea that bowel issues were such a concern.

As we got about two miles from the finish, I asked Doug if he wanted to run the full marathon next year. He gave me a dirty look and said, "Maybe life would be best if I could walk independently first."

It wasn't a no! I was joking in an attempt to distract myself from the blister forming on my foot, but I must have been delirious to ask such a risky question! Knowing how much time it took to train for this one and a torn ligament in my foot, I was in no way inclined to run a twenty-six miler.

The course designer was a joker as well. About the time we seemed to be getting close to the finish line, we flipped in the opposite direction—moving away from what we thought was the finish line. At this point, I was getting tired, and the blister on the bottom of my foot was making its presence known despite my best efforts to ignore it.

At last, as we were approaching the Higgins St. Bridge, we could see the finish line. People were crowded on either side of the bridge, cheering all of us on. The response was overwhelming! The announcer saw us coming and told the crowd about Doug's accident. Their deafening cheers of amazement and awe roared in our ears as they clapped their hands in support while we passed by. The support, encouragement, and affirmation was humbling. Holding back our tears was almost impossible because we were exhausted and experiencing such an outpouring of emotions. I quickly prayed for the ability to walk across the timing mat without falling. I especially didn't want Doug to fall at the finish after having done so well. I wanted him to finish strong to confirm his victory lap.

By God's grace, we conquered the half-marathon with only a few challenges. These were small trials in our book compared to what we have already been through and managed to overcome.

> "Human resources, however limited, when willingly offered and divinely empowered, are more than adequate to accomplish divine ends" (Stuart Briscoe).[59]

Deadman Still Walking

Doug continued to push toward walking without any mobility aids. He had been using walking sticks he made from shovel handles and cane tips on the bottoms. As truly wonderful and amazing as this was, the sounds of him falling were seared into my brain, and terror was barely held in check as I was torn between optimism and fear. I hoped I looked good in blue because I found myself holding my breath most of the time as he walked unassisted.

Fortunately, he was getting better about putting his hands out to break his fall, which was a significant improvement, but he still recently managed to faceplant on the hardwood floor almost exactly where he fell his very first time eighteen months before. Can you say flashback? Thankfully his head is *very* hard. He was okay, but I thought his rotator cuff may be torn. We went to the ER to get an MRI to find out.

He had also recently undergone another neuropsychological evaluation. This would be his last as far as he was concerned. He found them to be mentally and emotionally exhausting. This test showed little remarkable improvement from six months before, but it didn't show that Doug had learned skills to help him overcome many of his deficits, such as writing notes to offset short-term memory and meditating to reduce anxiety and ataxia, according to the neuropsychologist.

Despite all the progress Doug made, he was still very limited in his abilities. Accordingly, he was still far from being able to be completely independent. Not knowing when or if he would fall or how badly he would be injured after a fall undermined my assurance of his safety when left alone for any length of time. I continued to work at mustering my faith as I looked into the future, but my brain was overly efficient in finding evidence for depicting worst-case scenarios. I found myself becoming anxious, knowing we were getting down to the wire regarding a financial settlement with Work Comp. This would be merely for lost wages, those he lost since the accident up to his projected retirement date. His medical expenses relating to the accident would be covered until he expires for the last time! We heard this process could get very nasty, so we decided to get an attorney. I prayed hard from the beginning that this would not be our story; but having said that, we were prepared to take necessary measures to ensure a fair settlement in the end. But I also know God's ways are not our ways, so we simply desired that His way prevailed.

Our house was also officially for sale. To that point, there hadn't been much interest as this was not the best time to put a house on the market, but it took me all spring and summer to get everything ship-shape. And while we were disappointed with the appraisal, God knew what we needed, and once again, we had to trust Him for His best.

I had hoped to be moved before the first snow, but that wouldn't be happening. However, we were okay spending another winter here as Doug had improved significantly. We didn't want to be a burden for our friends and family by depending on them to help with firewood and snowplowing. Financially, we couldn't afford to pay anyone long-term to keep the wood supply stocked and the driveway plowed. However, we had been assured by family and friends, the snowplowing would be taken care of, and most of the firewood had already been supplied for that winter. In the end, though, we thought delaying the move may be best.

We believed that once we got our settlement, we would have a better financial picture of what our future would look like and what we could buy or build based on that information. I had to believe God was working in us, giving us the desire and the power to do what pleases Him (Philippians 2:13).

As long as God was still working in us, we were on the right path. I believed with divine guidance, we would eventually get where we were supposed to be, and we would be right on time.

"Traveler, there is no road; / you make your
own path as you walk" (Antonio Machado).[60]

Changes Over Time

January 17

Two years had already passed since the accident. So much had changed in our lives, and most of them had been for the best. We were better people for what we had been through, and we were able to encourage so many people along the way.

Since our winter had been so mild, we decided to get a head start with our training for the next Run Wild Missoula Marathon. Doug seemed to think he wanted to run the half-marathon that year. Funny how his mind changed once he had a chance to rest after the first race. His physical therapist and I explained to him perhaps it would be best if he walked this year without the walker before he attempted to run.

However, I recognized I could be wrong about him running because he was able to walk for more than an hour without a walker. But when Doug quit focusing on walking and started thinking, his brain short-circuited. Unfortunately, he did have a fall. When he walked, he walked; and when he thought, he thought. He just couldn't do both at the same time yet. Though, we both wondered if perhaps there was a day coming when he would prevail.

We were still waiting and contending with Work Comp to see what they decided about getting the wage part of the settlement over with. As foolish as we had been told we were not to have an attorney, we still did not have one. From our perspective, we didn't want to spend our future settlement on an attorney until we knew whether we really needed one. As Doug said, the case would not be settled until he signed on the dotted line. And for kicks, he was reading the

Workers' Compensation Law and Regulations book, believing it was to his benefit to be as educated to the laws as possible and, as he put it, "I have nothing better to do." He may have a brain injury, but he was not ignorant or slow to comprehend. In fact, his neuropsychological reports indicated he was brilliant.

After being told over and over how crazy we were not to have an attorney and how we needed to sue anyone and everyone we could, grabbing every penny we could, the bottom line was there was no one to sue. My frustration was coming out after two years of being told we needed to sue, we needed an attorney, and how stupid we were not to have one, or having the question asked, "Is he retarded?" while the question could better be asked, "Does he have mental limitations?" I do realize everyone has meant well, but unless you knew the full details and were walking the path, providing proper counsel was difficult at best.

> It is not the critic who counts; not the man who points out how the strong man stumbles, or where the doer of deeds could have done them better. The credit belongs to the man who is actually in the arena, whose face is marred by dust and sweat and blood.
>
> Theodore Roosevelt[61]

[/vc_row_inner]

We continued to be met with challenges in this journey called life. Our church had been some of our greatest cheerleaders in our fight of faith. However, Doug was finding himself overwhelmed with the large crowds, the loud worship music, and being the object of everyone's attention. Everyone meant well and were so thrilled to see the former dead man, particularly since they had prayed for several others who were not granted a miracle and entered eternal rest. Unfortunately for Doug, the combination was simply too much for him to handle. In tears, he often begged me to leave him home alone while encouraging me to go. This was not an option given his impulsivity and fall risk.

Perhaps we would need to find a new church but considering leaving our church was a very difficult decision for me and a potentially significant change for both of us. This church family stood by our side through the most challenging time of our life. We had truly done life and death together with those people. However, after much prayer, we felt led to move on. It was a tough decision. Not wanting to deal with my emotions during a conversation, I sent a letter to the pastor explaining our decision to leave.

There was little that could be done to change the situation for Doug. Music volume during worship is something many churches contend with, and we didn't expect it to be addressed just for Doug. He hadn't conveyed his sense of feeling overwhelmed by crowds in the moment, so we were not able to ask people to refrain from touching him. We quietly left without saying goodbye to everyone. Perhaps it was a coward's way out, but at the time, it seemed like the best option.

A co-worker suggested we check out the church she attended after hearing my concerns. This new church was so excited to meet the man they prayed so hard for after hearing about the accident that they made us feel like celebrities. We have been so blessed to meet many of the strangers who prayed for us long before they became family.

A Whole Lot of Shaking Going On

April 6

Doug had an EEG to determine if it was reasonable to reduce more of his anticonvulsants. Afterwards, the doctor was reluctant to tell us that the twitches and jerking movements Doug had been experiencing since his accident were small seizures. He explained it was like flipping a light switch, providing just enough of an interruption to cause the muscle to lose the message from the brain. This was not what we wanted to hear, but we finally had an explanation for the excessive movement.

"Instead of reducing the anticonvulsant, I would like to suggest you start taking Lamictal. It has a great track record of treating your kind of seizure." She went on to explain potential side effects, of which she indicated that .04 percent of people taking it react with a rash and die. *Really?*

I felt bile rising in my throat. "You do you remember that Doug is the guy that seems to be predisposed to having the rare reactions to many of the medications that he has tried, right? This one makes me really nervous!"

"Yes, I do remember that, but this is our only option."

We agreed to give it a try. Apparently, it takes four plus weeks to get a therapeutic dose into the system. This is also the time frame in which any reaction typically occurs. Needless to say, I was hovering like a mama bird watching his every move. Thankfully, there was no rash, and it did seem to be helping to control the seizures. He would revisit the doctor a few days later to determine whether he would stay on this one or not.

Upon hearing the news that Doug was still having seizures, Work Comp decided to renegotiate their original settlement offer after further assessment back at QLI for what his long-term needs would be.

The original offer was a monthly wage and a lump sum to cover the expense of a caregiver or institutional care. At the rate they were paying for his caregiver, the money would last for only seven and a half years. This time frame was not nearly long enough, and with the new information regarding these ongoing seizures, he would most likely need care for the rest of his life. So, we were off to Omaha.

Doug had mixed feelings about returning to Omaha. Knowing he needed to focus on the positive, I helped him see the opportunity he would have to reconnect with the staff at QLI, whom he missed and spoke of often, rather than focusing on being away from the comforts of home again. He took the bait and went on to say he could show them how much progress he had made. In the end, his attitude changed as he recognized the assessment from QLI was going to be to his benefit in regard to getting a fair settlement. He fully understood QLI had his back, ensuring he was not going to be medically cleared in areas in which he was still limited.

Selfishly, I was looking forward to some time alone once again. It would give me time to recharge my batteries now that QLI would be responsible for his care. I dutifully packed his bags, feeling confident this would be a much shorter stay than last time. We now had certainty as to the duration of his visit, whereas last time we were clueless with the exception of my inclination from the Holy Spirit that he would be there for seven months.

It was with open arms and loving hugs we were welcomed back to the QLI campus. Doug was ushered into a state of the art apartment. This room had all the latest in technology to provide disabled patients with the assistance needed to enable them to live with greater independence. Lights, window shades, and TV were all operated by voice commands. The setup was much homier than his previous room.

Once we were able to greet most everyone, Doug said he needed to rest. The traveling was exhausting for him. It was a quick trip for me because I needed to get back home to my responsibilities. I figured I would return in a month to bring him home, but at the conclusion of his stay, one of the QLI nurses took advantage of the opportunity to visit Montana and provide an in-person update on Doug's progress. She, along with the rest of the medical team, decided Doug would be a good candidate for a vagus nerve stimulator (VNS), which was implanted in early August. The VNS is somewhat like a pacemaker but sends electrical impulses to his brain instead of his heart, every five minutes for thirty seconds. The VNS would help rewire the brain and hopefully reduce his spasms, thereby reducing his falling. Bit by bit, we were seeing improvements, but we were still being very careful when walking knowing there was still the potential for falls.

October 19

At long last, we had a buyer for our house! We had to reduce our price considerably, but we always believed when one could no longer do the work required to maintain their home or afford to hire someone to do the work, it was time to make the necessary changes. So, we were making those changes.

We wouldn't have to make the long drive and deal with mud or as much snow anymore. We hoped Work Comp would get a settlement to us, and we would have the finances to remodel the house we were going to purchase, making it handicapped-accessible. I didn't love the new house, but it was one level; it could be remodeled to accommodate Doug's needs and to my liking. The property is five acres, mostly in pasture. It's a beautifully landscaped yard with mature trees, which would give us a greater sense of privacy. The location seemed perfect. It was only five miles from the edge of the city, so the hospital is minutes away instead of almost an hour. An added bonus for Doug was the nearby bike path, which I was sure he would take advantage of.

***

I found out I would no longer have a job with Western Montana Clinic. The doctor I had been working under was leaving, and my employers were selling the DEXA (X-ray) equipment I had been operating, and I would not be needed henceforth.

The timing couldn't have been worse! But the Good Lord must have felt that I was cut out for another challenge. I was not so sure I agreed, but again He says that trials develop character; at this rate, I figured I was going to be quite a character someday!

My priority was to get moved and then figure out what I wanted to be when I grew up. I was willing to go whatever direction He led me, but I was clueless! As I said previously, I have always believed that when one door closes, He always opens another. Perhaps this was my chance to explore other options.

Counseling always intrigued me to the point I went through training in spiritual inner healing through church ministry. I always read self-development books instead of novels. Co-workers and friends often said I should be a counselor. At this point, though, I just wanted to get settled in our new home and figure out how to create a new normal.

A week after moving into our new house, there was much to do. The kitchen was not what I was used to, and the bathrooms were a challenge for both of us. Doug was not able to get his wheelchair into either bathroom, which we knew was one of the most significant limitations of this house, but since he had been able to get around independently at times, we chose to take the risk. However, we were finding out firsthand exactly how challenging these obstacles really were. In choosing houses, it was not as though there were lots of options to meet our needs. With limited financing, we were required to settle for the best of what was available. Our prayers for a timely settlement escalated accordingly.

There is No Owner's Manual for a TBI

Now that we had moved and were somewhat settled in, I imagined life would settle down, and we would find a routine. Our lives had been in turmoil since the accident. We barely seemed to find a rhythm, and suddenly we had to change again with the big move.

According to an article entitled, *The Psychology of Daily Routine*, "When you regulate your daily actions, you deactivate your 'fight or flight' instincts because you're no longer confronting the unknown."[62] When we are able to turn off our fear instincts, we are actually able to enjoy life. Wow! No wonder I was having such a difficult time finding joy in my current state. It was beginning to make sense as to why I was desperately trying to return to the old ways of doing things. I was looking for the comfort I was accustomed to having in my normal everyday activities, regardless of whether they were mundane or not.

If I was struggling for lack of routine, I could only imagine how difficult it must have been for Doug to be tossed to and fro as he had been during this recovery process. I continued to have faith Doug would completely recover, but many days I had to settle for little bits of progress while on others, I had to take a step backwards.

Unfortunately, there is no owner's manual for traumatic brain injuries. Each is as unique as the creation God has made us. Perhaps He custom-designs our lives to grow us in the areas where we need it as these types of injuries are a challenge to the patient and the caregivers to discover the appropriate methods of thriving in the journey to recovery and beyond. It is our responsibility to look for the clues and resources He lovingly provides to illuminate the next step on our journey of faith.

Some days we get to spend lazing around green pastures and cool streams, while other times, we are required to trek across the fiery hot desert or up rugged, steep mountains where footing is treacherous at best. It is our internal GPS, otherwise known as the Holy Spirit, who is always there to guide us in the very next decision necessary. Despite our limitations, the Holy Spirit is always there to empower us to accomplish our personalized itinerary. Many may travel the same path, but each will have a different experience based on the Father's plan for our future.

I had been feeling discouraged that our life wasn't going to return to my understanding of normal any time soon. Doug still needed lots of help and supervision because he still battled with impulsivity. He often decided he was perfectly capable of a task and attempted it by himself, only to have a wreck—and several trips to the ER. Dishes and furniture were destroyed in the process.

It was hard to trust him to complete a task or remember a commitment because his short-term memory was compromised. Much like a person with dementia or Alzheimer's, he asked me the same question multiple times over the course of the day or even the hour. I had hoped the questions would decrease as his brain healed, but I was not seeing much improvement. I became disheartened and aggravated after having to remind him over and over what we just had discussed minutes before. As a result, I found myself becoming irritated and short with him in my response.

Of course, this was not what I wanted. I wanted to be patient and extend all the grace he needed, but I frequently failed—especially when he was cutting with the words he chose to use due to the damage to the emotional center of his brain. If he was angry, he struggled to hold it in check and spoke whatever was on his mind. He had always been outspoken. However, before his accident, he was able to use good judgment when expressing himself. This just wasn't the case anymore.

We were taught when you hit a pot and damage it, no amount of repair will ever put the pot back into the original shape. Our words have the same effect. Once the damage has been done, no amount of "I am sorry" or "please forgive me" will ever undo the damage.

I understood he wasn't in control of what was coming out of his mouth, but my heart was shattering with every angry word. I tried not to take his responses personally, but unfortunately, those poisonous darts managed to penetrate deeply despite my best efforts to deflect them.

As the poison seeped into my heart, it began to harden. I started building a wall around my heart as my relationship with Doug morphed into one of a caregiver and less of a wife. Between deflecting the ugly words and trying to manage the demands of meeting his needs in the daily grind of life, I could feel my spousal position eroding.

In talking with others in similar positions and from resources I read, I realized it was very common for the spouse to eventually default to more of a caregiver role. One must exercise great intentionality and energy to keep a marital relationship flourishing without the added complications of compromised mental and physical limitations.

I was running on fumes, and I knew I was in unchartered territory, so I kept doing what I knew to do, but this didn't seem to be working. I began researching solutions. It was clear to me that God was using those challenges to transform me. Jesus certainly suffered cruel words spewed at Him on more than one occasion, and He responded with the loving grace of His father. I wanted to do that too.

I prayed for grace when traveling the path God set before me. When I tried to see our situation from His perspective, I was able to change the way I lived each day. I knew that if I wanted to thrive in my relationship with my husband, I first had to thrive in my relationship with God, but it seemed I wasn't making my time with Him a priority at the time. There was always something else vying for my attention. In fact, if truth be told, at times, I resented just how much I was responsible for. After all, it didn't make sense I could spend time with Him and have enough to complete the priorities on my ever-growing to-do list. In reality, I had experienced the supernatural expansion of my time when I started my day in His presence.

There seemed to be a direct correlation between the amount of grace, patience, love, joy, kindness, peace, and gentleness I operated in to the amount of time invested with God.

> We can all draw close to him with the veil removed from our faces. And with no veil we all become like mirrors who brightly reflect the glory of the Lord *Jesus*. We are being transfigured into his very image as we move from one brighter level of glory to another.
>
> 2 Corinthians 3:18 TPT

[/vc_row_inner]

It was obvious to me that if I wanted to exemplify Jesus in my daily life, it was imperative I pull into His service station and get my tank filled up. It may have even been beneficial to schedule an oil and filter change. While Doug may have been suffering from not having a filter, I was aware my filter could be grimy, preventing me from getting the air necessary for premium performance. In fact, I was noticing my self-control was also determined by the amount of spiritual fuel in my tank. Knowing I was currently living in an "extra grace required" season of my life, I recognized the wisdom in prioritizing my pit stop.

Doug also gained considerable control over his emotions. Many times, throughout this journey, I have heard the Lord tell me to "trust the process." In as much as I chafed at having to wait, I knew seeds required germination. One day while driving, I heard this story on the radio about the growth process of bamboo. This story was a perfect illustration of waiting for signs of growth while developing patience in the process.

> The Bamboo is amazing. You water it and wait. You wait an entire year, and nothing appears. No bud, no twig, nothing.

So, you keep watering and protecting the area and taking care of the future plant. You wait another year. Still, nothing happens.

Another year passes, and still no sign of growth. It has been three years. Should you give up? Someone told you that it might take a while to really see the fruits of your efforts, so you keep on keeping on.

Another year passes. No plant.

You begin year number five with the same passion as day number one. You keep watering and keep waiting. Finally, after five years, the bamboo starts growing-and in six weeks, it grows to over 80 feet tall! Yes, eighty feet in six weeks! Well, not really. It is 80 feet in five years.

The point is simple. If you had given up for even the shortest period of time, there would be no Bamboo. It took almost impossible persistence. The plant is there for one reason and one reason only—because you never gave up on it.[63]

[/vc_row_inner]

God never gives up on us! He goes out of His way to meet us in our darkest, most desolate, and desperate of times. Often, we simply need a reminder to change our perspective and to trust the process of becoming who we were meant to be all along.

Job, Identity, and Relationship Losses

One would think that after seeing Doug lose his job of thirty-two years without being financially ruined or lacking in any way only then to have him die and be resurrected, I would have a surplus of faith to believe losing my job was no big deal for God. Instead, I found myself following the footsteps of the disciples, who witnessed many miracles firsthand and still struggled to keep their faith. Peter managed to muster enough faith to step out of the boat into the raging waters when Jesus called him, but it only took a moment before doubt crept in, and he began to sink. The Bible says Jesus rescued him and then rebuked him (Matthew 14:29-31). I wonder if the rebuke was more like firm encouragement. I imagine Jesus saying, "Pete, you know you are capable of doing this. Don't let fear keep you from reaching your full potential."

Even before Doug's accident, I loved to help others by sharing lessons I had learned or content from the latest book I was reading. Over the years, many people told me I should be a motivational speaker. Now that we had a significant testimony to share, those flames were fanned with those encouraging remarks.

After losing my job, I thought it might be the perfect opportunity to bring this dream to reality. However, writing and speaking is a great idea in theory, but not knowing how to get one's foot in the door made it financially lacking in reality—and, like Peter, doubts sank in.

Not working was barely financially doable, but we wouldn't starve because I was eligible for unemployment benefits. However, always looking to add insult to injury, the devil tried to cause more turmoil in our lives by conniving someone into stealing my identity and filing in my unemployment benefits, which added to my already stress-filled life taking a lot of time to resolve.

And on top of that, the job market for X-Ray techs in Montana was at an all-time low due to an increase of X-ray students being turned out than there were jobs in Montana cities. In fact, many new graduates had to leave the state to find work. It had become obvious I was going to need to trust my Provider to take care of us, and I needed the time afforded me to regroup after the long siege I had been under.

In this time of rest, I was able to do a better job of organizing the house and making it feel more like home. Soon, however, the enemy began to whisper to me I was a failure for not doing more to contribute financially. Even though I was taking a computer class through adult education, hoping to improve my chances of finding a job, it was not adding to our income at the moment. I began to feel guilty and wondered if I should find a part-time job while I worked on improving my computer skills.

Toward the end of my computer class, my previous employer, Western Montana Clinic, offered me a scheduling position. This position was part-time but included the appealing lure of much-needed health insurance. I'd be back in familiar surroundings among former co-workers, many of whom were like family. I immediately accepted this offer, despite the fact I would be making less than half the wages I made doing DEXA scans. I was confident, though, it was a divine provision. It was divine alright—another divine opportunity to grow.

In as much as I was welcomed back with warmth and excitement, I soon realized this position was not a good financial, physical, or mental fit for me. While performing DEXA scans, it was just my patient and me. I had the opportunity to get up and down from my desk as I accompanied my patient to and from the waiting room. I quickly discovered being tied to a desk and telephone, which required sitting most of the day, was wreaking havoc on my body.

The significant amount of background noise was also wearing on my nerves as I strained to hear what the person on the phone was saying. They were already fragile, and this chaotic environment wasn't helping them. I lasted about three and a half months before I resigned. It took Jonah three and a half days in the belly of the whale before he realized submission to God was a better option than to resist and go his own way. I can't imagine it should have taken so long, but I do know he and I are equally stubborn and slow to submit—no matter how smelly the situation.

I knew I needed to make more money, and believe it or not, cleaning toilets for others part-time was a much better solution than scheduling patients for doctor's appointments part-time. It wasn't glamorous work, but at least I could double the income I was earning and make a decent living doing it.

Financially, cleaning was the better decision, but socially, not so much. I thrive when I spend time with people. However, many of my clients were working during the day. Taking the time to chat with those who were at home cut into my productivity. I missed my DEXA job more than ever. It was a perfect fit, like Cinderella's slipper. How I longed to return to what was.

If I could get my foot in the door at St. Patrick Providence hospital, I thought there may be a chance I could eventually transition back into the radiology department and my beloved DEXA machine. So, when a neighbor mentioned the endoscopy department was looking for a tech, I decided this was my chance.

I assumed getting hired would be a simple process. After all, I had received my X-ray training with them and had a great work history, but the application and interview process was grueling. I jumped through what seemed to be endless hoops to find out the endoscopy job required working in dimly lit rooms while assisting the doctors during procedures. Even before applying for the job, I assumed cleaning the scopes used during the procedure was not going to be glamorous. I determined, however, if cleaning scopes would get me back to X-ray, I would roll up my proverbial sleeves and get to work, which I did. However, it was the lack of light during procedures that ate away at my mental well-being. It was as though the darkness seeped into my soul, extinguishing any glimmer of hope that life would improve. I already struggled with seasonal affective disorder, and now I was drowning in a pit of despair. An emotional plummet wasn't exactly what I was expecting when I put in for this job, and in my pride, I failed to see how God was fulfilling my needs.

Depression engulfed me. Its tentacles were wrapping tighter and tighter around my soul. I could perform my DEXA job in my sleep because I knew the routine so well. Now, I was making the mistakes of a newbie as I learned the ropes of a new endeavor. Each mistake threatened to erode my confidence.

I attempted to encourage myself with reminders of how many times Edison attempted to create the lightbulb before succeeding and stories of others who failed their way forward, but it didn't help that much. I'm not saying I was a complete failure at the job because that wasn't the case. I had gotten so comfortable with what I was doing, I was rarely challenged at work.

I also didn't realize how much of my identity was related to my job, but I was quickly learning. I thrived on the ability to bring encouragement to others while I was working. I also enjoyed the security of a good wage and the blessings it provided. Neither of the jobs I had gotten since being laid off allowed me to engage with other people to the degree I had previously enjoyed or brought in the income I was accustomed to for the work I did before. I was beginning to believe life was not worth living.

As my stress increased, my pain levels followed. And as the old adage says, "Pain seeks pleasure." Pleasure came in the form of food, especially ice cream. And alcohol. After consuming my poison of choice, I would be filled with guilt, shame, and self-condemnation. The devil was always quick to remind me what a failure I was for not being able to control how much I ate or drank. Cackling, he would say, *What makes you think you could ever motivate anyone else with your story now? Look at you, you're nothing but a glutton and a drunkard. Who is going to listen to you?* I allowed myself to wallow deeper and deeper, drowning in hopelessness and misery, but I knew in my heart this wasn't the creation that Jesus wanted me to become through this process. He hadn't died on the cross for me to live a life of desolation. He died to set the captives free.

The Spirit of the Lord is upon me, and he has anointed me to be hope for the poor, freedom for the brokenhearted, and new eyes for the blind, and to preach to prisoners, "You are set free!" I have come to share the message of Jubilee, for the time of God's great acceptance has begun.

Luke 4:18 TPT

[/vc_row_inner]

I was five months into this position when the thought of dying seemed far better than living. I knew Doug would be taken care of. In fact, in my current state, he would probably be better off without me. More than once I told God I wanted to die. However, He gently reminded me to trust the process.

The tipping point came one night when I was unable to sleep due to the physical pain I was in. Despite having taken Advil to ease the pain, relief never came. I tossed and turned for several hours. Frustrated and angry, I tossed back the covers, climbed out of bed at midnight, and tiptoed quietly to the living room, trying not to wake Doug.

I dropped to my knees, trying to choke back my sobs. *God, I can't do this anymore. There is no way I can continue working in a position, which is sucking the life out of me.*

I heard him clear as day. *Quit your job!*

I couldn't believe what I heard. *What?*

Once again, I heard him clearly. *Quit your job.*

God, we will be a $1,000 a month short of being able to pay our bills if I quit. Oh, and by the way, Doug is not on board with this idea.

Whenever I mentioned wanting to resign, he said I was foolish to quit a job, which provided health insurance, regardless of how miserable I was. He had been so adamant there was no excuse to quit, so I couldn't fathom there could be any way he would agree now. But if by some miracle he did, I would step out in faith and quit.

When we got up the next morning, Doug asked, "How did you sleep?"

"Not well."

He looked at me curiously. "Why not?"

"Leaning over those deep sinks cleaning scopes is causing my back so much pain it's making sleeping difficult. I have already told you my left leg is numb from sciatica. I can't feel a thing from my hip to my knee."

"Quit your job!"

You could have knocked me over with a feather. I was so shocked by his response. I said, "What did you say?"

"Quit your job."

I couldn't believe what I was hearing. God wasn't messing around. "Doug, I can't! Our financial situation won't allow for it. We need the money. I can't just quit."

He stopped and looked at me before he made his way to the bathroom. "God will provide."

God had put me on the spot. It was time to make good on my promise to quit my job if Doug agreed. In disbelief and a bit of fear, I left for work to give my notice. When I turned the key on in my car, the radio started playing, and the first words I heard were, "Oh what I would do to have / The kind of faith it takes to climb out of this boat I'm in," by *Casting Crowns*.[64]

I began to laugh and cry at what seemed to be confirmation to quit my job. Just like the prodigal son, I, too, had finally come to my senses and was ready to climb out of my stinky mess.

Within two weeks of giving my notice at work, I received a text from a young couple who had expressed interest in our last piece of property. In addition to the home we had lived in prior to selling and moving, we still owned bare acreage in the 9-Mile Valley, which Doug's parents had given us. Due to the steep terrain, this property would not have been suitable for us to build on unless Doug completely recovered. We knew we could use the money from selling it to pay off our vehicles, leaving us with just the house payment. This would make our finances more manageable without my income.

It made sense to sell it to someone who could appreciate it for the rustic lifestyle it would require. We couldn't help but remember we, too, had been young, adventurous, and up for the challenge of building remotely. The text said they were ready to move forward. They had a buy-and-sell ready to sign. I felt as though the weight of the world had been lifted from my shoulders. I breathed a huge sigh of relief. I could take some time to find employment suitable for my skills and personality. And little did I know God was opening another door of blessing.

The following week our attorney called and said he had received a settlement offer from Work Comp he felt we needed to accept. After receiving this news, I was giddy with joy and relief. I could now transition into being Doug's full-time caregiver and not have to worry about work until I felt compelled. We weren't going to have the income we had before his accident, but we would be debt-free, and with wise stewardship, we could manage.

I can't help but think how much suffering I may have saved myself from if only I would have believed God was more than capable and willing to provide for all my needs. Instead of forcing His will on me, He allowed me to go my own way, knowing I would learn. At last, we would be able to remodel the house and truly make it home. I could take over full-time caregiving, write this book, and have our privacy back. Don't get me wrong, having caregivers was a much-needed blessing. However, Doug and I had seldom had people in our home for extended periods of time before all this. It was a huge adjustment having a caregiver in the home to help with household chores, Doug's needs, and transportation. I felt I could seldom relax and let the dishes sit for the night or leave things laying around, knowing they would have to work around my mess. Even on the days I would go into work late, I felt as though I needed to be up, dressed, and ready to go instead of having a lazy morning reading with a cup of coffee. However, it was the caregiver who chose to go through and organize my underwear drawer without asking that really pushed my personal boundaries. Yes, I was looking forward to having my own personal space back.

You can have faith, or you can have fear, but you can't have both. If you want God to do something off the chart, you have to take your hands off the controls… If you aren't willing to let go, then you don't control whatever it is that you are holding on to. It controls you. And if you don't throw it down, your staff will remain forever a staff. It will be what it currently is. But if you have the courage to throw down your staff, it will become a lightning rod of God's miraculous power, not because you threw it, but because of the one who will change it… What you hold in your hand cannot multiply until you put it into the hands of God. But if you will let go, and let God, He will use it beyond your wildest imaginations.

Mark Batterson[65]

[/vc_row_inner]

Shortly before I lost my job, I was sharing our story with an older gentleman who had worked as an editor and publisher back east before retiring to Montana. He was spellbound as I told the story, and when I had finished, he said to me, "Young lady, write your book. Write your damn book. The world needs to hear your story!"

Despite all the encouragement I received, I was reluctant to put myself out there as an author. I was willing to dream but unwilling to chase my dream for fear of failure and for fear of what may happen to our quiet life if the book did sell as many had predicted it would. I allowed my limiting beliefs to keep me from fulfilling my full potential. I saw every obstacle as a giant while failing to see God had equipped me to be a giant slayer.

"Instead of believing you have a problem; believe you have a possibility for God to bring forth the provision necessary to overcome the problem" (Graham Cooke).[66]

As I was praying about finding a way to supplement our income, God gave me a vision of Cinderella being dressed by the birds, mice, and squirrels. She was in need of a dress suitable for the ball but didn't have the funds to buy one. Yet, a dress was lovingly and ingeniously fashioned for her out of items at hand by the creatures she cared for. The dress was stunning in its simplicity, and she outshone all the fancy expensive gowns.

Cinderella had a problem, which turned into a possibility, securing her future in ways she could have only dreamed of. This vision assured me that all of my needs would be taken care of once again. They might not arrive in the packages I believe they should, but I can count on His provision. For example, the Israelites had manna and the quail from heaven while they were in the wilderness for forty years to sustain them. When needing money to pay taxes, Jesus told Peter to go fishing. When he caught the first fish, Peter pulled a coin from the fish's mouth. It was exactly the amount needed to pay the taxes. There was no lack. God never leaves His children lacking.

> "I am convinced that my God will fully satisfy every need you have, for I have seen the abundant riches of glory revealed to me through the Anointed One, Jesus Christ!" (Philippians 4:19 TPT).

Broken Trust: Is This as Good as It Gets?

"Love is weakest when there is more doubt
than trust, but love is strongest when we learn to
trust in spite of the doubts" (Unknown).

Doug had always been a man of his word. If he told you he was going to do something, he made sure he followed through regardless of the cost to him.

After he returned from Omaha, I overheard him having a conversation with a neighbor regarding the scrap metal we were having cut up and hauled off. With words laced with irritation, Doug said to the neighbor, "It wasn't my idea to hire someone to cut it up. I am fully capable of doing it. I was forced into having to hire someone else to do the cutting."

This was a blatant lie. He was in no way capable of standing consistently without falling, let alone using a gas-fired cutting torch. He had agreed with me he was not yet able to cut the metal himself but willing to contract with someone else capable of doing it. I was completely dumfounded by the words I was hearing come out of his mouth as if he believed his words were the truth.

Doing my best not to let my anger, frustration, and confusion get the better of me, I carefully questioned him and eventually said, "You know what you are saying is not true. You told me you were fine with hiring someone to do it."

"Well, you know how stubborn I am," he said. "When things don't turn out the way I think they should, I have decided to say, 'That's not what I said.' Besides that, it was what he wanted to hear.

To know I am still capable of all that I could do before I got hurt. Anyway, I have a brain injury, so I can say whatever I want."

I was shocked. Brain injuries could significantly create personality changes, but so far, Doug was mostly on point. I was wrestling with many emotions as I processed his rationale for being suddenly dishonest.

I was starting to doubt my faith that he would truly be okay. He had been having short-term memory issues, but I never expected lying to be a side effect.

Since that event, I was quick to correct him whenever he had a conversation with someone and exaggerated his story. I felt bad about these corrections, but I also believed those he conversed with deserved to know the truth. Often, he told people how many miles he walked and how many days he walked during a week. Unfortunately, he tended to exaggerate both the number of miles and how many days he walked. He may have walked twelve miles two weeks before, but his brain seemed to struggle remembering it was two weeks ago and not yesterday he had the long walk. Bringing clarity without making him feel ashamed of the correction was a fine line to walk.

Not only did I have to monitor his words with others, I struggled to believe he would keep his word with me. On one occasion, I got a call from the hospital saying they had a patient who needed to have her apartment cleaned before she could return home, and they wanted to know if I wanted the work. I really needed the money, but I didn't have anyone to sit with Doug. He assured me he would be completely fine at home alone for a few hours so I should take the job. After much consideration, I decided this would be an opportunity to give him some independence. He promised me, as he put it, that he would "keep his butt in the chair."

I packed up my cleaning supplies, leaving Doug home alone while praying for angels to keep him safe. The cleaning job turned out to be far more than I had bargained for. The quick hour I had anticipated it taking turned into three. I was torn between finishing and returning home to check on Doug. Instead, I called and checked in, and he assured me all was well. I was greatly relieved, thinking perhaps we could finally gain some independence.

When I got home, all was well. We discussed my cleaning job and the woes of it. Soon Doug was asking me if I wanted to see what he had done to bless me while I was gone. He was so proud of himself, so I obliged, but I was perplexed and then immediately angry as he opened the door to go outside. I followed, not saying a word but thinking hundreds of them as I prayed for wisdom and grace. As we approached the flower beds, he showed me all the weeding he had done while I was gone. As it turned out, he had not kept his butt in the chair as promised me.

I was trying hard to hold my frustration in check and not yell at him or rip his head off like I wanted to do. Instead, I explained to him my fear of him falling and hitting his head on the rocks and needing help. "There is nothing I can do if you get hurt because you refuse to wear any type of fall alert. I understand you want more independence and how much you wanted to help, and I am grateful, but can't *you* understand how unnerving this is for me?"

"Well, I didn't fall. I didn't get hurt. So, you had nothing to worry about!" he said, clearly not understanding the message I was trying to send.

My other fear was that I'd be seen as a failure as a wife and caregiver if something did happen to him. How would I be judged if I didn't keep him safe? I knew I was becoming a helicopter wife, trying to ensure he didn't do more damage to himself, thereby complicating our lives even more. Perhaps, in my trying to keep him safe, I was hindering his growth and causing frustration.

I would have to find a balance between safety and growth and learn to trust God when I was struggling to let go. Counseling showed me I had been trying to protect myself from any more stress and trauma by trying to control Doug's behavior. In my needing to control Doug, I was not allowing any room for God to work. His timely word reminded me, "My grace is sufficient for you, for My power is made perfect in weakness" (2 Corinthians 12:9 NIV). This meant that once again, I needed to surrender Doug into God's capable hands. After all, He had gotten us this far, so surely He would sustain us the rest of our days.

However, believing that God would sustain us and living it out didn't always go hand in hand. I assumed Doug's recovery would take some time, but eventually, he would be back to functioning pretty much as he always had. As rapidly as he seemed to progress, I was confident he would be back on his feet, and we would resume life as normal. We also received several prophetic words telling us Doug would be whole once again and that God had huge plans for his life.

Was I wrong in my understanding, God? I keep holding out for his restoration to happen, but so far, it hasn't. I know You are the Author and Perfecter of our lives, and You have a much different plan or timetable that we do, but I wish You'd show us what's ahead.

2 Peter 3:8 (TLB) confirms this. "But do not forget this, dear friends, that a day or a thousand years from now is like tomorrow for the Lord." I wanted to see the evidence of Doug's restoration right then, and I didn't want to wait another day. Each day I was left waiting, I couldn't help but wonder if I needed to reconcile with the possibility that Doug may never fully recover and learn to be at peace with it.

I have observed many who have not come to terms with the adversity in their lives, allowing disappointment to give way to hopelessness, anger, and bitterness. Their souls become poisoned as they lose heart in the midst of their struggle. From their perspective, it seems as if life is against them, and a half-empty cup is their lot in life.

On the other hand, I have seen severely disabled individuals who seem to flourish and rise above their limitations. They are powerful examples of what it means to be an overcomer. It is in Christ we can all be overcomers, but we must be willing to surrender our plans in exchange for His. When disappointment and discouragement threaten our faith in God, it is then we must press into His immeasurable love, knowing if He is withholding something from us, it is for our greater good. For Psalm 34:10 (TPT) says, "Even the strong and the wealthy grow weak and hungry, but those who passionately pursue the Lord will never lack any good thing." I was trying hard to wrap my head around how Doug not being completely healed could be a good thing.

I believe with all my heart that God is good. Therefore, I have to trust Him at His word. By withholding healing, resources, or dreams, we are given an opportunity to develop a richer relationship with the Holy Trinity. If a deep intimate relationship with the Godhead is our greater good, it is what God will give us the opportunity to develop.

We attended a party with some of our 9-Mile friends. After being told how exhausted I looked, I shared my frustrations with them. They were quick to support me with words of encouragement and advice. However, when Doug arrived to join our conversation, my two friends didn't mince their words as they told Doug it was time for him to step up and help me out. I could see from the tightness in his jaw and narrowed eyes that he didn't appreciate their input.

As we were driving home from the party, the wine and exhaustion got the better of me as words fell from my mouth. I said, "Your unwillingness to sell the 9-Mile property to free me up from working right now makes me feel like the property is more valuable to you than I am. I am to the point that putting a bullet in my head seems to be a much better option than living right now."

My words were met with silence. His lack of response spoke volumes. The air was heavy with tension. It would seem my potshot hit the nail squarely on the head. I wished immediately I could retract those words. I knew better than to stoop to that level. I may have felt like he didn't care, but I shouldn't have chosen such poor timing to communicate my feelings.

Arriving at home, he went into the house ahead of me. I was in no hurry to head inside. I knew it would not be welcoming. Knowing I had to face the music sooner or later, I took a deep breath, opened the door, and took the plunge into what felt like the great abyss.

I could feel his anger as I walked into the living room. His eyes were narrow slits. Yet, I could still see the flashes of fury within. He said, "I have something to say to you. I want you to sit down and listen very carefully." With trepidation, I made my way to a chair as far away from him as possible to listen while wishing I had kept my mouth shut.

In all our years together, he had never used that tone with me. I had been present when he had used it with others, and it wasn't pretty. I knew he had reached his limits. I was scared, not knowing what to expect.

"Your drinking is getting out of hand. You need to stop. You are not allowed to drink anymore. Period. You need to decide between the alcohol and me."

I knew it was bad. How had I let it get so far out of control? I just wanted the pain to go away. I didn't want to be a drunk. I was taught that drunkards went to hell according to the Bible. "I am not leaving. I will give up the alcohol," I shamefully muttered.

A part of me desperately wanted to leave. I was tired of trying to meet his every need and of being his whipping post when he was frustrated with his limitations. I was tired of making sure his every need was being met while denying my own. And I was tired of being the one who had to maintain the yard, vehicle, budget, bills, cooking, and chauffeuring because he couldn't. I felt like I was the only one holding our life together, and I was sick and tired of it. I couldn't help but wonder if we were on our way to becoming the next TBI statistic?

Early on in Doug's recovery, we were told 95 percent of couples in our situation don't make it. The changes in the relationship coupled with dramatic limitations become unbearable, and they end up divorcing. We had been commended multiple times on our willingness to tough it out. This didn't change the pressure we were experiencing while trying to cope with all the changes.

Doug's counselor had suggested we start marriage counseling. "What are your thoughts about counseling?" I asked.

He replied, "I think we are doing okay. There is no reason to spend the money."

"Well then, why is your counselor suggestion we go?"

"I don't know," he replied.

Several months went by, and he again said his counselor suggested we would benefit from marriage counseling. We had the same conversation once again. Doug saw no reason for counseling. I was feeling suspicious. Why would his counselor suggest marriage counseling if he was telling her our marriage was "just fine"?

It was after meeting with the Work Comp Nurse Practitioner when she suggested counseling, we finally realized if our marriage was going to survive, counseling would be necessary. Her concern for us came through loud and clear in her words and tone. Doug's counselor was more than happy to provide a reference for us. Knowing I had reached the limits of my own self-development and inner healing training, I scheduled the appointment. I may not be doing the best job possible, but I wasn't willing to give up without a fight.

We went to our first appointment a couple of weeks later. It would seem by divine providence our counselor was a gentleman who had suffered his own brain injury and specialized in neurobehavioral counseling.

During our first session, I felt like a tattletale as I explained our circumstance. This was particularly true when I shared my resentment at the load of responsibilities I had while Doug had none. His life consisted of eating, sleeping, reading, watching TV, or exercising. That's about it. Occasionally, he would contribute in some small way by taking out the garbage or something similar, but then he expected to be patted on the back every time he did some small task. Keeping him emotionally propped up was exhausting. No one was patting me on the back for the endless hours I was putting in.

To be fair to Doug, there were things he couldn't do, nor did I expect him to do them. However, when he would offer to help, it was usually something risky where he could hurt himself. I couldn't win for losing.

As our first session came to a close, our counselor said to me, "You need to be careful of the tone you are using when talking to Doug. You don't realize how sharp you are being when speaking to him." Ouch! I knew I had my part to play in this game, but I didn't want to be reminded.

Then, leaning forward in his chair, the counselor looked sternly at Doug while shaking his head and said, "Buddy, if you don't step up to the plate and start helping out where you are able, you are going to lose your wife. She has carried far more than her share. It's time for you to give her a hand where you are able."

I was greatly relieved to have confirmation. I wasn't merely feeling sorry for myself and imagining my load was a tad on the heavy side. However, engaging in counseling created a particularly difficult season for us. Doug felt as though he was being ganged up on by me and the counselor. Due to the emotional portion of his brain being damaged, reasoning with Doug was difficult once he was upset. At one point, he exploded, yelling at me and the counselor, "Nothing I say or do is right! She can do nothing wrong! The two of you are making me look like the as*&$%! Feel free to keep on meeting if you want, but I won't be back. I refuse to return, knowing I am just going to take a beating."

He was acting like a child sitting there pouting with his arms folded across his chest. Dumbfounded, the counselor asked Doug, "What do you mean by saying you are the only one who is being corrected. I have brought several things to Tammy's attention that she needs to work on. It's not just you, Doug, who is being asked to change their behavior."

"That's not true," Doug angrily retorted. "You've hardly asked anything of her, but you keep telling me everything I do is wrong."

"I am sorry you feel that way," the counselor responded, "but that simply is not true. You are not hearing all that is being said to the two of you."

"Say what you want. I am not coming back!" With that, we left the counselor's office.

With tension still running high, we did our best to avoid each other as much as possible for the next several days. I was in my office while Doug was engaged in his Monday afternoon Restorative Yoga Therapy session when I overheard him tell his therapist, Serena, how angry he was with me and our counselor for asking him not to participate in the upcoming Run Wild Missoula Marathon.

Doug was in the process of weaning off more of the anticonvulsants. As a result, he was twitchier and was falling more often. Neither were helpful to the prospect of a successful injury-free marathon. It was a "lightbulb" moment. I now understood why he was so angry with us. The marathon represented a means of him proving to himself and to the world that he had value. We had taken away his sense of value.

I immediately called the counselor's office and explained my revelation to him. He agreed 100 percent. I also shared my intent to come to therapy alone. I would not even attempt to encourage Doug to attend so he could have some time to cool off.

After I returned from my individual session, I sat down with Doug to share what the counselor and I discussed. "Is there a chance your anger last week stemmed from us asking you not to walk the marathon?"

Surprised, he looked up at me and said quietly, "Yes. I have already proven I am capable of walking it. Now you have essentially emasculated me by telling me I can't walk it."

I replied, "I am so sorry. I had no idea how important it was to you. I just wanted to keep you safe. You have been really twitchy and falling more than you have been. I thought I was helping you, but I can see now I should have trusted God to protect you once again instead of trying to control the situation. Will you please forgive me?"

"Yes," he responded.

The atmosphere changed immediately. It was as though someone had released the air in a balloon, which had been overinflated. We were no longer holding our breath, waiting for the other one to pop.

Now that he had calmed down somewhat, he was easier to be around. The next week as I was preparing to leave alone for our scheduled marriage counseling session, he asked, "Am I welcome to join you for counseling today?"

"Of course," I replied.

During that session, we were able to iron out some of the existing wrinkles. However, there was still some underlying tension but not nearly as much as before the revelation. There certainly seemed to be a whole lot of potholes in this section of the road to recovery.

There were good days and bad days. I found, though, the more I focused on what he wasn't doing instead of what little he could do, the angrier I became. Even though God asked me to just love him, it was difficult for me to do when I was filled with anger and resentment. Counseling showed me that loving others is especially difficult when you don't love yourself, and I was definitely struggling to love myself.

I would later learn while attending The Life Coach School that I had a "manual" for Doug. We create manuals. These are instruction guides we have for people in our lives about

> how we would like them to behave so we can feel good and be happy. We feel that person should just know what to do and how to treat us. When they are not complying with our desires, we tend to go into Emotional Childhood with our emotions and behaviors even though we are mature adults. When we try to manipulate others into behaving in ways which they don't want to, we often created resistance and resentment.[67]

[/vc_row_inner]

My expectation that Doug would make me happy by doing what I expected him to do was having the exact opposite effect. I knew our thoughts have the ability to create our outcomes because Proverbs 23:7 (TPT) tells us, "For as he thinks within himself, so is he."

I had allowed my thinkin' to become stinkin'. I was no longer living with a glass half full or a grateful heart. I was not managing my mind; it was managing me. Our primal brain is always looking to protect us from harm or discomfort. It desires to experience pleasure with the least amount of effort as possible. It was terrific at showing me all the pain in my life and how easy it was to make the pain go away with ice cream and alcohol, etc. On the days where I had determined I was going to make changes, an urge to indulge would spring up. My primal brain would say, *I won't hurt just this once. You can always start tomorrow. Look at all you are going through; you deserve a treat.* It was obvious to me I was going to need help to move forward.

Even though Doug rejoined me in marriage counseling, I decided I could still benefit from—and needed—some ongoing individual counseling to help me navigate my personal and marital challenges. In my last appointment, my counselor brought up divorce as an option for me to consider. Part of me was appalled. The idea of a Christian counselor suggesting divorce for something other than adultery was unheard of to me. But I soon realized she was not suggesting divorce to convince me it was the right choice, but rather to help me see I was not stuck in marriage if I wanted to escape. I had options. Knowing there were options seemed to take some of the pressure off of me. I was making a choice to stay. No one was forcing me to stay.

Prior to consulting with this counselor, my understanding and conviction was infidelity was the only option permitting a Christian to divorce, as I had been taught in church. I must confess, I struggled to accept this teaching. How could a loving God sentence a spouse to a lifetime of commitment in an abusive marriage?

Later I read Matthew 19:9 (TPT), "But I say to you, whoever leaves his wife for any reason other than immorality, then takes another wife is living in adultery." The word "immorality" jumped off the page. Immorality is defined as immoral quality, character, or conduct; wickedness. Synonyms include wickedness, immoral behavior, badness, evil, vileness, iniquity, corruption, dishonesty, etc.[68]

I am in no way an expert, but it would seem to me abuse is immoral. Jerimiah 3:6-8 tells us God divorced Israel, so he obviously understands the pain and anguish divorce causes. It certainly is not an easy solution to a difficult situation. However, I believe it is up to each individual and their circumstances to go before the Lord and make peace with Him regarding their decision.

If He can forgive a murderer, certainly there must be forgiveness for someone who chooses to save their life through divorce rather than remain in an abusive situation and risk being beaten to death mentally or physically.

I believe divorce is a very private and personal decision that must be submitted to the Lordship of Jesus Christ. I know many dear friends who have been abandoned by their churches because they chose to divorce. As I recall, Jesus engaged the woman at the well who had been married five times, even offering her "living water," rather than denying her because of her immorality (John 4:18).

At times, divorce seemed like the perfect antidote to my misery. Many have marveled I have chosen to stay. However, I would guess others would be appalled if I opted to leave, deciding to believe I had abandoned Doug because he was disabled.

Truthfully, if I chose to leave, it would have been for my mental well-being. I am not so callous as to use his disability as an excuse to leave. When I allowed myself time to sit and ponder what I really wanted, I knew deep down in my heart of hearts, divorce wasn't it; nor did I believe it was what God wanted for me. We had already weathered some pretty tough storms, and we have always been totally committed to our "till death do we part" vows up to this point. Without exception, we have been willing to do whatever necessary to get through the difficult times together. I know this is a value of utmost importance to both of us.

I heard Devin Still (retired NFL player and Christian speaker) being interviewed on *In the Market* with Janet Parshall on Christian radio one day; what he said caught my attention. "Our values will determine how we live."[69] I thought to myself, *What do I value?* I valued my wedding vows. I valued my husband even though there were times I found it difficult to do so since his accident. I valued my relationship with Jesus. I wanted to live a life worthy of His sacrifice. I was grateful for this reminder. My values would empower me to live the life I was called to.

It's just like God to give me a sliver of hope when I thought I couldn't tolerate any more mental and/or physical pain. He lovingly told me if I continue to trust Him, life will improve eventually. He also reminded me if I will allow Him to do a work in me, He would also do a work in Doug. He continued to remind me that once I lay myself on the altar, life begins to shimmer with the hope of joy being restored.

The Remodeling

Imagine yourself as a living house. God comes in to rebuild that house. At first, perhaps, you can understand what He is doing. He is getting the drains right and stopping the leaks in the roof and so on; you knew that those jobs needed doing and so you are not surprised. But presently He starts knocking the house about in a way that hurts abominably and does not seem to make sense. What on earth is He up to?

The explanation is that He is building a quite different house from the one you thought of—throwing out a new wing here, putting on an extra floor there, running up towers, making courtyards. You thought you were being made into a decent little cottage: but He is building a palace. He intends to come and live in it Himself.

Clive Staples Lewis [70]

[/vc_row_inner]

When we built our home in 1996, I thoroughly enjoyed the process. I spent hours dreaming and drawing plans, working with precision to get every detail just right. However, with such careful attention to detail, there were a few things I wished I had considered. As a result, I relished the thought of having another opportunity to get a second chance to remodel or design and build another home.

It was also a relief to think it was my home I was renovating and not my life.

Apparently, God had other plans. It felt as though we had been stripped down to a few studs and a foundation. We had to leave our decent little cottage in the woods and settle for a 900-square-foot downgrade on the outskirts of the city. I should clarify, though, that this house had massive street appeal in Realtor-speak. It wasn't a dump by any stretch of the imagination. It just lacked some of the things important to me, such as a spacious and well-laid-out and efficient kitchen. The bathrooms were cramped as well. I knew it had potential; it just wasn't what I was accustomed to. I had to work on my attitude frequently, reminding myself how grateful I should be.

No, the new house wasn't as well planned out as the one I designed, but it was a significantly superior dwelling to what many others had. The downgrade is far from a cardboard box some people are forced to live in. In some ways, I felt as though God was asking me to put my beautiful house on the altar and settle for second best. I consoled myself with the hope of the possibility of being able to remodel the new house once Doug received his Work Comp settlement.

At last, we received the call from our attorney, Work Comp made an offer he felt we needed to accept. However, the settlement was not nearly what we had expected or had been told Doug's accident was worth. Well-meaning individuals exclaimed, "Your settlement will be multimillions of dollars." They went on to tell us about someone they knew who got a considerable settlement for a much less significant injury. As it turned out, if Doug had been able to continue working at the wage he had been making, he could have made the settlement's offer's value in merely three years.

Initially, Work Comp seemed to spare no expense in taking the very best care possible of Doug, which is why I was convinced it would continue. Since we started off with such an amiable relationship, I didn't see any reason we should be paying an attorney when it seemed we didn't need one. In my naiveté, I missed several opportunities for help and compensation for which our attorney said we had been eligible. I was told by one adjuster there was only a certain amount of money available for home improvement. If we used that money to improve the existing house, there would be no further money to improve another house if we moved. When I told the attorney how much money I had settled for on the home improvement portion of the settlement, he winced, saying that was not true and what they gave us was a fraction of what would have been available. After our experience, I would urge anyone in this situation to get counsel immediately.

Despite our disappointment in the settlement, the proceeds did allow us to have the necessary funds to remodel the house. I had been drawing plans shortly after we moved in, and God provided a contractor. In the end, the remodel turned out even better than I had imagined, I was blessed with a dream kitchen and wheelchair-accessible master bath. Yes, I did have to compromise in some areas, but my faithful Father provided the most important things.

Doug was being severely challenged with the extreme interruption to his normal routine. As a result, he began to get a lot twitchier, which made it more difficult for him to do things. I could tell he was not okay, but I couldn't help him if I didn't know what was wrong. He didn't want to do anything but read and watch TV. He began to get irritable for no apparent reason. The tension between us grew exponentially. Obviously, the house remodeling may have been over, but it was going to take a while for the dust to settle.

While the dust was settling in our physical house, it became apparent to me my mind was going to require some remodeling as well, after all. Proverbs 13:12 (TPT) says, "When hope's dream seems to drag on and on, the delay can be depressing. But when at last your dream comes true, life's sweetness will satisfy your soul."

I had been faithfully holding on to God's words, trusting Him to make Doug okay. It was obvious Doug was not yet okay. I was not okay either. I was depressed instead, feeling guilty because I should have been so grateful for how well Doug was doing. I was having difficulty reconciling my faith with my feelings, though. My soul seemed to be filled with more angst, anger, and bitterness than sweetness.

It would seem by divine appointment, I connected with a friend who attended my old church. She introduced me to the term "ambiguous grief." According to Google, ambiguous means "unclear or inexact because a choice between alternatives has not been made."[71] And grief means "sorrow, misery, sadness, distress, torment, suffering, heartache, etc."[72]

I felt as if I had been given a lifeline as I familiarized myself with the term, studies, and testimonies of other people's experiences. I was not alone. Nor was I mentally flawed. In one explanation I found on the internet,

> Ambiguous loss is different from the loss and grief of death because closure is not possible and your grief cannot be fully resolved while the person with dementia [in our case, TBI] is alive. But this ambiguity and the mixed feelings that it can stir up are a common and expected experience for caregivers of people with dementia.[73]

[/vc_row_inner]

Another article I read by Stephanie Sarazin explains:

> Grief, we have learned, is predictable: denial anger, bargaining, depression, and acceptance.
>
> But what if the common denominator isn't death? What if instead it was something far more nefarious that first takes our lived one away? Monsters like Alzheimer's Disease, Parkinson's Disease, Traumatic Brain Injury or Addiction. These life-altering diagnoses changes our loved one, and often resigned, we watch helpless as they slip further away from the person they once were to us. As the relationship dynamic changes, the grieving process begins. But often, the bereft are unaware. Since their beloved did not die a physi-

cal death, their grief doesn't neatly fit the 5 stages, though they may get lumped in anyway. Instead, their grief goes unnamed and untreated…

Grief is a dull aching pain that often shows up uninvited and hijacks your emotional being.[74]

[/vc_row_inner]

I had a warm body to remind me Doug was still alive. He was not cold and lifeless as he was before being resuscitated. Could I really grieve the loss of his former mental capacity and the physical abilities, which no longer resembled the man I had passionately loved and desperately hoped to have back someday? How could I hold on to the hope he may someday fully recover while learning to accept and embrace the reality of who he was at that very moment?

I would have to allow myself to let go of my hopes, dreams, and much of what was familiar. In Genesis 12:1 (NIV), God said to Abram, "Go from your country, your people and your father's household to the land I will show you." Abram left his country, but he took his father, nephew, and idols with him.

I was not the only one who wanted the promises of God while holding on to the comforts of what I had always known. I had left my church family, my home, and my job. The husband I married was no longer capable of doing many of the things I was accustomed to him doing previously. It would seem grief should be expected. Resisting it now seemed futile. In letting go, I was making room for what was to be. I had to relinquish what was in my grip to grasp the promises being offered through His hand.

Depression and Running on Empty

The Holy Spirit walks with us as we are, not as we are supposed to be or as we pretend we are on a Sunday, but as we are in our strong-willed blindness, independence, and judgment. And she [Krueger refers to the Hebrew word for Spirit, Ruach, a feminine noun] that works in the invisible world of the heart in order that we may encounter Jesus, and experience—against our own prejudices—the life he shares with us in his relationship with his Father.

Baxter Kruger[75]

[/vc_row_inner]

I was praying fervently for God to deliver me from the mess I created. I thought once the house was remodeled, I would be happy. However, it seemed as though happiness was elusive. It didn't come in a picture-perfect home, a fine wardrobe, a pint of ice cream, or the alcohol, which had found its way back into my life. Doug never once reminded me of his ultimatum—alcohol or him. Much to my surprise and chagrin, when he knew I was particularly stressed, he would suggest I have a drink to relax. I still felt like a fraud, though.

On the outside, I looked good—dressed in my Sunday best. I was not as trim as I wanted to be, but I was fashionably dressed, my makeup on point, and I had a trendy hairstyle. I was good at putting on a happy face, too. Occasionally, I would be vulnerable, taking off my mask to share my struggle regarding alcohol with a trusted friend, only to be met with words of disbelief. "Oh, Tammy, it can't be that bad! You are not that kind of person!" Others would tell me, "You deserve a drink or two to help you endure all you have been through."

The nights I had gone over my two-drink limit, I would lay in bed at night and silently beg God for mercy and forgiveness while the devil was shouting to me what a "fine" representative I was for the body of Christ. I frequently quoted scriptures to myself in an attempt to transform my mind and break free from the bondage of alcohol, but all to no avail. I was so ashamed of my behavior, I begged God to free me or take me. Despite my prayers, it often felt like God wasn't listening, but I knew He was. He is moved by obedience. In my state of cantankerousness, I was not willing to let go of my negative emotions or the alcohol necessary to deaden them. Instead, I erroneously believed this double shot of poison was better than the glorious transformation He was offering. The stench in my pigpen increased, as did the hardness of my heart.

Then one day, I heard the Holy Spirit reply to my prayers for freedom. *Trust the process, Tammy, this isn't just about you. You may not see the transformation you desire at this time, but it is coming.* What could He mean? How could my overdrinking be of benefit to anyone else?

Was it possible there was a message in my mess? Could I truly trust Jesus to take my guilt and shame and transform it into something beautiful? I felt a nudge from the Holy Spirt to read Song of Songs 2:10-13 (TLV):

> Get yourself up, my darling, my pretty one,
> and come, come! For behold, the winter has past,
> the rain is over, it has gone. Blossoms appear in
> the land, the time of singing has come, and the
> voice of the turtle-dove is heard in our land. The
> fig tree ripens its early figs. The blossoming vines

give off their fragrance. Arise, come my darling,
my pretty one, and come, come!

[/vc_row_inner]

My battered heart beat with optimism as I read these words of
love and encouragement. *Jesus, if there is any way for You to use my
transgressions for someone else's gain, then I am willing to trust Your
timing to deliver me from overdrinking.*

Desiring to live the abundant life the Bible says is available for
us to live, I promised myself I would somehow get free from the
alcohol. I wanted a life abounding in fullness of joy and strength for
mind, body, and soul. I read my Bible and devotionals daily. I prayed.
I read self-development books in an effort to gain control over my
flesh. Some days I was victorious, and other days I fell flat on my
face.

After a particularly tense and hurtful conversation with Doug,
I medicated my mental wounds with a bottle of wine, far exceed-
ing my two-glass limit. As you might imagine, the next morning I
wasn't feeling abounding at all. In truth, I was feeling pretty darn low
mentally, emotionally, and physically. I was disgusted with myself for
allowing Doug's hurtful words to disempower me, but I had responsibilities, so there was no time to wallow in my misery. I needed to
pull up my big girl panties and move on. Besides, Doug was waiting
for me to drive him to the gym, and so we went.

While he worked out, I passed the time by walking the dogs
in the neighborhood. Sidney, our Australian shepherd, is a magnet
for attention because he's a small puppy, not to mention a bundle
of cuteness. Therefore, I wasn't a bit surprised when a gentleman
approached to ask about him.

He wanted to know if we lived in the neighborhood, and I told
him we did not. I then explained why we were in the neighborhood.
Soon he was asking lots of questions about Doug's injury. It was
quickly obvious he was very familiar with traumatic brain injuries.
When I inquired about his knowledge, he said he worked in health
care and was a brain rehabilitation specialist. It was nice to meet

someone that spoke the language, but soon he needed to leave. Before he did, he said to me, "You're not just surviving your husband's accident, you're thriving in your circumstances."

I was absolutely dumbfounded. How could a complete stranger say such a thing? These were intimate details only someone who knew us would be aware of. I, therefore, responded, "Excuse me?"

He repeated himself and went on to say, "I see you juggling a calendar, a cake, a chainsaw..." He said something else, but I didn't hear it. I am sure my jaw hit the pavement in surprise and wonder at the exchange, which had taken place. How could he possibly know how much I would identify with those descriptions? It couldn't possibly be a coincidence! Was it possible the Holy Spirit was trying to encourage me?

> "Here is a God who sees me and knows me just as I am as well as all that concerns me" (Ray Steadman).[76]

Little else was said before this man, or rather as I now recognized him as the messenger of God, turned to leave. As he walked away, I headed back to the gym to pick up Doug, all the while wondering, *Is it possible I am indeed thriving? What is God seeing that I'm not?*

Looking back now, I can see I was indeed flourishing. What I failed to comprehend is the pinching back and pruning of plants forces the roots to grow deep and wide, providing a greater opportunity to acquire nutrients, which then produces greater blossoms and fruit. Simply because I was experiencing a season of struggle didn't mean I was not growing. It was quite the opposite, actually. I was experiencing accelerated growth!

However, with growth comes growing pains, and I was experiencing them big time. I realized I was not as selfless as I imagined myself to be. On a few occasions, to my shame, my patience grew beyond thin and sometimes completely vanished. In those moments, I found myself thinking if Doug had died, my life would be so much easier.

So much for "In sickness and health, for better or for worse."

The one redeeming thing about these thoughts was no sooner than the evil idea entered my mind, I was immediately engulfed with guilt and shame for thinking it. As a God-fearing Christian woman, I wondered how I could possibly think something so depraved about the man I loved.

I've learned that thoughts like these are not uncommon for a caregiver to have once they have reached the end of their proverbial rope. A friend shared her story of caring for her husband with a terminal condition while she was working full-time and raising children. She came home from work and was exhausted from the multitude of responsibilities she was carrying. As she walked through the door, her husband asked her if she would adjust his pillows. In her extremely depleted state, she snapped emotionally, picked up the pillow, covered his face as if to smother him, and asked, "Is that better?"

Like me, she was mortified by her behavior because she loved her husband dearly. Shame, guilt, and self-condemnation were quick to persecute her.

I shared my frustration and unburdened my soul with Doug's yoga therapist, Serena, and she responded, "Oh, Tammy, how human of you! Of course, you are having these feelings. You wouldn't be human if you weren't."

Feeling a measure of gratitude and relief but not yet feeling fully confident, I asked, "Are you sure it is normal to feel this way?" My friend was the only person I had heard of to confess their feelings of desiring their loved one's demise. But then, who wants to share these heinous thoughts with others? No one wants to expose themselves to be judged harshly. As I allowed myself to be real and share my depravity with others, I found I was far from alone in my circumstance. Others have confided to me that they, too, have felt the very same but were afraid to speak it out. Through their tears of shame and gratitude, they have hugged and thanked me for my vulnerability, much to my relief and amazement.

Instead of your shame you will receive a double portion, and instead of disgrace you will rejoice in your inheritance. And so you will inherit a double portion in your land, and ever-lasting joy will be yours.

Isaiah 61:7 NIV

[/vc_row_inner]

Hidden emotions cannot be healed. I believe as we bring our shameful thoughts and deeds to Jesus, He lovingly restores us, rather than condemn us. Ephesians 5:13 (NIV) says, "But everything exposed by the light becomes visible—and everything that is illumi-nated becomes a light."

As I have opened up and shared with others about my "wishing Doug had died" moments and my overdrinking, I found myself and others finding freedom and relief when no longer bound by guilt and shame. Instead, we were being restored and set free.

In my moments of wishing either Doug or I were dead, it seemed my dreams of using our story to encourage others were dying as well. I struggled to believe anyone would believe in the goodness of God when they saw the depravity in my heart. Apparently, I needed to be encouraged and have my faith buoyed, so a friend sent me a YouTube video of Pastor Steven Furtick preaching a message on the devil steal-ing your dreams.[77] He referenced the story of Elijah's prayers for rain and his confrontation with Jezebel (1 Kings 18:41-46, 19:1-18).

Through Pastor Furtick's message, God helped me see how the devil caused me to doubt I could ever achieve my dream. The devil's goal was for my dream to be destroyed. When I managed to muster enough faith to pursue my dream, and it began to evolve, the devil told me my dream would never amount to anything.

As I overcame his deception by trusting God and His Word, I continued to increase my faith, providing the fuel for my dreams to flourish. Once success was achieved, however, I found that the devil then attacked with fatigue, depression, and discouragement in an attempt to destroy the dreams' longevity.

Pastor Furtick gave the example of Elijah praying for rain, and the small cloud the size of a man's hand appeared. Elijah continued to pray in faith until heaven opened, and there was a deluge. In supernatural strength, Elijah even managed to outrun Ahab's chariot (1 Kings 18:41-46).

Next, we find Elijah holed up in a cave hiding from Jezebel, feeling sorry for himself despite having defeated a multitude of false prophets. This single woman, Jezebel, had the power to disempower the man of God, immediately after he had gone toe-to-toe with the enemy and won! So why was he so beaten down?

Pastor Furtick went on to explain that what Elijah failed to understand was, even though he had soundly beaten the enemy during the obvious battle, the enemy is relentless. There is some-times no resting from his persistent harassment. Elijah found him-self exhausted, depressed, and disillusioned, no longer believing he was empowered to overcome. He had incorrectly assumed once he defeated the prophets of Baal, the battle was won, and the fighting was over.

I have done the very same thing as Elijah. I assumed all was going to be well once we got moved and settled in, so I let my guard down. I got hit by a virus of some sort and was sick for weeks. I had become the victim instead of the victor. I didn't feel like I could allow myself time to rest and recuperate. But instead of admitting my weakness and allowing Jesus to be my strength, I put my shoulder to the plow one more time applying for jobs. I mistakenly believed it was up to me to secure an income even though my severance pack-age and unemployment benefits were sufficient for the time being. I should have taken a lesson from Elijah, remembering how God sent the ravens to supply his food (1 Kings 17:4-6).

In hindsight, I now believe God was offering me a season of rest and further training in His supernatural provision. Not recognizing His intentions, I failed to humble myself by not taking the time to crawl into the arms of my Father and rest.

The Making of Diamonds and Butterflies

When we are living a life submitted to Christ, following his path and dying to self, we realize that it is his power enabling us to it all. He works within us to make more room for himself. He does not only lay out the path for us and give us the instructions, he actually lives his life in us, empowering us by his Spirit to do what we cannot do on our own.

Catherine Skurja[78]

[/vc_row_inner]

I have witnessed the Spirit's power at work in Doug, enabling him to come to terms with his limitations. Doug does what he can to advance his recovery, but he has made peace with where God has him. When we were approximately a year and a half into his recovery, he told me he believed God had actually blessed him through the accident. In disbelief, I asked him to repeat himself and then define what he meant. Repeating himself as requested, he then went on to explain how he absolutely hated traveling for work since it meant being away from home for up to six weeks at a time. Now that he was not able to work anymore, he got to stay home with me.

I was having a hard time processing this news. Doug had been such a workaholic before the accident. He rarely slowed down. He was seemingly independent and seemingly indestructible. I had a difficult time believing he could possibly be at peace with his limitations. Nor could I believe he enjoyed being at home when there had been as much discord as we had. I didn't even enjoy my own company some days. How was it possible he was able to? Nonetheless, he does the majority of the time, much to my relief and amazement.

Still needing clarification, I continued to question him. "So, you are willing to trade being completely healed and fully capable of doing whatever you want for being disabled and limited in your activities so you can spend all your time at home?"

His response was an adamant "Yes, I missed being with you and wouldn't trade wholeness for living away from you!"

I was shocked. I truly love Doug, but I have always functioned best when we have some time apart. (He worked shiftwork for the first twenty-five years of our marriage, so I was accustomed to having two weeks a month with evenings home alone.) In fact, having him home all the time since returning from Omaha had been one of the biggest challenges for me to overcome. Before the accident, we had been like best friends.

We looked forward to time spent together hiking, skiing, floating the river or driving mountain roads looking for wildlife. I know the last six-week tour he had in Alaska the summer before he got hurt was difficult to endure. I managed well for the first few weeks he was gone taking advantage of alone time to catch up with friends or read, but after that, I missed him terribly. He didn't fare as well living in a man camp. He would call me each evening and talk for hours.

Knowing we had enjoyed a relative harmonious relationship before the accident and now that it was frequently filled with discord, I was taken aback by his attitude. I was blessed by his comment, and, filled with guilt and remorse, I couldn't match his sentiments exactly. I immediately offered up a silent prayer asking for the Holy Spirit to change my hardened heart to match that of Doug's.

Baxter Kruger says:

> She [the Spirit] is alive and powerful, and
> constantly moving... She inspires witness to
> Jesus and works within the deepest trenches of

the human heart and its wounds. Or, perhaps I should say, she works within the root systems of the gardens of our souls.

While she can be lied to, resisted, tested, grieved, insulted, quenched, and blasphemed, she is remarkably comfortable with the sinful mess we have made of ourselves and our lives.[79]

[/vc_row_inner]

The garden of my soul seemed to be overrun with weeds, choking out the desirous plants in my life. Yes, there was much good still growing. However, I often struggled to see the good because the growth was regularly compromised and shrouded by the weedy vines, which entangled my heart.

However, I was sitting with Jesus one morning, and He reminded me of the parable of the wheat and tares (Matthew 13:27). Tares are considered to be a noxious weed, barely discernible from the wheat until maturity. When ripe, the tares stand erect while the wheat heads bow down with heaviness making the difference easily discernible. The contrast has been likened to pride versus humility.

In this parable, the master tells his servants not to pull the weeds but to let them grow. Otherwise, there is a risk of damaging or uprooting the wheat in the process. Gently, the Holy Spirit helped me understand my weedy mess didn't bother Him. In fact, He was delighted to allow me time to mature, knowing there would be a bountiful harvest of goodness when the time was right. I may not have been comfortable with the noxiousness of my garden, but I had hoped it would someday be bountiful, fragrant, and glorious.

"We learn the most about ourselves when we are uncomfortable" (Dr. Joe Dispenza).[80]

As I continued pressing into God, wondering when I was going to have a breakthrough, He gave me a vision of a finger with a large splinter. The skin around the splinter was red and inflamed, hot to the touch, and painful. I felt Him say He knows I am miserable right now, but soon the splinter will easily pop right out, and the wound will be healed shortly thereafter. My compassionate Father was telling me there was a maturation process taking place in my life. Yes, there were weeds and infections, but eventually all things run their course. Abundant life and healing were eminent.

> Come, let us return to the Lord. He has torn us to pieces but He will heal us; He has injured us but He will bind up our wounds. After two days He will revive us; on the third day He will restore us, that we may live in His presence. Let us acknowledge the Lord; let us press on to acknowledge Him. As surely as the sun rises, He will appear; He will come to us like the winter rains, like the spring rains that water the earth.

> Hosea 6:1-3 NIV

[/vc_row_inner]

Counseling showed me it is normal to experience the myriad of feelings I have had since the accident. Even though I knew I was doing an excellent job caring for Doug and holding our lives together, I still struggled to see all the good I was doing while feeling like I should have done more and done it better. I constantly compared myself to others, quite sure if I wasn't doing all they were doing in addition to caring for Doug, I was somehow less-than. I unwittingly played into the enemy's hand once again, with self-flagellation being the weapon of choice.

And while I know now all of this is normal, I also know it's extremely destructive. In my stubbornness, I found myself wildly galloping around, believing if I got everything right, my life would be blissful. But I now recognize my life was never meant to look like everyone else's. We are all given specific—and different—assignments in His kingdom.

Adam and Eve were convinced they were missing out on something good when God told them not to eat of the tree of knowledge. But when God finished creating the heavens and the earth and mankind, He said, "It is good" (Genesis 1:31). This means He was well-pleased with the adequacy of what and whom He created. In fact, the word "good" in Hebrew is defined as "precious,"[81] which means it is of great value and should not be treated carelessly. Accordingly, Adam and Eve didn't need anything He hadn't already provided for them, and yet, they didn't see it that way. They focused on their seeming lack and sinned against God.

Likewise, nowhere do I find God telling us we are lacking. In fact, having been created in His image (Genesis 1:27), Scripture tells us we lack nothing. But we have been lied to by Satan since the beginning of time, creating a sense of lack and confusion about our identity as children of God—the perfect provider and Father.

Graham Cooke, author and prophetic minister, says, "When you don't step into the identity that God created for you, it is an insult to Jesus. When we discover who we truly are, we will behave accordingly."[82] Jesus thinks I am precious and loves me enough that He willingly died so I may fully experience abundant life, and yet, I continued to deny myself this gift. I was living in a mindset of poverty by denying my full identity in Christ.

I have been told I am a Renaissance woman because I am capable of many things. I can fix a fabulous meal, bake a decadent dessert, change the oil in my car, and operate heavy equipment. Yet I disdained these gifts, thinking I should be something more. I looked to the leading ladies in Christian ministry such as Beth Moore, Joyce Meyer, Christine Caine, Amy Grant, and Darlene Zschech and believed I fell far short of having anything of value to contribute to the world. I spent years chasing all I thought would propel me into my destiny when my destiny was already inside of me, waiting to be discovered.

"Be who God meant you to be and you will
set the world on fire" (St. Catherine of Siena).[83]

The time had come for me to crawl out of my cocoon of limiting beliefs. Like the butterfly, I, too, wanted to soar and experience all my Father had prepared for me. But I was clinging to the past, afraid I may experience more pain in risking growth. I knew I couldn't keep looking back at what I used to have in my old life. In looking back and wishing I still had the many things that I left behind, I failed to see the blessings God was pouring into my life.

In my grief, I failed to see that fulfilled promise was only on the other side of a change of heart. I needed to embrace the "new thing" God was doing in my life (Isaiah 43:19).

Pastor and author Mark Batterson says, "Unless we commit to a new course of action, we will maintain our current rhythms and routines."[84] God was increasing the pressure in my life to bring about the change He greatly desired for me.

***

Doug forgot my birthday. I tried to brush it off and chalk his forgetfulness up to the brain injury, but his failure to acknowledge my special day five years post-injury still hurt. I guess this was the first time he had forgotten or didn't have a caregiver to remind him. It was obviously my problem that I was hurt, not his. After others called to offer me birthday wishes, he realized his faux pas and offered to take me to dinner at one of our favorite places.

Prior to that, I told him I would take him to the gym so we both could work out when I got done cleaning a house for a friend. He agreed and said he would be ready to go when I got home shortly after noon.

I was driving home after I was done cleaning and saw Doug walking alongside the snow-covered road miles from home. He progressed significantly over the years and had gained some independence. This was wonderful, but I was still anxious when he went out on his own, particularly knowing he still had the propensity to fall now and then.

I questioned his judgment to walk along the snow-packed roadside. My concern for his well-being morphed into anxiety and frustration, but I knew he would be angry with me if I tried to reason with him. So, I drove home, deciding I would walk the dogs instead of going to the gym because he probably wouldn't have the energy to go with me. While walking the dogs, I ran into a neighbor who told me how amazed she was to see Doug walking all the way down by Walmart, which was five miles from our house for a round trip total of ten miles. My frustration gave way to full-blown anger as I contemplated, once again, the treacherous road conditions and his safety or lack thereof.

Doug finally arrived home an hour later, giving my vexation a chance to reduce from boiling to a simmer. I asked him if he had forgotten our gym date, and he sheepishly said he had and that he was sorry. It didn't make me feel any better, but I held my tongue and did my best to move on, trying to avoid another conflict. After all, what use was there to try to explain the danger he put himself in when I knew he would argue that he knew what he was doing and was confident of his safety.

Over dinner, he explained he made the long walk into town earlier because he felt terrible for missing my birthday and wanted to get me something special from my favorite jeweler.

My stomach knotted up as I considered our precarious financial situation. I immediately wondered how much he had spent. I saw the excitement and pride in his eyes as he then told me he had bought me a diamond solitaire necklace. "I know you have said you don't want any more diamonds, but this one is an investment, and I wanted you to have it."

My consternation increased with his every word. I tried to enjoy this special dinner as I ruminated about the cost of the gem. I found it difficult to swallow my food because anxiety was knotted up in my throat.

He said I would have to wait until Monday when the store opened to pick up my new jewel. The next day I was wrestling with my emotions. I finally mustered up the courage to ask him how much this new acquisition cost us. It was an exorbitant expense, just as I had feared it may be. He had no business making financial decisions without consulting me since I was the one managing what little we had at the time.

How could he be so irresponsible to spend so much money? I was sick. I had very carefully saved money from the remodel to paint the exterior of our house. Now it seemed my plans would be detained. I did not want to hurt his feelings with my contempt toward his lavish gift. Therefore, I quickly made some excuse to go for a walk, hoping to burn off some of the steam I was feeling. I needed to have a discussion with God.

As I was pouring out my frustration to God about all the things we *should* have used the money on, including paint for our new home, I suddenly heard God intervene, *What if I wanted you to have the diamond?*

Had I heard Him right? *What?*

What if I wanted you to have the diamond? God was clear.

If you really want me to have the diamond, then I will accept it, but I'm still not happy about having to give up the paint money for a stone I never wanted in the first place.

But I knew if I returned the diamond like I wanted to, Doug would feel rejected. In one of Joyce Meyer's books, I read years ago, she said, "When you reject the gift, you reject the giver."[85] It's true. I knew it would crush him, so I settled my conversation with God and thanked Doug for his thoughtfulness when I got home.

I wore the glittering diamond necklace to church the following Sunday. While at church, I decided to ask a friend who is a counselor what she would have done under the circumstances. After I explained the story, she immediately teared up and said I was supposed to keep the diamond. She also felt there was something prophetic about the diamond that God would reveal to me in time.

I went back to my seat, tears streaming down my face and onto the floor as God whispered to my heart again, *Tammy, all you can see is the wrong things you have done, but all I can see is the jewel that you have become. This is why I want you to have the diamond as a reminder of what you have become.*

I was undone as I realized the depth of His love for me in the middle of my brokenness. With tears streaming down my face, I whispered a promise to wear the diamond proudly.

The more time I spend in His presence, the more polished I become. Hebrews 4:12 (TPT) says:

> For we have the living Word of God, which
> is full of energy, and it pierces more sharply than

a two-edged sword. It will even penetrate to the very core of our being where soul and spirit, bone and marrow meet! It interprets and reveals the true thoughts and secret motives of our hearts.

[/vc_row_inner]

I can visualize His word cutting the many facets into the rough stone. Removing the excess to reveal the dazzling quality within. I liken meditating on the Word to the polishing process, the place where we begin to reflect the very nature of Christ Himself.

In my ever-growing relationship with God, one day I asked Him what He loved about me. *I love that you are multifaceted and can do so many things.*

My heart exploded as these words of edification penetrated my soul.

During my struggle to come to terms with the changes in our lives, I know now that God wasn't punishing me. He was preparing me for my destiny. The heat and pressure were creating the diamond, the new creature I was meant to be. He had to cut away everything, which prevented me from being perfectly faceted.

He wanted me healthy, whole, and fully surrendered to His will so I could reflect His glory. I have not fully arrived. I am still a work in progress. But I know God is faithful to complete what He starts. He continues to "polish" me at every opportunity. I can see now, what the devil thought would break and mar me has only caused me to shine brighter.

May His light in me give hope to others walking in the darkness.

"You are praying that God will change your circumstance, but He is waiting for you to change your perspective" (Tony Evans).[86]

Finishing Strong

Transformation is a "change in form, appearance, nature or character."[87] While courage is "the quality of mind or spirit that enables a person to face difficulty, danger, pain, etc., without fear; bravery."[88]

When we used to dream about our future and growing old together, a life-altering accident was never part of the dream. Of course, no one ever dreams of such a thing. Dreams are typically reserved for optimism, things of beauty, aspirations of prosperity, and the like. Dreams turn into nightmares when they become thwarted and filled with angst. Even though our dreams took a detour through hell, or so it seemed, we have learned, if you are willing to embrace the challenge and all the changes that come with it, there is an opportunity to grow. Great and wonderful opportunities will frequently present themselves.

> "A man's mind plans his way [as he journeys
> through life], but the Lord directs his steps and
> establishes them" (Proverbs 16:9 AMP)

I know with every fiber of my being, I would have never been able to cope with Doug's accident as well as I was able if it were not for the sovereign presence of Jesus in my life. If you have struggled to believe He is a loving Father, I hope my story has helped clear up any doubt you may have. I once believed He was an angry God just waiting to spank me for my every wrong. I now know He waits patiently and lovingly for us to come to our senses, to realize He wants us to live to the fullest—empowered by the Holy Spirit to overcome our battles.

If you have never asked Jesus to be a part of your life, I invite you to do so now. It is as simple as saying, "Jesus, I believe You are the Son of God. I believe You died and rose again so I may spend eternity with You. I am sorry for the wrong things I have done; please forgive me." Perhaps you have turned your back on God and walked away from Him. Now is a perfect opportunity to get back on track. He is waiting for you with outstretched arms. Tell Him you are sorry, and He will gladly forgive you. Ask Jesus to show Himself to you and be on the lookout for the many ways you will begin to see evidence He is at work in your life.

Next, you will benefit greatly by getting plugged into a church family that can help you grow in your faith. If going to church intimidates you, then start by checking them out online. If you have prayed this prayer, I want to be the first to welcome you to the family of God. Now you have the same power to overcome as I have. It's the best decision you'll ever make, and I know He will help you along in your journey—whatever it may hold.

We are certainly not a perfect example of how to overcome tragedy, but perhaps in our sharing you will learn from our successes and mistakes. I am reminded of some lyrics written by country music singer/songwriter John Michael Montgomery. "Life's a dance you learn as you go. / Sometimes you lead, sometimes you follow. / Don't worry 'bout what you don't know, / life's a dance, you learn as you go."[89] We must continue dancing, trusting in the One who directs our steps and makes provision as we follow Him.

Prior to the accident, I would first look to Jesus for direction before looking to Doug for confirmation. Now that Doug was no longer capable of making consistently sound decisions, the responsibility was mine. I had to trust what I understood Jesus to be conveying to me before informing Doug of the plan. This was one of the areas in which we struggled the most. I know he resented not having more input into decisions that needed to be made.

When I would try to include him by asking his opinion, he responded with irritation and sarcasm, "What does it matter? You are going to do what you want anyway." I knew his words came from his injury and even more so from his inability to fully contribute to our well-being. Nonetheless, over time his angry words created festering wounds of resentment and irritation in my soul. I didn't have the tools to deflect his emotional eruptions or the venom spewed forth. Neither of our souls were prospering (3 John 1:2).

Counseling was helpful but expensive, and it did not seem to provide the resources I needed to manage my thoughts. Thought management would come when I was introduced to The Life Coach School (TLCS) by a friend. I learned how thoughts are ours to choose about any given circumstance. Thoughts create feelings, which create actions, which create results. The quality of a result is completely dependent on our thoughts.

I may not have liked what Doug was doing or saying, but if I chose to let that upset me, I now recognized I was giving my emotional power away to him. I learned to quit reacting to his behavior and instead spend time focusing on what I wanted the outcome to be for any given situation. In essence, I chose to set my mind on things above (Colossians 3:2). This has not been an easy or a quick fix because it takes consistent work to manage one's mind, but I have found it to be completely worth the effort.

Thought and urge management were the tools I also used to gain control of my overeating and drinking. In her book *This Naked Mind Control Alcohol*, author Annie Grace quotes Albert Einstein, who said, "The world we have created is a process of our thinking. It cannot be changed without changing our thinking."[90] Annie shows her readers how we have been conditioned by society to believe alcohol relieves stress and brings happiness. In fact, the alcohol industry spends billions of dollars to convince us we can find pleasure and relief in a bottle. It was as though God was driving this point home when I saw a delivery truck for a particular alcoholic beverage emblazoned with the words, "Delivering Happiness!"

As I educated myself on the negative aspects of alcohol, I began to understand how my drinking didn't take away my stress and anxiety. Instead, it only added to the problem. Not only was alcohol increasing my despondency, but it was also robbing me of the ability to experience joy in my life fully. When you use a "numbing agent," it deadens your ability to feel both the good and the bad life has to offer. As Annie writes, "Alcohol is a physical depressant that poisons your body and ensnares your brain. It destroys you physically and mentally. It deadens your senses. Thereby deadening all your survival instincts. It takes the happiness of this beautiful life with it."[91] As I read her words, I couldn't help but wonder how the quality of the last several years could have been significantly improved for Doug and me if I hadn't bought into the lie, I could find relief in alcohol.

I was already exhausted, overwhelmed, and discouraged. I could see how adding alcohol to the mix was clearly the reason I suffered depression and fatigue. I knew alcohol was a depressant, I just didn't realize how powerful its effect was. It was as though I was caught in a vortex, unable to get out. But by the grace of God, I was thrown a lifeline. He delivered me. Never once has He condemned me. Rather, He has lavished His love on me. Like the prodigal's father, He was biding time until I came to my senses. He was patiently waiting to show me He has already supplied all I need to navigate this journey called life successfully.

> The Lord himself is my inheritance, my prize. He is my food and drink, my highest joy! He guards all that is mine. He sees that I am given pleasant brooks and meadows as my share! What a wonderful inheritance! I will bless the Lord who counsels me; He gives me wisdom in the night. He tells me what to do.
>
> I am always thinking of the Lord; and because He is so near, I never need to stumble or fall.
>
> Heart, body, and soul are filled with joy. For You will not leave me among the dead; You will not allow your beloved one to rot in the grave. You have let me experience the joys of life and the exquisite pleasures of Your own eternal presence.
>
> Psalm 16:5-11 TLB

[/vc_row_inner]

I believe one of the most valuable lessons I have learned over the last eight years is to embrace the pain of life. I have spent my life trying to anesthetize it with food, alcohol, people-pleasing, and a host of other things, not comprehending I was only covering up the pain. I wasn't acknowledging it or allowing it to be processed. Through TLCS, I learned to sit with my emotions and feel them for better or worse. Once you can sit with your emotions without having to deny them, they eventually pass, and you retain your emotional power. And as Brooke enlightened me, no one will die or get pregnant by feeling their emotions.

Is it uncomfortable? Yes. To the point of death? No. Do I fail? Yes. Every day. But I am discovering I have what it takes to be victorious. Again, neither one of these processes happens quickly. Rewiring the brain takes repetition. Habits are developed through repetition and, therefore, must be undone consistently and mindfully to make positive changes. As I have worked on managing my thoughts, my emotions are no longer in control of my life. I am in the driver's seat most days. I have been able to use my tools to help Doug manage his emotions as well.

As we are being more mindful of our emotions and the words coming from our mouths, we are slowly rebuilding the trust in our relationship. I would be lying if I told you we are living a life filled with passion and romance as we did early on. Doug's anger-laced words were like deadly torpedoes, wreaking havoc in my heart. Every hostile word decimated my rapidly waning trust and affection towards him. Even though I recognized the downward spiral in my affection toward him, my desire to protect my heart was far greater than my willingness to risk the pain of further injury by opening my emotions to him. Feeling guilty, I retreated from his advances.

I was introduced to the work of speaker and author Alison Armstrong by one of my TLCS classmates, and I experienced an aha moment. Alison explains that when a woman meets a man, psychologically, she determines if he is a predator or protector. Upon determining he is a protector, the woman engages with the man. However, the protector turns predator when threatened or angered, with loud, volatile outbursts (a common way men express anger). The woman is now afraid of the man, her former protector, and therefore she retreats.[92]

After studying her work, I understood why I was emotionally pulling away from Doug. Every time he got angry and erupted verbally, I felt myself withdrawing, trying to shelter myself from his emotional shrapnel.

Not only were we dealing with the challenges of the TBI, but both of us were also dealing with the hormonal changes the aging process brings with it. I knew I was dealing with the ups and downs of perimenopausal symptoms but never considered Doug may be dealing with his own hormonal changes until Alison Armstrong described the effects in a YouTube video I was listening to.[93] Doug and I were in opposition to each other hormonally. As my estrogen levels dropped, so were my levels of compassion and patience. After having lab work done, I also found my testosterone levels were extremely low, which likely contributed to my being exhausted much of the time. Frankly, my "give a darn" was busted. Getting my hormone levels in balance definitely improved my sense of well-being. My ability to manage my emotions was enhanced. I say all of this not to give you our medical history but rather to share my insight in hopes it may help you, my reader, possibly find a comparable resolution to your circumstance if needed.

Peace and laughter have mostly replaced the tension and resentment in our relationship as his brain continues to mend and as we continually discover new ways to further improve the quality of our life.

Years ago, I spent time educating myself on the psychological differences between the sexes in order to improve my marriage. However, in the midst of trying to survive the storm created by Doug's accident, I had neglected to use the knowledge I had gained when it could have benefited me most. Once again, God was faithful to provide what I needed through Alison's reminder of the difference between men and women.

My love for Doug has morphed over these last several years from one of youthful passion to that of maturity, steadfast commitment, and devotion during these years of recovery. As Doug's brain continues to heal, thus increasing his independence, he is able to contribute more to our daily existence, thereby lessening his dependence on me. This has reduced some of my day-to-day responsibilities, allowing more time for me to care for my own well-being.

Many folks dream of being financially well off, believing money will eliminate life's problems, but as I have looked around, it seems this belief isn't true. Doug and I are finding ourselves much richer mentally, emotionally, and spiritually despite our income being significantly reduced. While I will agree, money can't buy happiness, having enough for the basics in life increases peace of mind and reduces stress.

I have also learned I can trust in the goodness of God as my provider.

> ...yet he has never left himself without clear evidence of his goodness. For he blesses us with rain from heaven and seasons of fruitful harvests, and he nourishes us with food to meet our needs. He satisfies our lives, and euphoria fills our hearts.

> Acts 14:17 TPT

[/vc_row_inner]

The depth of satisfaction we get in helping others learn how to navigate their own rocky road far surpasses all the money in the world. I seem to forget the immense agony I have experienced over the course of this journey when I am able to impart a measure of hope to those who are in the midst of their own suffering. The apostle Peter said, "I don't have a nickel to my name, but what I do have, I give you: In the name of Jesus Christ of Nazareth, walk!" (Acts 3:6 MSG).

We have learned to walk by faith, not by sight or feelings. Yes, we have stumbled and fallen many times on this turbulent journey of faith, but by the grace of God, we have gotten back up to try again and again. Our prayer for you is you will trust God to give you the faith, hope, and strength to get up every day, believing the best is yet to come. Some days believing will be far easier than others. You will have days where nothing turns out as you had hoped; and you will have evenings unexpectantly spent in the emergency room instead of relaxing at home. In hot tears of anger and frustration, you will want to throw in the towel. Instead, remind yourself that through Christ's strength, you have what is necessary to carry on.

Encourage yourself by reading stories like Job and testimonies of others, especially throughout Scripture, who have overcome the odds. They will spur you on to rise above the adversity. While you may find it hard to believe, there are many others counting on you to succeed. Your story will be the antidote to someone else's suffering because God doesn't waste our pain (2 Corinthians 1:3-4, Romans 1:12).

Faith is like a muscle, it must be stretched and strengthened through resistance, while hope is a torch, shining light into the darkness, illuminating your next step.

May our faith spark an increase in yours and our hope kindle your aspirations.

> Arise [from spiritual depression to a new life], shine [be radiant with the glory and brilliance of the Lord]; for your light has come, and the glory and brilliance of the Lord has risen upon you.
>
> "For in fact, darkness will cover the earth and deep darkness will cover the peoples; but the Lord will rise upon you [Jerusalem] and His glory and brilliance will be seen on you.
>
> Nations will come to your light, and kings to the brightness of your rising.
>
> Isaiah 60:1-3 AMP

[/vc_row_inner]

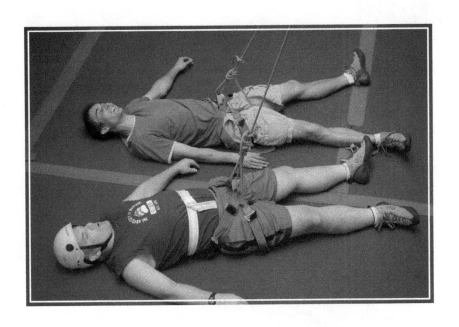

295

Endnotes

Introduction
1 Brené Brown, *Rising Strong: How the Ability to Reset Transforms the Way We Lead, Love, Parent, and Lead* (New York: Random House, 2017), 5.

Chapter 1
2 Good Reads, s.v. "Winston Churchill," accessed September 8, 2020 <https://www.goodreads.com/quotes/22166-there-is-something-about-the-outside-of-a-horse-that/>

Chapter 3
3 Sarah Young, *Jesus Calling: Enjoying Peace in His Presence* (Nashville: Thomas Nelson Publishers, 2004), 358.
4 Napoleon Hill, *Outwitting the Devil: The Secrets to Freedom and Success* (New York: Sterling Publishing Company, 2011), 86.
5 Hill, *Outwitting the Devil*, 99-100.
6 Hill, *Outwitting the Devil*, 106.

Chapter 4
7 Amy Carmichael, *Candles in the Dark: Letters of Hope and Encouragement* (Fort Washington: CLC Publications, 1981), 57.

Chapter 5
8 Intubation is the placement of a flexible plastic tube into the trachea to maintain an open airway or to serve as a conduit through which to administer certain drugs. Wikipedia, s.v. "trachial intubation," accessed December 1, 2019 <https://en.wikipedia.org/wiki/Tracheal_intubation/>
9 PICC line is a central intravenous catheter that can be used to administer medications. Mayo Clinic, s.v. "PICC line," accessed May 20, 2020 <https://www.mayoclinic.org/tests-procedures/picc-line/about/pac-20468748/>

Chapter 6
10 Hope is an optimistic attitude of mind, based on expectation or desire. Accessed December 1, 2019 <https://www.goodreads.com/book/show/46928456-she-holds-onto-hope-for-he-is-forever-faithful-1-corinthians-1/>

11 Faith is the confidence or trust in a person or thing or a belief not based on proof. Dictionary.com, s.v. "Faith," accessed December 1, 2019 <https://www.dictionary.com/browse/faith?s=t/>

Chapter 7
12 Graham Cooke, brilliantbookhouse.com
13 Hill, *Outwitting the Devil*, 80.

Chapter 9
14 Young, *Jesus Calling*, 24.

Chapter 10
15 Bill Gaultiere, "Dallas Willard's Definitions," *Soul Shepherding*, <https://www.soulshepherding.org/dallas-willards-definitions/>
16 Lillian B. Yeoman, *His Healing Power: Four Classic Books on Healing, Complete in One Volume* (Springfield: Gospel Publishing House, 1966), 152.

Chapter 11
17 Flint Rehab, "7 Recovery-Boosting Essential Oils for Brain Injury," November 26, 2019 <https://www.flintrehab.com/essential-oils-for-brain-injury/>
18 The Ethics and Religious Liberty Commission of the Southern Baptist Convention, "The Accuser in the Mirror: The Danger of False Guilt," erls.com, July 25, 2014 <https://erls.com/resource-library/articles/the-accuser-in-the-mirror-the-danger-of-false-guilt/>
19 Young, *Jesus Calling*, 21.

Chapter 12
20 My MS, s.v. "Tremor and Shaking," accessed September 8, 2020 <My-ms.org/symptoms_tremors.htm/>

Chapter 13
21 Oswald Chambers, "May 24: The Delight of Despair," <utmost.org/the-delight-of-despair/>
22 Good Reads, s.v. "Martin Luther King Jr," accessed September 8, 2020 <https://www.goodreads.com/quotes/78209-but-i-know-somehow-that-only-when-it-is-dark/>

Chapter 14
23 This is the author's own translation of Psalm 23.

Chapter 15
24 Young, *Jesus Calling*, 27.

Chapter 16
[25] Young, *Jesus Calling*, 34.
[26] Young, *Jesus Calling*, 38.

Chapter 17
[27] Gilbert K. Chesterton, *G.K. Chesterton's The Head of Caesar and Other Stories: The Way to Love Anything is to Realize That It May be Lost* (Digital: Miniature Masterpieces, 2013), cover.
[28] Max Lucado, *The Devotional Bible: He Still Moves Stones* (Nashville: Thomas Nelson Publishers, 2003), 1490.
[29] David Wilkerson, *God is Faithful: A Daily Invitation into the Father Heart of God* (Ada: Baker Books, 2012), 247.
[30] Lysa Terkeurst, *It's Not Supposed to be This Way: Finding Unexpected Strength When Disappointments Leave You Shattered* (Nashville: Nelson Books, 2018), 45.
[31] Jeffery Tacklind, *The Winding Path of Transformation: Finding Yourself Between Glory and Humility* (Downers Grove: InterVarsity Press, 2019), 93.

Chapter 18
[32] Civilla D. Martin and Charles H. Gabriel, *His Eye is on the Sparrow,* 1905 <https://www.umcdiscipleship.org/resources/history-of-hymns-his-eye-is-on-the-sparrow/>

Chapter 19
[33] Ataxia, which is typically defined as the presence of abnormal, uncoordinated movements. It manifests as an impairment of muscle control or coordination of voluntary movements, such as walking or picking up objects. <https://www.mayoclinic.org/diseases-conditions/ataxia/symptoms-causes/syc-20355652/>
[34] Young, *Jesus Calling*, 106.
[35] Good Reads, s.v. "John F. Kennedy," accessed September 15, 2020 <https://www.goodreads.com/quotes/42653-we-must-find-time-to-stop-and-thank-the-people/>

Chapter 20
[36] Drug titration is the process of adjusting the dose of a medication for the maximum benefit without adverse effects. When a drug has a narrow therapeutic index, titration is especially important, because the range between the dose at which a drug is effective and the does at which side effects occur is small. Wikipedia, s.v. "drug titration," <https://en.wikipedia.org/wiki/Drug_titration/>
[37] Andrew Womack Ministries, "God's Man, Plan, and Timing," <http://www.awmi.net/reading/teaching-articles/gods_man/>
[38] Young, *Jesus Calling*, 110

39 Larry A. Brookins, *The Detox Series: Seven Sermons on Decontaminating the Soul* (Bloomington: Author House, 2014), 62.

Chapter 21
40 Young, *Jesus Calling*, 121.
41 Young, *Jesus Calling*, 125.
42 PBS, "Snowbound: Animals of Winter," January 11, 2017 <https://www.pbs.org/wnet/nature/snowbound-animals-winter/14857/>
43 "If I Don't Have You," Spotify, track 6 on Love and the Outcome, *These are the Days*, Word Entertainment LLC, 2016

Chapter 22
44 Young, *Jesus Calling*, 128.

Chapter 23
45 "Enemy's Camp," Spotify, track 2 on Lindell Cooley, *Revival at Brownsville*, Integrity Music, 2010.
46 Ann Voskamp, *The Broken Way: A Daring Path into the Abundant Life* (Eugene: Zondervan Publishing, 2016), 147.
47 Tony Fahkry, "Why It's Important To Rediscover Joy When Life Hurts Most," February 22, 2018 <https://medium.com/the-mission/why-its-important-to-rediscover-joy-when-life-hurts-most-36bae1eac415/>
48 Andy Andrews, *The Noticer: Sometimes, All a Person Needs is a Little Perspective* (Nashville: W Publishing Group, 2009), 13.
49 Timothy Paul Green, *Today and Tomorrow: A Daily Devotional for the 21st Century Christian* (Murfreesboro: Sword of the Lord Publishers, 2004), 309.

Chapter 24
50 Mark Batterson, *The Circle Maker: Praying Circles Around Your Biggest Dreams and Greatest Fears* (Grand Rapids: Zondervan, 2011), 110-111.

Chapter 26
51 John Bevere, *Relentless: The Power You Need to Never Give Up* (Colorado Springs: Waterbrook Press, 2011), 4, 10.

Chapter 27
52 Bevere, *Relentless*, 138.
53 Young, *Jesus Calling*, 305.
54 Bevere, *Relentless*, 186.
55 Steve McVey, "Why Doesn't God Rescue Us From Pain?" *stevemcvey.com*, July 20, 1016, <http://www.stevemcvey.com/doesnt-god-rescue-us-pain/>

Chapter 28

[56] Sarah Young, *Jesus Today* (Nashville: Thomas Nelson, 2012), 76.

[57] Young, *Jesus Calling*, 372.

Chapter 30

[58] Good Reads, s.v. "St. Francis of Assisi," accessed September 15, 2020 <https://www.goodreads.com/quotes/14329-start-by-doing-what-is-necessary-then-what-is-possible/>

[59] Richard Sharpe Jr., review of *Brave Enough to Follow: What Jesus Can Do When You Keep Your Eyes on Him*, by Stuart Briscoe, June, 2012, <http://www.smallchurchministries.org/brave-enough-to-follow/>

Chapter 31

[60] Antonio Machado, "Traveler, Your Footprint," poem in *There is No Road* (White Pine Press, 2003). <https://www.poetryfoundation.org/poems/58815/traveler-your-footprints/>

Chapter 32

[61] Theodore Roosevelt, Wikipedia, s.v. "Citizenship in a Republic," accessed September 13, 2020 <https://en.wikipedia.org/wiki/Citizenship_in_a_Republic/>

Chapter 34

[62] Breanna Wiest, "The Psychology of Daily Routine," ThoughtCatalogue.com, October 13, 2018 <https://thoughtcatalog.com/brianna-wiest/2015/10/the-psychology-of-daily-routine-7-reasons-why-people-who-do-the-same-things-each-day-tend-to-be-happier-than-those-who-chase-adventure/>

[63] Noah St. John, "Why I Hate the Bamboo Story," *EarlytoRise.com*, March 17, 2011 <https://www.earlytorise.com/why-i-hate-the-bamboo-story-2/>

Chapter 35

[64] "Voice of Truth," Spotify, track 3 on Casting Crowns, *Casting Crowns*, Reunion Records, Inc., 2003.

[65] Mark Batterson, *All In: You are One Decision Away from a Brand New Life* (Grand Rapids: Zondervan, 2013), 132.

[66] Graham Cooke, <Brilliantbookhouse.com/>

Chapter 36

[67] Brooke Castillo, The Life Coach School Certification Program Curriculum, accessed September 13, 2020 <https://thelifecoachschool.com/certification/>

[68] Dictionary.com, s.v. "Immorality," <https://www.dictionary.com/browse/immorality?s=t/>

[69] Devin Still, "Pressing On," interview by Janet Parshall, *In the Market with Janet Parshall*, January 19, 2019 <https://moodyaudio.com/products/best-market-pressing/>

Chapter 37
[70] Clive Staples Lewis, *Mere Christianity* (San Francisco: Harper Collins, 2001), 205.
[71] Google.com, s.v. "Ambiguous," accessed September 15, 2020.
[72] Google.com, s.v. "Grief," accessed September 15, 2020.
[73] Alzheimer Society Canada, "What is Ambiguous Loss?" <https://alzheimer.ca/en/Home/Living-with-dementia/Grieving/ambiguous-loss-family/>
[74] Stephanie Sarazin, "5 Signs You Might be in Ambiguous Loss," *ThriveGlobal.com,* July 9, 2018 <https://thriveglobal.com/stories/5-signs-you-might-be-in-ambiguous-grief-and-what-you-can-do-about-it/>

Chapter 38
[75] Baxter Kruger, *The Shack Revisited* (New York: Faithwords Publishing Hatchette Book Group, 2012), 86.
[76] Ray Stedman, "Genesis 16:13, June 11," <https://www.raystedman.org/daily-devotions/genesis-12to25/the-god-who-sees/>
[77] Steven Furtick, <*youtube.com/*>

Chapter 39
[78] Catherine Skurja, *Paradox Lost: Uncovering Your True Identity in Christ* (North Plains: Imago Dei Ministries, 2012), 223.
[79] Baxter Kruger, *The Shack Revisited*, 87.
[80] Joe Dispenza, "How to Control Your Mind, Anxiety and Stress," *garylite.com*, <https://garylite.com/2019/07/28/how-to-control-your-mind-anxiety-and-stress/>
[81] Hebrew Good
[82] Graham Cooke, <Brilliantbookhouse.com/>
[83] Good Reads, s.v. "St. Catherine of Siena," accessed September 15, 2020 <https://www.goodreads.com/quotes/20893-be-who-god-meant-you-to-be-and-you-will/>
[84] Mark Batterson, *All In*, 111.
[85] Joyce Meyer,
[86] Tony Evans,

Chapter 40
[87] Dictionary.com, s.v. "Transformation," accessed September 15, 2020 <https://www.dictionary.com/browse/transformation?s=t/>
[88] Dictionary.com, s.v. "Courage," accessed September 15, 2020 <https://www.dictionary.com/browse/courage/>

89 John Michael, *Life's a Dance*

90 Annie Grace, *This Naked Mind: Control Alcohol, Find Freedom, Discover Happiness and Change Your Life* (New York: Avery Publishing, 2018), 21,

91 Grace, *This Naked Mind*, 169.

92 Alison Armstrong,

93 Alison Armstrong, "The Secrets to Building Happy and Healthy Romantic Relationships," interview by Mike Dillard, *Self Made Man*, February 10, 2017 <https://www.youtube.com/watch?v=U9tq_QuBnig/>

94 AgingCare.com, "Thirty Percent of Caregivers Die Before The People They Care for Do," October 2007 <https://www.agingcare.com/Discussions/Thirty-Percent-of-Caregivers-Die-Before-The-People-They-Care-For-Do-97626.htm/>

95 Jack Frost, shiloplace.org

96 QuoteSeed.com, s.v. "Henry Ward Beecher," accessed September 15, 2020 <http://quoteseed.com/quotes/henry-ward-beecher/henry-ward-beecher-the-difference-between-perseverance-and/>

97 Good Reads.com, s.v. "George Mueller," accessed September 15, 2020 <https://www.goodreads.com/author/quotes/5825213.George_M_ller/>

Appendix A

Tips for Caretakers

It has taken infinite courage for me to stand up to the medical community, to hold fast to my faith and believe my husband would survive, to face my demons, and to be completely vulnerable and open to sharing my failures. But I do this all to let you know you are not alone in your struggles.

Here are some tips for you, the caretaker, finding yourself in a similar story to my own and desiring a change for the better in your life.

1. Remember, you won't get it all right.

As I considered the cost of sharing and the inevitable judgment that comes with doing so, Jesus reminded me he had enough grace to forgive Paul, who had persecuted and slaughtered Christians. Therefore, his grace was more than sufficient to forgive me in my many sins and shortcomings.

2. Lean on those who have gone before you.

Others have gone before us to light the path to freedom. Reach out to anyone who resonates with you. They may be able to give you insight into your situation. While their story may not be exactly the same, each one may have a nugget of truth you need to hear. There is an abundance of books, support groups, and other resources available. An outside perspective, while not always welcome, may be the insight you need for a positive outcome.

3. There are others who need to hear your story.

I do not believe God allows us to experience pain without a purpose. There is always someone who needs to hear your story. Your testimony may be the avenue, which finally provides hope for someone that they, too, may find wholeness and victory. As we have shared the miracle of Doug's recovery with many others, we heard over and over through tears, "I really needed to hear this. I finally have hope for my situation."

4. Accept your circumstances as they are and have hope for a better tomorrow.

Part of our character testing came in the form of learning to accept the limitations our life now presented. We could have easily allowed ourselves to become bitter and resentful in our circumstances, as many do. However, for the most part, bitterness and resentment are not in either mine or Doug's nature. We are mostly "glass half full" people. That is not to say, at times, we have had to be very mindful about looking for the silver lining in the grey clouds as they poured a deluge and hurled lightning bolts on our parade. Early on, while Doug was at QLI, we were given countless opportunities to count our blessings as we met many individuals and their families who were far more disabled than Doug was.

5. Don't be too proud to ask for help.

Even though Doug was not sent home with an "Owner's Manual" to help prepare us for the future, there are many resources available. In my stubborn independence, I failed to ask for the help I needed at times for fear of inconveniencing or being a burden to others. But getting help is important to sanity preservation. You are not a failure in caring for your loved one if you ask for help. You will thrive when you have the help and rest you need. Counseling has been a critical component in the preservation of our sanity and marriage. Crises tend to destroy even the strongest of relationships.

6.   Take care of yourself.

Caregiving for a loved one can be extremely taxing on the relationship. Especially if there is little to no respite for the caregiver. Respite care is critical for the well-being of the caregiver and, in turn, the loved one. One article I read stated:

> Rough statistics show that 30% of caregivers die before those they are caring for. Some studies show deaths higher. Illness that doesn't lead to death is rampant, as well—depression and auto-immune diseases are high on the list. Caregivers often don't find time to go to their own doctor appointments. They put them off, because they are too busy, or are just plain sick of sitting in clinics with their loved ones. Then things like breast cancer, which could be caught at an early stage, aren't found until the illness is much worse or even life threatening. Caregivers are as important as the people they care for. If they abuse their bodies, minds and spirits while caring for others, no one wins.[94]

[/vc_row_inner]

Making the decision to let go of things near and dear to our hearts is tough, but sometimes those hard decisions must be made to preserve our own well-being.

Years ago, I heard Jack Frost, charismatic author and a Bible teacher, say that without God at the center of your marriage, it is like having two ticks and no dog. We suck the lifeblood out of each other when we expect our spouse to fully meet our needs and fill us up. Only God can fill us, thereby enabling us to pour into others.[95]

I believe this is true; we can't give to others what we don't have ourselves. Self-care has been one of my greatest challenges throughout this journey and has created relational trials for us. However, as time goes on, I am doing significantly better in caring for my mental, physical, and spiritual well-being, and can readily recognize the benefits in doing so. I have a much better perspective and significantly more grace when I am in a healthy place than when I don't prioritize my own care.

7. Don't give up. Continue to bloom where you are planted.

As we continue to challenge ourselves, we continue to grow. Even though there are many things Doug can no longer do, we attempted and discovered many new things he could do. The brain can and will rewire itself if one is willing to put forth the effort.

> "The difference between perseverance and obstinacy is that one comes from a strong will and the other from a strong won't" (Henry Ward Beecher).[96]

I guess, I have a strong will of my own, which, combined with my faith, allowed me to stand and be courageous during our season of testing.

> "The greater the difficlty to be overcome, the more it will be seen to the glory of God how much can be done by prayer and faith" (George Mueller).[97]

Bibliography

AgingCare.com. "Thirty Percent of Caregivers Die Before The People They Care for Do," October 2007 <https://www.agingcare.com/Discussions/Thirty-Percent-of-Caregivers-Die-Before-The-People-They-Care-For-Do-97626.htm/>

Armstrong, Alison. "The Secrets to Building Happy and Healthy Romantic Relationships," interview by Mike Dillard, *Self Made Man*, February 10, 2017 <https://www.youtube.com/watch?v=U9tq_QuBnig/>

Alzheimer Society Canada. "What is Ambiguous Loss?" <https://alzheimer.ca/en/Home/Living-with-dementia/Grieving/ambiguous-loss-family/>

Andrew Womack Ministries. "God's Man, Plan, and Timing," <http://www.awmi.net/reading/teaching-articles/gods_man/>

Andrews, Andy. *The Noticer: Sometimes, All a Person Needs is a Little Perspective*. Nashville: W Publishing Group, 2009.

Batterson, Mark. *All In: You are One Decision Away from a Brand New Life*. Grand Rapids: Zondervan, 2013.

Batterson, Mark. *The Circle Maker: Praying Circles Around Your Biggest Dreams and Greatest Fears*. Grand Rapids: Zondervan, 2011.

Bevere, John. *Relentless: The Power You Need to Never Give Up*. Colorado Springs: Waterbrook Press, 2011.

Brookins, Larry A. *The Detox Series: Seven Sermons on Decontaminating the Soul*. Bloomington: Author House, 2014.

Brown, Brene. *Rising Strong: How the Ability to Reset Transforms the Way We Lead, Love, Parent, and Lead*. New York: Random House, 2017.

Carmichael, Amy. *Candles in the Dark: Letters of Hope and Encouragement.* Fort Washington: CLC Publications, 1981.

Chesterton, Gilbert K. *G.K. Chesterton's The Head of Caesar and Other Stories: The Way to Love Anything is to Realize That It May be Lost.* Digital: Miniature Masterpieces, 2013.

Dispenza, Joe. "How to Control Your Mind, Anxiety and Stress," *garylite.com,* <https://garylite.com/2019/07/28/how-to-control-your-mind-anxiety-and-stress/>

Fahkry, Tony. "Why It's Important To Rediscover Joy When Life Hurts Most," February 22, 2018 <https://medium.com/the-mission/why-its-important-to-rediscover-joy-when-life-hurts-most-36bae1eac415/>

Gaultiere, Bill. "Dallas Willard's Definitions," *Soul Shepherding,* <https://www.soulshepherding.org/dallas-willards-definitions/>

Grace, Annie. *This Naked Mind: Control Alcohol, Find Freedom, Discover Happiness and Change Your Life.* New York: Avery Publishing, 2018.

Green, Timothy Paul. *Today and Tomorrow: A Daily Devotional for the 21st Century Christian.* Murfreesboro: Sword of the Lord Publishers, 2004.

Hill, Napoleon. *Outwitting the Devil: The Secrets to Freedom and Success.* New York: Sterling Publishing Company, 2011.

Kruger, Baxter. *The Shack Revisited.* New York: Faithwords Publishing Hatchette Book Group, 2012.

Lucado, Max. *The Devotional Bible: He Still Moves Stones.* Nashville: Thomas Nelson Publishers, 2003.

Machado, Antonio. "Traveler, Your Footprint," in *There is No Road.* White Pine Press, 2003 <https://www.poetryfoundation.org/poems/58815/traveler-your-footprints/>

McVey, Steve. "Why Doesn't God Rescue Us From Pain?" *stevemcvey.com,* July 20, 1016 <http://www.stevemcvey.com/doesnt-god-rescue-us-pain/>

PBS. "Snowbound: Animals of Winter," January 11, 2017 <https://www.pbs.org/wnet/nature/snowbound-animals-winter/14857/>

Sarazin, Stephanie. "5 Signs You Might be in Ambiguous Loss," *ThriveGlobal.com,* July 9, 2018 <https://thriveglobal.com/sto-

ries/5-signs-you-might-be-in-ambiguous-grief-and-what-you-can-do-about-it/>

Sharpe Jr., Richard. Review of *Brave Enough to Follow: What Jesus Can Do When You Keep Your Eyes on Him*, by Stuart Briscoe, June, 2012 <http://www.smallchurchministries.org/brave-enough-to-follow/>

Skurja, Catherine. *Paradox Lost: Uncovering Your True Identity in Christ*. North Plains: Imago Dei Ministries, 2012.

Stedman, Ray. "Genesis 16:13, June 11," <https://www.raystedman.org/daily-devotions/genesis-12to25/the-god-who-sees/>

Still, Devin. "Pressing On," interview by Janet Parshall, *In the Market with Janet Parshall*, January 19, 2019 <https://moodyaudio.com/products/best-market-pressing/>

St. John, Noah. "Why I Hate the Bamboo Story," *EarlytoRise.com*, March 17, 2011 <https://www.earlytorise.com/why-i-hate-the-bamboo-story-2/>

Tacklind, Jeffery. *The Winding Path of Transformation: Finding Yourself Between Glory and Humility*. Downers Grove: InterVarsity Press, 2019.

Terkeurst, Lysa. *It's Not Supposed to be This Way: Finding Unexpected Strength When Disappointments Leave You Shattered*. Nashville: Nelson Books, 2018.

The Ethics and Religious Liberty Commission of the Southern Baptist Convention. "The Accuser in the Mirror: The Danger of False Guilt," *erls.com*, July 25, 2014 <https://erls.com/resource-library/articles/the-accuser-in-the-mirror-the-danger-of-false-guilt/>

Voskamp, Ann. *The Broken Way: A Daring Path into the Abundant Life*. Eugene: Zondervan Publishing, 2016.

Wiest, Breanna. "The Psychology of Daily Routine," ThoughtCatalogue.com, October 13, 2018 <https://thought-catalog.com/brianna-wiest/2015/10/the-psychology-of-daily-routine-7-reasons-why-people-who-do-the-same-things-each-day-tend-to-be-happier-than-those-who-chase-adventure/>

Wilkerson, David. *God is Faithful: A Daily Invitation into the Father Heart of God*. Ada: Baker Books, 2012.

Yeoman, Lillian B. *His Healing Power: Four Classic Books on Healing, Complete in One Volume*. Springfield: Gospel Publishing House, 1966.

Young, Sarah. *Jesus Calling: Enjoying Peace in His Presence*. Nashville: Thomas Nelson Publishers, 2004.

Young, Sarah. *Jesus Today*. Nashville: Thomas Nelson, 2012.

CPSIA information can be obtained
at www.ICGtesting.com
Printed in the USA
BVHW071511170621
609823BV00002B/156